WRITING
FROM THE
INSIDE OUT

CHRISTOPHER C. BURNHAM
New Mexico State University

HARCOURT BRACE JOVANOVICH, PUBLISHERS

San Diego   New York   Chicago   Austin   Washington, D.C.
London   Sydney   Tokyo   Toronto

Requests for permission to make copies of any part of the work should be mailed to: Permissions, Harcourt Brace Jovanovich, Publishers, Orlando, Florida 32887.

"Chair Chat" by Jon Carroll © San Francisco Chronicle, 1983. Reprinted by permission.

"Get Drunk!" by Charles Baudelaire from 20 Prose Poems of Baudelaire translated by Michael Hamburger. Reprinted by permission.

"My Papa's Waltz" by Theodore Roethke copyright 1942 by Hearst Magazines, Inc. Reprinted by permission of Doubleday & Company.

"My War" from The Boy Scout Handbook and Other Observations by Paul Fussell. Copyright © 1982 by Paul Fussell. Reprinted by permission of Oxford University Press, Inc.

"Nobel Prize Address" from Essays, Speeches and Public Letters by William Faulkner reprinted by permission of Random House.

"Notes and Comment" reprinted by permission; © 1986 The New Yorker Magazine, Inc.

"Were Dinosaurs Dumb" reprinted from The Panda's Thumb, More Reflections in Natural History, by Stephen Jay Gould, by permission of W. W. Norton & Company, Inc. Copyright © 1980 by Stephen Jay Gould.

ISBN: 0-15-597865-9
Library of Congress Catalog Card Number: 87-82786

Printed in the United States of America

PREFACE

TO THE INSTRUCTOR

Writing is a powerful tool for developing personal identity, for discovering ideas and learning about subjects, for creating and communicating knowledge, and for persuading audiences to believe and act in particular ways. *Writing from the Inside Out* is a textbook for instructors who take this broad view of writing and who want to collaborate with their students, helping them become confident and successful writers in their personal, academic, and professional lives.

This textbook contains structured academic and personal journal exercises and a sequence of seven formal essay assignments that introduce students to writing in various contexts for various purposes. Students learn the power of writing by writing for themselves and for various audiences to accomplish various purposes.

Writing from the Inside Out applies the commonsense principle that what is written begins inside a writer as a vaguely defined insight, then is articulated and evaluated to make sense to that writer, and finally is structured and styled according to the writer's particular purpose and audience. In short, we write from the inside out, first to ourselves, then to others.

Writing from the Inside Out develops through three major sections. In Part One, "Writing for the Inside," students learn how to write for and to themselves in academic and personal journals. They discover, develop, and evaluate ideas, and gain a comprehensive sense of themselves, especially their personal values and beliefs. In Part Two, "Writing for the Outside," students learn a process for developing and structuring essays to accomplish particular purposes for particular audiences. Specifically, they learn to write essays to describe, to inform, to interpret, to argue, and to persuade. In Part Three, "Writing the Inside Out," students write an expanded, "ethical" essay. This essay originates in the long tradition of reflective writing exemplified by Montaigne, Thoreau, Merton, and others. Using the thinking, writing, and researching skills learned in the first parts of the book, they declare and defend their membership within a particular community, an academic discipline, a religious or philosophical tradition, or a profession.

Having completed these exercises and essays, students have experienced writing as a means of exploring self; discovering, creating, and communicating knowledge; and articulating and defending personal values and beliefs. An appendix, "The Writer's Resources," provides instruction in fundamental writing skills such as invention, grammar and mechanics, and sentence style. After completing this book, students are prepared to write successfully for themselves and for their academic and professional careers.

In developing this writing program, *Writing from the Inside Out* employs these significant features:

1. Structured academic and personal journal exercises emphasize *writing to learn*. These activities teach *critical and reflective thinking*, the higher-order thinking skills fundamental to effective writing.

Students learn how to keep an academic journal, a Learning Log, through which they create a record of their learning in this and any course. Working in the Learning Log, they learn how to read aggressively, how to develop a critical sense of what they are reading, why they are reading it, what they are learning, and what they can do with what they learn.

Students also complete a Personal Development Journal (PDJ), a sequence of 14 structured journal exercises. This programed sequence requires them to review their past and its influence on their present, to examine their present by determining where they are in relation to what they want for their future, and to speculate about their future in order to establish direction and set goals they can accomplish. Each exercise requires students to complete a mini composing process. They must generate information, shape it into a particular journalistic or literary form such as an obituary or dramatic dialog, and finally evaluate what they have produced. This last step requires students to determine what they have learned by writing the exercise and what they are going to do to put that knowledge to work for them.

The goal of the PDJ is to introduce students to intensive journal keeping as a means of becoming aware of the personal values and beliefs that, implicitly or explicitly, guide their actions. Awareness allows evaluation; evaluation allows choice and growth. Understanding themselves, they can more clearly present their ideas in writing to audiences. Finally, the PDJ serves as a "subject bank" to which they will return throughout the course to find ideas and issues they will develop in their formal essays.

2. A *writing-process approach* within a *collaborative learning framework* teaches students to manage writing assignments effectively.

Having learned "Writing for the Inside," students turn to "Writing for the Outside." They practice by writing formal essays, each with its own purpose and audience. They learn the full scope of the writing process by composing a personal narrative essay based on an incident first discovered in the PDJ. They learn concrete and specific techniques for solving problems while writing. They devote time to *discovery*, learning how to recognize and develop what they want to say and why they want to say it. They learn ways to manage *drafting*, the struggle to get words and ideas into a shape complete and coherent enough that a working draft can be shown to a test audience. They learn how to complete peer critique exercises in which they try out their drafts on the real audience of a small peer group. They learn self-evaluation strategies that will help them use peer responses while *revising* their writing. Understanding the writing process gives students the opportunity to produce noteworthy writing that explores significant ideas and issues.

3. Essay assignments teach *rhetorical awareness* by emphasizing specific purposes and audiences.

Having gained a sense of the complete writing process, students work through essay assignments that teach them how to accomplish different purposes in their writing. Specifically, they learn to describe, to inform, to interpret, to argue, and to persuade. Each assignment provides specific instructions on discovery, drafting, and revising, as well as a peer critique exercise tailored to the specific rhetorical problems inherent in their purpose or related to the specific audience they are addressing. In addition, students complete various self-evaluation exercises, including essay mapping, that allow them to use the criticism from their peers while revising their essays. The complete sequence teaches the thinking and writing skills required to produce thoughtful and persuasive essays.

4. The accompanying Instructor's Manual discusses the theory behind the teaching method and gives suggestions for using the text in class and for evaluating and grading students' work.

Many freshman-composition teachers decry the dearth of ideas in student writing. Others complain that the ideas that do appear are superficial; they lack either conviction or substance. *Writing from the Inside Out* starts with the individual student, proving that each one has significant ideas worthy of development and expression. Then it provides a method for developing and expressing those ideas so both the student and the idea receive serious consideration. In this way, teachers and students become partners in a process that enables students to assume responsibility for their personal, academic, and professional development, and that allows teachers to take pride in the instrumental role they play in initiating that process.

ACKNOWLEDGMENTS

Far too many people have contributed to the making of this book to recognize each individually. However, a few deserve special note. I owe much to the many writing students I have taught in Rhode Island, New Jersey, and New Mexico, especially to those who have allowed me to use their writing here. My students remind me constantly that writing can be learned, and that it can be learned with pleasure.

Several colleagues deserve special credit. Penelope Dugan, of Stockton State College, taught me to pay close attention to teaching and to students. Royce Burton, formerly of Stockton State, showed me how to keep growing. Robert Parker, of Rutgers University, introduced me to the theory of language and learning that informs this book. At New Mexico State University, Bill Bridges helped me draw all that I knew together and showed me that it was a book. Kevin McIlvoy listened patiently, helping me shape emerging ideas on long runs through the desert. Ann Rohovec and Maja-Lisa Moran read closely, tested and confirmed much of this material, and helped me sharpen my focus.

Paul Nockleby, my editor at Harcourt Brace Jovanovich, listened patiently, providing support. Lue Hawk, Shirley K. Rose, Mary Kay Tirrell, and John Snapper reviewed the text with very sharp pencils. Robert Watrous, Kim Svetich, Cathy Reynolds, and Lesley Lenox turned a manuscript into a book.

I thank my parents, Charles and Penny Burnham, may they rest in peace.

Most of all, I thank my wife, Kelly, "the sweetest, wisest soul of all my days and lands." Her confidence in me and her close reading and criticism made the book possible.

TABLE OF CONTENTS

INTRODUCTION

Writing from the Inside Out has one purpose: to help you learn to write effectively for yourself, for school, and, later, for your work.

The approach is based on common sense. Whether a term paper in a history class, a letter of application for law school, or a personal letter expressing joy at the good fortune of someone you love, what you write starts inside you and then works its way out, finding a specific structure and style determined by your purpose and audience.

The approach is practical. Because the best way to learn to write is by writing, you will write frequently. And because there is great diversity in writing styles and purposes, you will practice many different kinds of writing.

Finally, the approach works. The writing exercises and formal essays that make up *Writing from the Inside Out* have already helped many students from various backgrounds and with different interests learn to write. In fact, this book is their legacy.

WHY LEARN TO WRITE?

You are taking this course to learn how to write. Why? The answer is simple but worth examining. Becoming an effective writer will make a difference for you personally, academically, and professionally.

Personally, writing can help you become a successful life-long learner and problem solver. Writing can also contribute to your own spiritual and emotional development. Frequent, self-initiated, personal writing—generally in journals—is a practice often used by the most creative and productive people in our culture. Their use of writing suggests its power.

Academically, writing can contribute to your intellectual development and accomplishment. In college, notetaking, summarizing, and asking and answering questions in writing are tools effective learners use to master material of all kinds. In addition, writing is a means you can use to distinguish yourself. Through essays and written exams, you can demonstrate your ability to learn and communicate what you have learned in your classes. Your skills will be rewarded with good grades.

Professionally, writing can help you not only to land a job but also to prosper in that job. When you finish school, you will find that employers consider the ability to communicate effectively in writing a prerequisite, a minimum qualification, for hiring. In addition, once you start working, you will find writing to be the key to successfully completing many of your duties. More importantly, studies have discovered that effective writing and communication skills are crucial factors in determining promotions. Last and surely not least important, with well-developed writing and thinking skills, you will be secure in your job and, therefore, more likely to enjoy your work. Because we work much of our lives, feeling secure and satisfied in our jobs will enrich our lives.

There are abundant personal and professional rewards for learning to write effectively. Keep these rewards in mind as you work through this course. Let them motivate you to do your best.

THE PLAN: WRITING FROM THE INSIDE OUT

Just as this approach to learning writing is based on common sense, so also is the structure of the book. It begins by addressing the fundamental question "What makes writing good?" This discussion of the factors on which that answer depends, like purpose and audience, will establish some of the characteristics of good writing. This information will help you set goals and establish criteria for judging your own writing performance.

Writing for the Inside

Having set some goals, you will then practice writing for yourself. The personal writing you do—collecting and connecting information in the process of learning, reflecting upon your experiences and dreams, and discovering and developing your sense of self—is WRITING FOR THE INSIDE. After you have practiced this kind of writing, you will begin to move your writing out, from the inside to the outside, from self to others, from the private to the public.

You will practice this private and personal writing in several forms. First you will practice keeping an academic journal. It will help you investigate the relationship between writing and learning and provide the opportunity to take advantage of the writing-learning connection. You will learn specific procedures for collecting your class notes and reading responses, so you can use them to your best advantage. The purpose here is to develop an aggressive attitude toward learning. This attitude will help you make the most of your education in general and of this course in particular. .

Second, you will learn how to keep a personal journal. Specifically, you will complete a 14-day cycle of exercises in a Personal Development Journal and learn how journal keeping can enhance your self-development. The exercises will help you establish a sense of self and personal identity, gain a sense of the context of your life, and decide on some directions for the future. Being aware of and secure in your identity—knowing yourself—will contribute to your ability to write well. In addition, the personal journal will serve as a subject bank. Throughout the course you will be developing formal essays from work begun in the personal journal.

To summarize, the first part of this text will deal with WRITING FOR THE IN-SIDE, writing to and from the self to aid learning, to enhance personal development, and to create subjects for subsequent writing.

Writing for the Outside

Equipped with this repertoire of specific techniques for writing to and from yourself, you will then learn procedures, structures, and analytic techniques to help you begin WRITING FOR THE OUTSIDE. While writing a personal narrative, we will investigate how experienced writers write, and we will establish a model composing process. The model composing process will be divided into three major phases—discovery, drafting, and revising. You will learn how to use this sequence of activities to take an idea from its earliest stages to its final form as an essay submitted to an instructor for evaluation.

You will put this process to work WRITING FOR THE OUTSIDE by completing seven formal essays and other exercises. Writing these essays will give you extensive practice using the basic structures and specific writing skills you will need to write in school and, later, in your work. You will write essays of narration, description, interpretation, analysis, argument, and persuasion. Complete the formal essays following the instructions provided. Writing each essay will be broken into assignments including specific activities. Some ask you to analyze the structure of an essay as it is taking shape. Some require you to dissect paragraphs or analyze segments of an essay to evaluate how effectively they are accomplishing their particular purpose for their specific audience. Often these exercises require you to work with peers, who will serve as a real audience, allowing you to test and revise essays before submitting them to your instructor. The assignments give you the opportunity to work systematically through the composing process, making sure that you are not forgetting to do something which will ultimately improve the quality of your essay. Finally, you will submit your essays to your instructor who will provide response and evaluation.

In addition, an appendix at the back of the book, "The Writer's Resources," provides supplemental information on a variety of subjects important to WRITING FOR THE OUTSIDE. The appendix will first introduce you to invention, which is the process of discovering and analyzing subjects for writing. Then it will provide discussions of crucial skills such as using dictionaries and thesauruses to increase your vocabulary, developing effective editing and proofreading techniques, using a grammar handbook to improve your skills in basic grammar and mechanics, and developing effective sentence style through practice with sentence combining. Many teachers will assume you already have these basic skills and know how to use these resources. If you are inexperienced or unsure of your abilities in these areas, "The Writer's Resources" will provide you with information and exercises that you can work through independently. Some instructors may prefer to work through the appendix as part of the class.

Writing the Inside Out

Having practiced writing for the self and having practiced writing formal essays for specific purposes to audiences beyond the self, we will turn finally to the greatest challenge writers confront—WRITING THE INSIDE OUT. The final assignment, writing an ethical essay, will require you to choose a subject of great personal interest, determine why it is personally significant, and master it through research and writing. You will establish personal authority and articulate and defend your beliefs and conclusions in a longer essay. Doing this you will have completed the process begun at the beginning of the book—you will have learned WRITING FROM THE INSIDE OUT.

KEEPING A LEARNING LOG

In order to work through this course, you will need a loose-leaf binder and plenty of loose-leaf paper. The binder will become your Learning Log, the academic journal of this course, the place where you record and store all that you do and learn. Save all that you write for this course in your Learning Log—including class notes, doodles, complaints, handouts supplied by your instructor, and the required writing. The required writing includes the seven formal essays and exercises as well as two other kinds of exercises—the Personal Development Journal and Log Exercises.

The Personal Development Journal will include the 14 separate exercises in Chapter 2. Be sure to follow the sequence exactly because it is designed to help you systematically explore your past, present, and future. Complete each exercise as instructed in order to gain its maximum benefit. The Personal Development Journal will become one distinct section of your Learning Log. You will be referring to it frequently throughout the course.

Log Exercises are another kind of writing you will be doing for this course. The Log Exercises are informal writings that are completed mostly for yourself. You are your own audience. These exercises are not to be worked through as if they were formal essay assignments. They will not be evaluated as finished pieces of writing. If they are evaluated, they will be checked only for completeness and productivity.

Spread throughout the text, often at the beginning of chapters or when we are changing from one topic to another, Log Exercises prepare the way for new material. The Log Exercises should help you in two ways. First, they will get you ready for new material by warming up your mind. Like the runner's calisthenics or the ballet dancer's routine at the *barre*, they make you stretch, so you do not strain as you work through the material that follows.

Second, they help you discover how much you already know about the material that will follow. We know much more about many things than we think we do. Much of our knowledge is stored deep in our memories. We need prompts to force that stored knowledge back into our immediate awareness. The Log Exercises provide the prompts. When we bring existing knowledge to our immediate awareness, we are better able to understand new information. Warmed up and aware, we can fit old and new together into a coherent whole. The Log Exercises will help you learn by reducing the strangeness of new material.

Your instructor will collect some of these exercises as you complete them in order to check your progress in the course. Your instructor may or may not want to inspect the complete Learning Log at the end of the course. In any event, remember that this is writing you are doing for yourself, to help you learn the most you can from this course. Keep all the materials from the course well organized in your Learning Log as a complete record of this course. You can then use it for future reference when you are writing for other courses.

COLLABORATION AND COMMUNITY

This course works on the principle that, like most important activities in life, writing is best learned as a collaborative activity. Many students believe that writing is a solitary act, a slow, sometimes torturous, form of punishment, which is about as enjoyable as a toothache. Those who have learned to write alone suffer through an assignment playing a guessing game, wondering whether they are doing the right thing, wondering whether they are making sense and communicating. The result of this guessing game is frustration.

One way to end this frustration is to write as part of a small peer group. Group members collaborate in order to help each other produce the best writing possible. Throughout this course, you will complete exercises in pairs or in small groups formed by you or by your instructor. You may be working with the same people all the time, or you may be working in various groups in order to learn different points of view. Follow your instructor's directions. Your peers will serve as a "real" audience on which you can test your writing as it is taking shape. They will give you specific information to improve your writing. And you will do the same for them.

Learning to write in collaboration with peers is important for two reasons. First, a great deal of the writing done in the work-world is done by collaboration. An engineering project report is completed in segments with the various members of the project team contributing pieces that are then compiled and revised as a single report. Managers, scientists, lawyers, and many other professionals often write in the same way. Thus, by writing in collaborative groups you will be gaining experience that will help you in your subsequent work.

A second important reason for writing in groups relates to how humans learn best. We learn best in a supportive environment where we feel part of a group in which each member is cooperating to accomplish a valuable task. In this case, you will be writing and sharing your writing in a cooperative community whose purpose is to help all its members become the best writers they can become. The class, a writing community, will provide real audiences and real responses that will help each writer grow and learn.

Your instructor will serve as an experienced writer, a model you can imitate. Your instructor understands the process of writing and knows about finding and using information, about structuring arguments, and about editing and proofreading to make sure an essay follows the rules of grammar and mechanics. Your instructor will guide you through the process and will strive to establish an open and cooperative environment where you can take chances and fail, find help, try again, and succeed.

The need to feel that you can fail is important. Failures provide opportunities for learning, growth, and success. Failures are steps along the pathway to learning. You, your classmates, and your instructor are part of a community in which all the members work together not to be stymied by failures but to push forward to realize potential.

LOG EXERCISE: What Is Good Writing?

An ancient Chinese proverb reminds us that the longest journey begins with the first step. The first step you must take as a writer is to define "good writing."

Begin by brainstorming a list of the characteristics of good writing. A brainstorm is a record of your thinking for a short time on a particular subject. When brainstorming, set a time limit, in this case ten minutes, and record as quickly as possible whatever comes to mind on the subject of good writing.

To begin your brainstorm on the characteristics of good writing, take a sheet of loose-leaf paper, record the date, put "Good Writing" at the top of the sheet as the title, and write whatever comes to mind. Do not worry about writing complete thoughts or grammatically correct sentences. Your job is to get as many ideas about good writing on the sheet as possible. Make the list legible enough that you can make sense of it when you are finished. Your list can include items as different as "letter from Pete about the new

baby brought tears to my eyes," "has complete sentences," "communicates clearly," and "impressive vocabulary."

If you are having a hard time getting started, think about something you have read that had a great impact on you. It could be a novel or short story, a personal letter, a poem, or maybe a book about science, history, or religion. It does not matter. What does matter is that you can remember its impact, so you can start brainstorming on good writing.

After ten minutes you should have a fairly long list of phrases and ideas about good writing. Review the list, and boil it down to two or three absolute fundamentals. From these write a one- or two-sentence definition of good writing.

Your definition will be a personal one which will probably differ from the definitions of others. Do not worry about getting the "correct answer." In this and in the other Log Exercises there is no single "correct answer." There are only productive responses.

GOOD WRITING DEFINED

Since good writing takes different shapes for different people at different times, no single definition covers all cases. However, writers like you have produced various general definitions. Here are a few:

Good writing is purposeful; it says something and says it
   correctly.

Good writing has "voice" and "energy."

Good writing is thoughtful and thought provoking.

Good writing communicates an important message clearly to
   its intended audience.

Good writing expresses the writer's self honestly and evokes
   a personal response in the reader.

Most often the specific definitions experienced writers create reflect the way writing fits into their work and lives. Engineers and scientists will emphasize brevity and conciseness; they want specific information communicated without the interference of opinion or ornate language. Lawyers will emphasize clarity and succinctness; they want the legal issue in question stated as simply and directly as possible. Philosophers will emphasize thoughtfulness. Poets will emphasize the harmony of sound and sense.

These definitions and varying emphases stress certain key variables, certain basics. They include the writer's sense of purpose and control of subject matter, the writer's sense of audience and its needs, the writer's control of language and use of structure to aid communication. In each instance, the "writer" forms the center of the definition. The writer must determine what is appropriate in terms of the purpose and audience for the writing. In short, good writing depends on a writer's choices.

Writing from the Inside Out assumes that good writing can be studied, practiced, and learned, and that you can learn to recognize alternatives and choose the best among them.

PART ONE

WRITING FOR THE INSIDE

CHAPTER 1

Keeping an Academic Journal

INTRODUCTION

Descriptions of good writing like those we just discussed often focus on the message communicated, on the "something" the writer said and why it was important. The message is most often what readers respond to. Who would disagree? But what such discussions of good writing fail to address is the process through which messages are discovered and then communicated. The first task in learning to write, then, is understanding and practicing the process of discovering things to write.

We will undertake two separate efforts. First, we will consider the close connection between writing and learning. To be successful in this writing course and in our personal and professional lives we must develop an aggressive, self-sufficient attitude toward learning that lets us make the most of what we know and are studying in school. In "Keeping an Academic Journal," we will discuss what it means to learn and examine ways we can use writing to and for ourselves to become aggressive learners.

Second, we will take the writing-learning interconnection very seriously and use it to make ourselves the subject of our own investigation. In "Keeping a Personal Journal," we will learn how to use writing to start paying close attention to ourselves so that we can discover who we are and begin to exert some effective control over where we are going. Mastering these two uses of WRITING FOR THE INSIDE, writing to learn about the world and writing to learn about ourselves, is the first step toward becoming a knowledgeable and confident writer who can then work on writing to communicate with readers.

LOG EXERCISE: The Learning Process

You have been about the business of your education for a long time now. In most cases, you have already spent twelve years in school and, in addition, have had many life experiences from which you have also learned. But have you ever taken time out to evaluate that education? The purpose of education is to promote learning, but many of us have never really thought about what it means to learn. This will be our subject in this exercise.

Your job now is to think and write your way to an informal definition of learning. A good way to get started is to think back over situations in which you remember having learned something. Think back over your schooling. Do you remember a particular class in which you learned a lot? What did you learn? How did you learn it? How do you know you learned it? If you can't remember learning much, think back over particularly bad courses and determine why you did not learn. What was missing?

The purpose of this exercise is to make you think about learning. Try especially hard to answer this question: "How do I know when I have learned something?"

Write this exercise in your Learning Log and be prepared to discuss your response and your conclusions with your classmates.

WRITING AND LEARNING

Long ago, Francis Bacon wrote, "Reading maketh a full man; conference a ready man; and writing an exact man." Bacon is writing about the various ways people prepare themselves to live in the world. We read and through reading gather information about subjects and situations far beyond our limited personal experience. We conference, talk, and argue with trusted friends and teachers, seeking their opinions, their wisdom, and the benefit of their experiences. And we write. Bacon placed special value on writing. In his terms, writing makes us "exact" because it empowers us, making us precise, fully knowledgeable, and able to control our lives.

To understand how writing does all this for us, we must consider what happens as we write. For most of us, writing is a struggle to understand and to make sense. Conceiving an idea in writing is something like being on the beach and staring out at the horizon. Far away there is a speck so poorly defined it could be anything. The speck moves closer and starts to take shape. In fact, it takes several shapes depending on what we associate with its vague outline. At one moment it seems to be a huge oil tanker; at the next, a solitary whale. Finally it is close enough for us to see clearly: it is a sea gull flying just above the waves.

As we write, we think and find our minds filled with sensations, impressions, and memories. But like the speck on the horizon, these assume no immediate shape. We glimpse some sort of an outline and direct ourselves to a particular subject, then the mind's energies—the sensations, impressions, and memories—organize themselves into a thought about something.

But the process is not complete. A slight shift in perspective will cause us to lose focus, and another image then takes shape. We refocus and recapture the original idea, but we have no reason to believe it has value by itself unless we expand the thought and connect it with others to create a more complete picture. Thus we must give our thoughts a recognizeable structure.

Once we structure them and make sense of them for ourselves, then we can try them out. We test them. We put them to work and see where they succeed and fail. We add what works to the bank of ideas from which we will build our final product. We dismiss thoughts that do not work or reshape them and test them in other ways to see if they have any value worth saving. We repeat this process until finally we have something, an essay or journal entry, perhaps only a paragraph or sentence. But we have something where before we had nothing. This is the miracle of writing.

The process of writing requires generating materials, connecting and structuring them, and evaluating and applying them. This is the same process as learning. We perceive or receive information, connect it to what we already know, test it by putting it to work in our lives, store what works, and dismiss or reevaluate what does not.

This is what you discovered in your Log exercise. Thinking about a rewarding class, you probably remember experiencing pleasure at encountering new information. You probably felt even better when you connected it with other information and came to understand how it made sense in itself and in various contexts. But the true feeling of accomplishment finally came when you put the information to use. In fact, some would say that you have not really learned something until you have put it to use. If you could not remember learning much in a class, you probably remember the confusion and frustration which came from having new information but not having a way to make sense of it or put it to use. If you remember only boredom, you're reacting to the absence of a sense of purpose. The class was pointless. Considered in these terms, the struggle to make sense—which is the process of writing—clearly resembles the process of learning—the collecting, connecting, and applying of information.

How far can we go in a comparison of writing and learning? Your own experience teaches that unlike most learning, or unlike what we remember about learning, writing is a slow and deliberate activity. Writing is not the same as reading. When reading, the brain registers information almost as quickly as our eyes move across the line of print. Neither is writing like daydreaming in which the mind jumps with lightning speed from subject to subject. Nor is writing like skating where we may once have had bruises to attest to our struggle to learn, but now don't even use our conscious memory while gliding around the rink. Writing is special because it is so slow and deliberate.

What is the point? Very simply, writing mimics the process of learning, but, because it is so slow and deliberate, it tames and concentrates the mind. Writing can be a powerful instrument for learning. Not only a way to collect and record what others have learned, it is also a way to make the connections, evaluations, and applications that are characteristic of learning.

ACADEMIC JOURNALS: THE WRITING-LEARNING CONNECTION

What does all this highfalutin talk about writing and learning have to do with you now? That's a good question, and here's the answer.

As a student in the early stages of your academic career, you are involved in the process of becoming generally educated. You are mastering fundamental skills like writing, oral expression, analytical reading and interpretation, basic mathematics, and others. You are accruing a broad range of basic information and discovering interrelations between various bodies of knowledge. History teaches you the relationships between past and present. Economics explains why supply and demand affect cost. Literature helps you appreciate the human struggle and the nobility of the human character. Every subject contributes to your store of knowledge. Each is like a single strand in a giant spider's web of knowledge and understanding.

Your job as a student is to master skills and learn information which you can put to work for yourself in your life. Much of your success later on will depend on your ability to fit the information into a coherent whole and to use your skills to show mastery of content and situations. Writing that you do for and by yourself about your courses and your reading can help you learn more and learn more effectively; they can give you the edge that allows you to disinguish yourself as a student now and to succeed later.

A well-kept academic journal, such as the Learning Log you are already keeping in this course, can serve as both an instrument for and a record of your learning and growth as a student. In an academic journal, you use writing to keep and organize records, to plan and set goals, to define and solve problems, and to reflect upon and evaluate the personal significance of the material and content of any course. Using the writing-learning connection, you can become an active and purposeful learner rather than a passive and directionless bystander. Using the writing-learning connection, you can explore, personalize, integrate, and master information and achieve understanding. The rest of this chapter will discuss ways you can develop good learning habits by keeping an academic journal for any course.

KEEPING AN ACADEMIC JOURNAL

To use an academic journal effectively, you must discipline yourself to pay attention and organize yourself to be productive. To this end, use flexible materials. A loose-leaf binder with plenty of paper is all you need to keep an academic journal. The binder makes collecting materials easy. You can conveniently move information from one section to another. You can add information and materials as they become available. You can reorganize and recombine as you learn more or take subsequent courses in the same area.

In the loose-leaf binder you will collect three kinds of writing: in-class materials, self-initiated responses, and personal commentaries, or what we will call "private papers." These three sections can encompass everything from lecture and class notes, to responses to readings and lectures, to personal complaints and applications of your learning. Successful learning requires aggressive participation, and keeping an academic journal promotes such participation.

Your academic journal is a kind of gymnasium where ideas play around and compete with one another as they define themselves and assume shape. Use it to develop the habit of paying attention. Keep yourself ready to learn. The origin of an insight might be a reading assignment, a class activity, or a comment by the instructor or a classmate. Be ready to write. Important breakthroughs sometimes come as lucky accidents: while you are eating breakfast one morning, a thought may form which helps you apply information learned in a class to some experience in your life. Record the event in your journal. Remember, you are responsible for making these connections and capturing them in writing. You are responsible for your own learning.

In-class Materials

The first kind of writing in an academic journal, in-class materials include lecture and class notes, handouts, formal exercises, returned exams and papers— everything that is part of the official record of the course. Remember, one of your purposes in keeping an academic journal is to amass a *complete* record of the course. Whenever an instructor distributes a handout, note the date and place a heading on it so you can identify it later, punch holes in the sides, and place it in the binder. Collect the in-class materials according to the chronology of the course. Because this chronology generally reflects the organization of topics in the course, you will have all the materials on a particular unit together. Your goal is to have easy reference to the materials of the course.

Keep your lecture notes with the in-class materials. Take notes with the idea that you will be coming back to them later, oftentimes with more information and understanding than you have while you are making them. While you are taking notes, consider the function of the information the instructor is providing. Is it new material supplementing what is available in readings or does it merely repeat what is available elsewhere? Is it factual so that you will have to remember it precisely? Is it conceptual so that you will have to be able to summarize and explain its significance? Don't record every word. Listen, consider the function, and record the information so you can use it to your advantage later.

For practical convenience, leave room on the sheet to revise and expand. Many students find it helpful to keep notes on only one side of a sheet of paper. This allows them a blank facing page in the binder to make more notes later. Some even draw a line down the middle of each sheet and keep their lecture notes only on the right side of that line. The blank space on the left gives them room to make more notations when they review their notes and reflect on the material. You might try similar techniques.

Most good learners review their notes immediately after a lecture. Go back over your fragments and phrases and bring them together. When you are reviewing, summarize key points. Write the summary in blank space next to the notes. Putting new or seemingly strange concepts into your own words—translating them from someone else's language into your own—will help you understand the concepts more effectively.

Just as important, while you are reviewing, evaluate how well you understand the material, how well you can fit the pieces together. If you do not understand the material, read or study more. Failing this, get whatever help you need when it can do some good. Don't wait until it is too late. Consult the instructor, a tutor if one is available, a friend who has already taken the course, or an informed classmate. Understanding a lecture is your responsibility.

Self-initiated Responses

The second kind of writing in an academic journal includes self-initiated responses to the materials of the course. Throughout a course, you can use informal writing of various types to come to master the material. Collect self-initiated responses wherever they fit in the chronology of the course.

One of the best reponses to new material is a form of intellectual doodling. Take some time to make yourself comfortable with new ideas and soften the anxious edge that often comes when dealing with unfamiliar materials. Attack a new topic or concept by brainstorming short informal statements of what you already know about it. You may discover that you already know quite a bit and that the new information does indeed connect with information you already have. Armed with a sense of familiarity and control, you will have an easier time fitting the various parts of the puzzle together.

Many students use their academic journals to review large blocks of material and to test and evaluate themselves before exams. You can do the same. Anticipate questions the instructor might ask and write answers for them. Share these potential questions and answers with classmates who have also created questions and answers. If the instructor provides study guides or practice exams, use them actively by planning and writing specific answers. Create outlines from study guides, commit the outlines to memory, and use them as skeleton answers you can expand upon during the exam. The very act of having already written the answer will help you remember more and do well on the exam. Do everything you can to prepare yourself in advance. Discover what you know and do not know, and devise plans to help you understand material if it is not clear. All these are techniques employed by successful students.

Aggressive Reading

Self-initiated responses also include writing about the reading you do for a course. One of the great benefits of keeping an academic journal is becoming a more effective reader. An instructor has too little class time and too much material to teach to permit spoonfeeding information to you. Thus, you are responsible for completing a process that only begins in the classroom. Instructors provide supplemental reading so you can fill in the rather sparse picture drawn in a class or lecture. This is how college works. One problem with this system, however, is that too many students do not know how to read aggressively and learn independently. The academic journal is the ideal place for you to respond to reading materials and use them to your maximum benefit.

Journal writing provides ways you can attack reading assignments and establish their significance and application. The flexibility of the loose-leaf binder allows for many possibilities. Reading notes can be compiled in a section separate from the class notes, or they can be placed in chronological order along with other materials in the journal as the semester progresses. However you place them into the journal, make sure they are clearly identifiable, so you can find them when it is time to go back and review.

The following journal activities for aggressive reading assume that you can read for basic comprehension, that you can identify main ideas and distinguish the details being used to support or elaborate them, and that you understand specialized vocabulary or know how to find the meaning of unfamiliar words. These activities force you beyond simple understanding toward true learning; they require interpreting, criticizing, and applying the information offered in a reading assignment. These exercises take you well beyond the "basics" of reading. If you have difficulty reading, or if you feel you read slowly and do not remember what you should, get some help from your college's learning center or reading lab. Many colleges offer short self-improvement courses to bolster basic skills. Take advantage of them if they are available. There is no shame in getting help. The shame is in failing when failure is avoidable. A little bit of time and effort now can have huge payoffs later.

These activities, explanations, and examples have been developed and used successfully by students keeping academic journals in various courses:

1. Preview the Text

Use the title, introduction, conclusion, headings, graphics and other visual aids, topic sentences of paragraphs, review questions, and so forth to preview a reading assignment and prepare yourself for the information to follow. Such a preview will let you know what to expect as you read the material.

After the preview, formulate two specific questions you want to be able to answer after completing the reading. When reading for a science course, you might ask how certain particulars fit together; for example, "How does the structure of the vertebrate brain reflect the general principles of evolution?" When reading for a literature course, you might ask questions concerning characters: "What drove Roderick Usher crazy in 'The Fall of the House of Usher'?" Productive questions are not difficult to phrase. As you read, look for the answers to your questions.

After reading, spend time writing answers in your journal. This previewing, questioning, and answering procedure will make you an active reader and greatly improve the quality of your learning.

2. Mark the Text

As you read, mark the text for difficult concepts, important points and definitions, or points you agree or disagree with. Mark these areas with a check mark or star. Do not spend a lot of time underlining. Do not try to understand everything as you read through for the first time. Often problems of understanding will be solved as you continue reading. Excessive underlining often retards comprehension rather than aiding it. After you complete the reading, go back to the spots you have marked and make notes. Now underline important information you missed the first time through. Record information like definitions in your journal. This procedure will help make you a more efficient reader.

3. Assess Your Understanding

Stop in the middle of a reading assignment, especially when the writer is moving from one important point to another, and assess what you have already learned or question what is about to follow.

While keeping an academic journal, you must learn to pay attention to the signals writers provide to help you through a reading. For example, in the middle of a reading, when it is time to review and reflect, the writer will often provide a new heading or some extra white space or an obvious transitional sentence signalling a shift from one idea to another. In a sense, the writer is providing you with a traffic signal, something like a stop sign. Recognizing this sign, you must slow down, stop, look both ways, then, having determined the road is clear, you can proceed with caution. A good way to do this is to underline a phrase or sentence from the reading, write it out in your journal, and then respond to it in your own words. Saving the quote by copying it into your journal and responding to it in your own words will help you remember both that idea and the whole reading assignment.

For example, responding to the paragraph above, you might underline and recopy the phrase "the writer is providing you a traffic signal, something like a stop sign," and respond:

> Reading requires more than being a passenger on a train — the train can only lead where the tracks take it. No, it is more like driving a car — I am the driver and I determine where it is going and how fast I want it to go. Of course, the idea is to stay on the road and arrive safely where the road — the reading — is directing me.

Note how this short reflection on a particular quote not only applies to the article in question but also is a generalization about reading and studying in all situations. Academic journals work best when you use them to connect your personal experience with the lessons your courses and readings offer.

4. Distill Key Points

After completing a reading assignment, brainstorm a list of its important points. Determine which points are most important and use them to write a two- or three-sentence summary of the entire assignment. Then, again briefly, address why the article has significance for you.

Pat Mease wrote the following distillation in response to one of the sections of Thomas Merton's *Wisdom of the Desert*, a book she was reading in conjunction with a writing and philosophy course in which she kept an academic journal. Note how she moves from a general summary to analysis of significance, especially in terms of what she might do with an idea "borrowed" from Merton.

Summary:
Don't try to remove all pain and trouble from your life, but learn how to constructively battle temptations and evil. The soul is only matured through turmoil.

Significance:
Illustrates the problem of seeking something which doesn't help you grow, but makes you feel 'perfect,' which isn't always desirable. Shows how to make conflict & problems work for you. Would make a good short story subject theme.

5. Evaluate Key Points

After reading, spend some time thinking and writing about how the main points of the article either affirm or contradict your experiences. How does this new information relate to things you already know? What have you discovered that is new?

It is important to connect what the reading has to offer with your own experience. For example, Jack Rogers uncovered some important insights about Hawthorne's *The Scarlet Letter* and the current controversies surrounding TV evangelists and their private lives and habits.

I'm sitting in my room trying to read while my roommate is glaring at the news on the TV tube. I'm distracted. They are interviewing a young woman who seems to have been one of the main entertainments at the Rev's big party in Florida. While I am watching, I see an "A," a big scarlet "A," taking shape on her chest. I know that this is not really happening – but I see it anyway.

Amazing.

It's 1987 and we are making the same mistakes and reacting to human sin and imperfection in the same way. No child will be born from this incident, but the sin has been preserved forever in videotapes.

Rev. Dimmesdale's pulpit is no longer held within a single church in Salem. Now he enters every home hooked up to cable. And the scorn and disappointment people feel when they learn that their preacher has strayed, despite his fine words and public piety, is increased in magnitude. It is a public issue, a national concern. News!

America and her people – not much has changed; everything has gotten bigger, no one seems to be able to hide dirty laundry very well. What's the lesson? I know I don't like it. Some things are private and should remain between the person and God alone or kept in the confessional.

Jack's response to *The Scarlet Letter* is interesting on several levels. First and most important, we must note that he's taken contemporary incidents and personal experience and connected them with Hawthorne's novel, which he was studying in an American literature course. Jack was using the academic journal to pay attention to the world, using what his education is offering him. The more we can see connections between our lives and what we study in school, the more we will learn and understand. In addition, Jack was remarking on the continuing human problem of public piety and private imperfection. Although the scorn and disappointment may be more in him than in Hawthorne's book, he makes a good point, "America and her people—not much has changed." Of course, the insights are not fully developed, but this response is a piece of sand in an oyster which in time and with more development could become a pearl of a paper for that literature class. The academic journal, when used to pay attention and speculate freely about the relevance and application of school learning to living, can become a bank of insights.

6. Question the Author

After reading, formulate two questions you would ask the writer if you were given the opportunity. Write an informal letter, asking the questions as specifically and precisely as possible. Then think through your questions, do some research, or consult with the instructor to find the answers to your questions.

Margie Zalinka worked through *Walden* in an advanced composition course. She asked Thoreau a very specific question about an allusion in the text which she did not understand:

> Dear Mr. Thoreau:
>
> You don't know me and it's likely we will never meet, but I wanted to tell you that your book Walden has made a great impression on me. Since reading it through the first time, I have returned to it again and again, and each time I see something that had escaped me before. It seems to contain more distilled truth and beauty than any other book I have read.
>
> I'm sure you must be plagued by readers with questions about your work and yourself.

At the risk of adding just one more voice to the babble, may I ask you one question?

In the section "Economy" is a paragraph which begins: " I long ago lost a hound, a bay horse, and a turtledove, and I am still on their trail." What is the significance of these three animals?

For me, many of the wonders of <u>Walden</u> are found in the different levels of meaning underlying apparently simple statements. In this instance, though, I don't know where to look for understanding. Is this an allusion to myth? Is it a classical reference? Is it to be taken literally?

I confess I cannot see where this passage comes from or where it goes. There, I promised only one question but ended asking four.

I won't take any more of your time, but I look forward to your explanation of this (for me, at least) most puzzling paragraph.

Most respectfully,

Margie Zalinka

When Margie mentioned this letter and the question it contained in class, many students admitted the same curiosity. They had learned one of the lessons of *Walden*, that appearances can be deceiving, that as readers we need to look closely and pry deeply.

In fact, all through *Walden*'s history readers and critics have speculated about those three animals. The speculations range far and wide. Some are interesting, some are not. The point is, however, that in raising this question as she did, Margie allowed the instructor to guide the students through the various speculations, thus providing them more information and insights about *Walden*. The questions, especially as they are framed in journal letters, can greatly aid learning and understanding.

You also should realize that writing a letter often results in receiving a letter back. If you are reading a living writer's work, consider sending the letter you wrote. You might get an answer. Generally, you can reach the writer by sending the letter in care of the book's publisher. (If you have any questions for me, write me at Box 3E, English Department, New Mexico State University, Las Cruces, NM 88003. You may not get a response within two weeks, but you will get a response.)

7. Apply a Key Point

After reading an assignment, devise a specific application of one of its key points. How will it change the way you have thought about or dealt with the material previously? If your application involves doing something, try it, and evaluate its success after your attempt.

The following academic journal entry by Cathleen McLane illustrates just how writing can circle around several points, ultimately coming to a resolution and application which may have huge implications. In this excerpt, she is responding to Robert Pirsig's *Zen and the Art of Motorcycle Maintenance*, which she was reading in a philosophy and writing seminar. She was moved by the predicament that confronts and almost destroys Chris, the young son of the book's narrator, because it is similar to a situation she herself had experienced. By comparing the real and the fictional, by developing a tangible application of information offered in the book, she comes to know both better. She questions why many people act as they do, and then she resolves to change the way she acts.

> Coming back to *Zen and the Art of Motorcycle Maintenance* is like coming home for Christmas vacation. The fifth time through it starts to grow on you; you start to get less and less bogged down by the philosophy and more into the honest-to-God humanity of the book....
>
> I saw Chris as nothing more than an innocent bystander to the whole process. In Chris I saw myself over nine years ago trying to understand how my father had died and my mother had gotten so ill within the space of 1 month. Chris reacted and behaved as I had when I was

under the care of my brother, or in the limbo between one family that had been exploded and another one. I was going at speeds so astounding I can't remember half of what I said or did....

Never did I realize how close to the edge Chris must've been, I must've been in that year. Only now through the healing distance of time has anything begun to make sense.

... I cannot countenance a world where there are so many people around us who can help, but don't. I wonder why my friends aren't always there when I need them, why I'm not always there when they need me.... Are they blind, am I blind, and why? Why does our society let people have the freedom to hurt themselves when there are so many of us around to throw out a lifeline....

For every time bomb walking among us there are a thousand potential diffusers who never go into action. People get so pent up making themselves into rugged individualists that they forget they aren't, and can never hope to be true Robinson Crusoes. We all need our Man Fridays, our support groups — not encounter groups, but support groups — that can tell us when we're taking ourselves too seriously, and when we're not taking ourselves seriously enough.

The fine minds that reside in the Pirsigs, the Kerouacs, and others of the world should come down out of their books if they can and tell us that they really did live among us. I want to see more of them on talk shows and news programs turning the vast wasteland of our media into an oasis. No more of the absolute shyness which oftentimes sets them up as "oh so ethereal and oh so intellectual."

> *I mean they need to come down to us and make us stop analyzing their books and tell us to start living our lives in a way that will keep us from concentrating on the unproductive pursuit of individualism, in a global community. We must refuse to let our fellows fall by the wayside so long as we see or suspect that they are stumbling.*

Experiment with these exercises designed to make you an aggressive reader and a more effective learner. The academic journal, as a place for recording, summarizing, focusing, centering, questioning, and interpreting, is one of the student's most valuable resources. Use it to make your reading worthwhile.

LOG EXERCISE: Aggressive Reading

To gain some practice with aggressive reading strategies, complete the following exercise as a class activity. The following essay, "Were Dinosaurs Dumb?" comes from Steven Jay Gould's *The Panda's Thumb* (New York: Norton, 1980), a collection of Gould's monthly columns from the journal *Natural History*. "Were Dinosaurs Dumb?" is a particularly wide-ranging essay that uses the logic, method, and theories of biology, paleontology, and archaeology to question and attack some of the popular myths about dinosaurs. As a result, Gould helps us understand our role as human beings in the great drama of nature.

The essay provides opportunities for each of the "aggressive reading" exercises we have discussed. For convenience, a list of the exercises follows:

1. Preview the text
2. Mark the text
3. Assess your understanding
4. Distill key points
5. Evaluate key points
6. Question the author
7. Apply a key point

For this exercise, complete three of the seven activities. Compile the work in your Learning Log and be prepared to share the results in small groups or with your class.

WERE DINOSAURS DUMB?

1   When Muhammad Ali flunked his army intelligence test, he quipped (with a wit that belied his performance on the exam): "I only said I was the greatest; I never said I was the smartest." In our metaphors and fairy tales, size and power

are almost always balanced by a want of intelligence. Cunning is the refuge of the little guy. Think of Br'er Rabbit and Br'er Bear; David smiting Goliath with a slingshot; Jack chopping down the beanstalk. Slow wit is the tragic flaw of a giant.

2   The discovery of dinosaurs in the nineteenth century provided, or so it appeared, a quintessential case for the negative correlation of size and smarts. With their pea brains and giant bodies, dinosaurs became a symbol of lumbering stupidity. Their extinction seemed only to confirm their flawed design.

3   Dinosaurs were not even granted the usual solace of a giant—great physical prowess. God maintained a discreet silence about the brains of behemoth, but he certainly marveled at its strength: "Lo, now, his strength is in his loins, and his force is in the navel of his belly. He moveth his tail like a cedar. . . . His bones are as strong pieces of brass; his bones are like bars of iron [Job 40:16–18]." Dinosaurs, on the other hand, have usually been reconstructed as slow and clumsy. In the standard illustration, *Brontosaurus* wades in a murky pond because he cannot hold up his own weight on land.

4   Popularizations for grade school curricula provide a good illustration of prevailing orthodoxy. I still have my third grade copy (1948 edition) of Bertha Morris Parker's *Animals of Yesterday,* stolen, I am forced to suppose, from P.S. 26, Queens (sorry Mrs. McInerney). In it, boy (teleported back to the Jurassic) meets brontosaur:

> It is huge, and you can tell from the size of its head that it must be stupid. . . . This giant animal moves about very slowly as it eats. No wonder it moves slowly! Its huge feet are very heavy, and its great tail is not easy to pull around. You are not surprised that the thunder lizard likes to stay in the water so that the water will help it hold up its huge body. . . . Giant dinosaurs were once the lords of the earth. Why did they disappear? You can probably guess part of the answer—their bodies were too large for their brains. If their bodies had been smaller, and their brains larger, they might have lived on.

5   Dinosaurs have been making a strong comeback of late, in this age of "I'm OK, you're OK." Most paleontologists are now willing to view them as energetic, active, and capable animals. The *Brontosaurus* that wallowed in its pond a generation ago is now running on land, while pairs of males have been seen twining their necks about each other in elaborate sexual combat for access to females (much like the neck wrestling of giraffes). Modern anatomical reconstructions indicate strength and agility, and many paleontologists now believe that dinosaurs were warmblooded.

6   The idea of warmblooded dinosaurs has captured the public imagination and received a torrent of press coverage. Yet another vindication of dinosaurian capability has received very little attention, although I regard it as equally significant. I refer to the issue of stupidity and its correlation with size. The revisionist interpretation, which I support in this column, does not enshrine dinosaurs as paragons of intellect, but it does maintain that they were not small brained after all. They had the "right-sized" brains for reptiles of their body size.

7   I don't wish to deny that the flattened, minuscule head of largebodied *Stegosaurus* houses little brain from our subjective, top-heavy perspective, but I do wish to assert that we should not expect more of the beast. First of all, large animals have relatively smaller brains than related, small animals. The correlation of brain size with body size among kindred animals (all reptiles, all mammals, for example) is remarkably regular. As we move from small to large animals, from mice to elephants or small lizards to Komodo dragons, brain size increases, but not so fast as body size. In other words, bodies grow faster than brains, and large animals have low ratios of brain weight to body weight. In fact, brains grow only about two-thirds as fast as bodies. Since we have no reason to believe that large animals are consistently stupider than their smaller relatives, we must conclude that large animals require relatively less brain to do as well as smaller animals. If we do not recognize this relationship, we are likely to underestimate the mental power of very large animals, dinosaurs in particular.

8   Second, the relationship between brain and body size is not identical in all groups of vertebrates. All share the same rate of relative decrease in brain size, but small mammals have much larger brains than small reptiles of the same body weight. This discrepancy is maintained at all larger body weights, since brain size increases at the same rate in both groups—two-thirds as fast as body size.

9   Put these two facts together—all large animals have relatively small brains, and reptiles have much smaller brains than mammals at any common body weight—and what should we expect from a normal, large reptile? The answer, of course, is a brain of very modest size. No living reptile even approaches a middle-sized dinosaur in bulk, so we have no modern standard to serve as a model for dinosaurs.

10   Fortunately, our imperfect fossil record has, for once, not severely disappointed us in providing data about fossil brains. Superbly preserved skulls have been found for many species of dinosaurs, and cranial capacities can be measured. (Since brains do not fill craniums in reptiles, some creative, although not unreasonable, manipulation must be applied to estimate brain size from the hole within a skull.) With these data, we have a clear test for the conventional hypothesis of dinosaurian stupidity. We should agree, at the outset, that a reptilian standard is the only proper one—it is surely irrelevant that dinosaurs had smaller brains than people or whales. We have abundant data on the relationship of brain and body size in modern reptiles. Since we know that brains increase two-thirds as fast as bodies as we move from small to large living species, we can extrapolate this rate to dinosaurian sizes and ask whether dinosaur brains match what we would expect of living reptiles if they grew so large.

11   Harry Jerison studied the brain sizes of ten dinosaurs and found that they fell right on the extrapolated reptilian curve. Dinosaurs did not have small brains; they maintained just the right-sized brains for reptiles of their dimensions. So much for Ms. Parker's explanation of their demise.

12   Jerison made no attempt to distinguish among various kinds of dinosaurs; ten species distributed over six major groups scarcely provide a proper basis for comparison. Recently, James A. Hopson of the University of Chicago gathered more data and made a remarkable and satisfying discovery.

13   Hopson needed a common scale for all dinosaurs. He therefore compared each dinosaur brain with the average reptilian brain we would expect at its body weight. If the dinosaur falls on the standard reptilian curve, its brain receives a value of 1.0 (called an encephalization quotient, or EQ—the ratio of actual brain to expected brain for a standard reptile of the same body weight). Dinosaurs lying above the curve (more brain than expected in a standard reptile of the same body weight) receives values in excess of 1.0, while those below the curve measure less than 1.0.

14   Hopson found that the major groups of dinosaurs can be ranked by increasing values of average EQ. This ranking corresponds perfectly with inferred speed, agility and behavioral complexity in feeding (or avoiding the prospect of becoming a meal). The giant sauropods, *Brontosaurus* and its allies, have the lowest EQ's— 0.20 to 0.35. They must have moved fairly slowly and without great maneuverability. They probably escaped predation by virtue of their bulk alone, much as elephants do today. The armored ankylosaurs and stegosaurs come next with EQ's of 0.52 to 0.56. These animals, with their heavy armor, probably relied largely upon passive defense, but the clubbed tail of ankylosaurs and the spiked tail of stegosaurs imply some active fighting and increased behavioral complexity.

15   The ceratopsians rank next at about 0.7 to 0.9. Hopson remarks: "The larger ceratopsians, with their great horned heads, relied on active defensive strategies and presumably required somewhat greater agility than the tail-weaponed forms, both in fending off predators and in intraspecific combat bouts. The smaller ceratopsians, lacking true horns, would have relied on sensory acuity and speed to escape from predators." The ornithopods (duckbills and their allies) were the brainiest herbivores, with EQ's from 0.85 to 1.5. They relied upon "acute senses and relatively fast speeds" to elude carnivores. Flight seems to require more acuity and agility than standing defense. Among ceratopsians, small, hornless, and presumably fleeing *Protoceratops* had a higher EQ than great three-horned *Triceratops*.

16   Carnivores have higher EQ's than herbivores, as in modern vertebrates. Catching a rapidly moving or stoutly fighting prey demands a good deal more upstairs than plucking the right kind of plant. The giant theropods (*Tyrannosaurus* and its allies) vary from 1.0 to nearly 2.0. Atop the heap, quite appropriately at its small size, rests the little coelurosaur *Stenonychosaurus* with an EQ well above 5.0. Its actively moving quarry, small mammals and birds perhaps, probably posed a greater challenge in discovery and capture than *Triceratops* afforded *Tyrannosaurus*.

17   I do not wish to make a naive claim that brain size equals intelligence or, in this case, behavioral range and agility (I don't know what intelligence means in humans, much less in a group of extinct reptiles). Variation in brain size within a species has precious little to do with brain power (humans do equally well with 900 or 2,500 cubic centimeters of brain). But comparison across species, when the differences are large, seems reasonable. I do not regard it as irrelevant to our achievements that we so greatly exceed koala bears—much as I love them—in EQ. The sensible ordering among dinosaurs also indicates that even so coarse a measure as brain size counts for something.

18   If behavioral complexity is one consequence of mental power, then we might expect to uncover among dinosaurs some signs of social behavior that demand coordination, cohesiveness, and recognition. Indeed we do, and it cannot be accidental that these signs were overlooked when dinosaurs labored under the burden of a falsely imposed obtuseness. Multiple trackways have been uncovered, with evidence for more than twenty animals traveling together in parallel movement. Did some dinosaurs live in herds? At the Davenport Ranch sauropod trackway, small footprints lie in the center and larger ones at the periphery. Could it be that some dinosaurs traveled much as some advanced herbivorous mammals do today, with large adults at the borders sheltering juveniles in the center?

19   In addition, the very structures that seemed most bizarre and useless to older paleontologists—the elaborate crests of hadrosaurs, the frills and horns of ceratopsians, and the nine inches of solid bone above the brain of *Pachycephalosaurus*—now appear to gain a coordinated explanation as devices for sexual display and combat. Pachycephalosaurs may have engaged in head-butting contests much as mountain sheep do today. The crests of some hadrosaurs are well designed as resonating chambers; did they engage in bellowing matches? The ceratopsian horn and frill may have acted as sword and shield in the battle for mates. Since such behavior is not only intrinsically complex, but also implies an elaborate social system, we would scarcely expect to find it in a group of animals barely muddling through at a moronic level.

20   But the best illustration of dinosaurian capability may well be the fact most often cited against them—their demise. Extinction, for most people, carries many of the connotations attributed to sex not so long ago—a rather disreputable business, frequent in occurrence, but not to anyone's credit, and certainly not to be discussed in proper circles. But, like sex, extinction is an ineluctable part of life. It is the ultimate fate of all species, not the lot of unfortunate and ill-designed creatures. It is no sign of failure.

21   The remarkable thing about dinosaurs is not that they became extinct, but that they dominated the earth for so long. Dinosaurs held sway for 100 million years while mammals, all the while, lived as small animals in the interstices of their world. After 70 million years on top, we mammals have an excellent track record and good prospects for the future, but we have yet to display the staying power of dinosaurs.

22   People, on this criterion, are scarcely worth mentioning—5 million years perhaps since *Australopithecus,* a mere 50,000 for our own species, *Homo sapiens.* Try the ultimate test within our system of values: Do you know anyone who would wager a substantial sum, even at favorable odds, on the proposition that *Homo sapiens* will last longer than *Brontosaurus?*

Private Papers

Have you ever felt mentally fogbound and wished a strong wind would come along to blow that fog away? Writing is a good way to create some wind and clear the air. Sometimes the fog comes up in the middle of a course or a reading assignment, and we need to clear the air and get ourselves unstuck. Private Papers provide just that opportunity. It is the third and last kind of writing kept in an academic journal.

Private papers contain personal entries focused on a particular subject or on problems associated with the course. Writers use private papers to complain about how much work they must do, how lost they feel, how little they understand, how sure they are that they will do poorly on an upcoming exam, how the exams are unfair, how the instructor dislikes them personally, how the lectures are boring, and so on. You get the point. In private papers, students get things off their chests; the writing clears the air so they can get back to work.

However, often there is more than mere ranting and raving. Often a private papers entry uncovers a problem you can solve. For example, you're writing an entry about how famished and distracted you get during a class at a time that is normally your lunch hour. You get so hungry that you can't pay attention to the discussion. You only want the class to be over so you can go and eat. While writing about this, you realize that you can bring something to the class to eat so you can survive until lunch without any problem. You would no longer be distracted and could pay better attention. Writing a private papers entry allowed you to discover and solve a problem and helped you become a more effective student.

Some students keep private papers with other class notes and entries in the regular chronology of their academic journals. Because they are not really part of the official record of the course, you might prefer to keep them in a separate section in the back of your binder. Later you can determine whether to put them into the journal or to throw them away.

Conclusion

Now that you have a sense of all that you can do in an academic journal, try keeping one in each of your courses. The journal will help you learn more and learn more efficiently. Through it you are creating records that document your learning. What a valuable reference tool these journals can become later! Look at them as something you do for and by yourself, as a celebration of learning and growth through WRITING FOR THE INSIDE.

CHAPTER 2

Keeping a Personal Journal

INTRODUCTION: WRITING AND PERSONAL DEVELOPMENT

Now that you have used personal writing to learn about the world in an academic journal, it's time to use personal writing and the writing-learning connection to make yourself the subject of your study. This chapter will demonstrate how writing can be used for personal development. It presents a sequence of exercises designed to help you come to know yourself. You will be writing about you and for you. You will be WRITING FOR THE INSIDE. This is the next step toward WRITING FOR THE OUTSIDE. Moving from the inside out requires that you know yourself as well as the world.

The Past and the Present

Most of us recognize the platitude "to thine own self be true." According to Polonius in Shakespeare's *Hamlet*, if we remain true to ourselves, we can "not then be false to any man." But what is this self to which we must be true? What influence does it exert on our lives?

Think of the self as what stands between our past experience and the world of the present and future. The self is a collection of patterns of behaviors and habits that we have developed from our past experiences to organize our lives and help us manage new experiences. That self is comprised of many elements—our biology, our family, our schooling, our culture, and more.

In large part, the self determines how we respond to new experiences based on how it has responded to previous experiences. We act as we have been taught to act by previous experiences. For many of us this fact causes a problem. We are so involved in living our lives in the present that we really are not aware of our past experiences and how they influence us. Or we have given considerable thought to our past experiences, but, dulled by habit, we fail to apply their lessons to our present needs. The result, the problem, is that we act in the present without understanding why we do what we do. We too often act without purpose and control. Disregarding the influence of past experiences on the present, we overlook the influence of the present on the future. Even now the present is becoming our past and the future our present.

Developing self-awareness can help us solve this problem. We need specific activities through which we can examine our past experiences, understand their influence, control them, and use them to our advantage. We need to come to know ourselves, learn to be true, and begin to live our lives the way we want to.

KEEPING A PERSONAL JOURNAL

Keeping a personal journal helps us develop awareness of the various influences directing our behavior. With awareness can come control. A personal journal helps us monitor our personal and psychic health. It causes us to pay attention, note imbalances, and try to correct them. It lets us reflect and soothe the wounds of day-to-day life. It lets us relive victories. It lets us puzzle over life's mysteries. It lets us celebrate our love for life and for one another.

But most people do not take advantage of the benefits a personal journal offers. Some do not know how to start keeping a personal journal. Others start one but do not know how to continue it productively. The program presented in this chapter will provide you a thorough introduction to keeping a personal journal. Working through the Personal Development Journal (hereafter referred to as the PDJ) will start you keeping a personal journal. You will experience its joys and benefits. Having finished the PDJ, you will be prepared to keep a personal journal in whatever form you want for the rest of your life. You will also be writing about experiences, personal concerns, and issues which will become the subjects for essays later in this course.

THE LENS OF SELF

Keeping the PDJ is a technique we will use to begin to come to know ourselves. Consider for a moment that the self stands between the past and the future in the same way that the lens of an eye stands between the inside world of our minds and the outside world. Writing the PDJ is something like having an eye examination. We will be looking closely at the composition of the self to discover imperfections in our vision. The death of a beloved grandparent, for example, may have distorted the lens, causing us to need glasses to see clearly.

We will look to see if there are not some specks of dust and smudges collecting on our lenses as we live our lives. Missing a close friend is like a speck of dust interfering with our vision. A fight with a loved one creates a smudge, clouding everything in our view. Through the PDJ, we will be working on the lens of the self, learning how to wash and care for it to maintain clear vision. Coming to know ourselves truly will take our whole lives, but writing in the PDJ can begin the process and make it manageable and enjoyable. The PDJ will help us see ahead and allow us to choose a clear path.

Over the next two weeks, this program of exercises will show you all that personal journal keeping can do for you. Through the 14-day cycle, you will learn things about yourself that you did not know, and you will start establishing real goals you can begin working to achieve. You will encounter problems and ways to solve those problems. You will discover interests and perhaps begin a life-long study. You will find subjects to use later when writing essays. You will also have created verbal "snapshots" that you can pull out from time to time to look over and reminisce. You will finish the PDJ with a greater sense of self, and an understanding of how journal keeping can contribute to your sense of self. You can use or later adapt the journal-keeping program as you choose.

THE PERSONAL DEVELOPMENT JOURNAL: OVERVIEW

There is rigor involved in keeping the PDJ. You will need to find a quiet and restful place where you can write for one hour on each of the next 14 days. Follow the cycle exactly, writing the exercises in the sequence suggested. Write only one exercise per day. The cycle will end when you have written every exercise. Also, do not skip an exercise. One feeds into another. If you are having difficulty with a particular exercise, do not walk away from it. Give it your best shot and do all that you can to complete it.

Consider these exercises as a type of directed freewriting. Write for yourself. Your job is to get as many ideas down on paper as possible. Do not let spelling, word choice, or the conventions of grammar and mechanics interfere with getting the ideas down. But remember to take enough care with each exercise so that you will be able to come back and make sense of it. The final exercise requires you to review and evaluate all you have done in the PDJ. Make sure you will be able to understand what you will be going back to.

There are four kinds of exercises in the program cycle. The first kind, **Centering**, asks you to write about your present. You will brainstorm on all the sensations you are experiencing, distill from them a metaphor that describes you in relation to these sensations, and, finally, reflect upon and evaluate the significance of the sensations and the metaphor. The **Centering** exercises allow you to establish a solid base, a "center." They help you learn who you are right here and now so you can reflect productively upon your past and future.

The second kind, **Reminiscence**, directs you to think and write about your past and what it means to you. You will write first about a place, then about a person. Both of these must have great meaning for you because this meaning will provide the energy that enables you to write the exercises. Next, you will create a dialog, something like a scene from a play, in which you discuss your current life with someone from your past. Finally, you will write a myth or a fable about your family or one of your ancestors. The **Reminiscence** exercises will make you aware of your past and how that past shapes your values and beliefs. These values and beliefs create the conscious or unconscious code that guides your everyday behavior. Each exercise will end with an analysis designed to help you make positive use of the influence the past has on you. Awareness can lead to control and allow you to make purposeful choices about your life.

The third kind, **Cinema,** invites you to write about your future. You will write a "milestone," an imaginary obituary, in which you present the major accomplishments of your ideal life and suggest their significance. You will write a scenario dealing with the near future in which you are featured as a successful person who has achieved control and is enjoying life. You will write an "acceptance speech" to deliver when you receive an award of great distinction in your field. Finally, you will write another scenario, this time as a contented person nearing the twilight years of life. The **Cinema** exercises allow you to project an ideal future. The analytical sections in each exercise ask you to consider whether your dreams are realistic and what you might do now to begin accomplishing them.

The complete cycle of the PDJ is designed to help you ascertain where you are, where you have been, and where you would like to be going. With this perspective of present, past, and future, you can examine yourself, decide what roads you might want to follow, and start out. The final exercise, **Reflections,** will ask you to review and assess all that you have done in the PDJ. Its purpose is to make you focus, evaluate, and draw some conclusions.

Privacy, Support, and Evaluation

Many students who are asked to keep journals frequently ask about their privacy and about how the journal will be evaluated. Although the PDJ is written for the self and about the self, writers sometimes find it difficult to probe deeply toward the truth because they suspect their writings might be read and evaluated by the instructor. They consider such reading an invasion of privacy, and they wonder how an instructor could say one journal is adequate, another inadequate, and yet another distinctive. To solve the problem, writers sometimes purposely avoid certain important but potentially revealing or embarrassing subjects. They stick close to the surface. They refuse to take chances because they are concerned about their safety, about what might be done by others with the information they reveal. At the same time, however, these writers deny themselves much of the benefit of the journal-writing exercises.

There are several ways to solve the problem of privacy. The first is to maintain absolute privacy and show the PDJ to no one. This is not a good way to work through the program. Many journal-keepers want to share their feelings and findings, either by talking or by sharing actual journal exercises with others, including the instructor.

Often sharing helps the process of self-discovery and personal growth. Sometimes as a journal-keeper you may feel entirely alone and isolated, that you are the only one in the entire cosmos who must confront problems. Talking with some-one else often allows you to discover that others are dealing with problems too, sometimes with the same problems. Knowing this, you no longer feel isolated or strange and find comfort and hope in being like others.

In addition, if you encounter a particularly difficult problem, one that you can-not resolve for yourself, you may need to talk with someone else. In such instances, your instructor can be very helpful. As a concerned person, your instructor will be able to give you some help, especially by knowing whom you should see for coun-seling, if necessary. If you do not feel comfortable talking with your instructor about this kind of problem, search out other available resources like your college's coun-seling center. Remember, there is nothing wrong with getting help. In fact, getting help is healthy.

The typical way of dealing with the PDJ in a class context is to complete the exercises as instructed, organize and prepare it neatly in your three-ring binder, and submit it to your instructor for inspection. Often instructors will advise writers to clearly identify particular parts that are not to be read. An exercise can be taken out of the binder and a sheet inserted explaining why the exercise is missing. An exercise can be folded in half and stapled or taped shut. This allows an instructor to see that the exercise was done but it is not to be read. Sometimes writers are particularly happy with an exercise, and they want it read. They note this so the instructor will read and perhaps respond.

The instructor will not read all of your PDJ. You wrote it for yourself. The in-structor will spot check to see that it is complete and that you took the exercises seriously. The instructor will evaluate the PDJ with these two criteria in mind: Is it complete? Is the writing serious? Meeting these criteria, your PDJ will be consid-ered successful, and you will be given credit. That is all the evaluation there nor-mally will be. The payoff, after all, is for you, the writer, who has worked on the inside, who has created a firm foundation for learning to write for the outside. And you have uncovered a wide range of subjects for subsequent writing.

Remember, the PDJ is an invitation to a journey, a journey inside toward the discovery of self. Begin in high spirits, like the poet Walt Whitman, who took a similar journey:

> Afoot and light-hearted I take to the open road,
> Healthy, free, the world before me,
> The long brown path before me leading wherever I choose.

AN INTENSIVE PERSONAL JOURNAL PROGRAM

SCHEDULE

The 14-day cycle of exercises follows. You will receive complete directions, and, where appropriate, examples for each day's exercise. Write all the exercises on loose-leaf paper and collect them in your three-ring binder as a separate section of your Learning Log. The full schedule of the exercises is arranged like this:

Day One—Centering One
Day Two—Reminiscence: Place
Day Three—Cinema: Milestone
Day Four—Centering Two
Day Five—Reminiscence: Person
Day Six—Cinema: Noonlight
Day Seven—Centering Three
Day Eight—Reminiscence: Dialog
— Day Nine—Cinema: Acceptance Speech
Day Ten—Centering Four
— Day Eleven—Reminiscence: Myth
Day Twelve—Cinema: Twilight
Day Thirteen—Centering Five
Day Fourteen—Reflections

DAY ONE—CENTERING ONE

The cycle begins with an exercise derived from widely known principles of relaxation and meditation. In the **Centering** exercises, you will probe your immediate context—where you are and what you are doing. In the process, you may make some discoveries and gain some control. Here is an outline of the **Centering** procedure followed by an example you can use to help you get started.

There are three parts to the exercise. *First*, find a quiet place in which you can write without distraction. Make yourself comfortable. Take a sheet of loose-leaf paper, write the date, time, and place of the writing, and title it "Centering One: Brainstorm." Then, close your eyes and relax. Clear your mind of its everyday clutter. Breathe deeply and slowly. When you are relaxed and clear of mind, start brainstorming a list of the sensations you remember from this immediate period of your life. The list should include both the sensations and their sources. For example, "frightened—a new school, all these strange faces," or "tender—I think I really love Joanne." Continue brainstorming until you have a substantial list, perhaps ten or fifteen entries.

Second, after brainstorming, take another sheet of paper and label it "Metaphor." Review your brainstorm and select what seems to be the dominant sensation or write one sensation that seems to summarize your brainstorm. Write it on the sheet and use it to develop an image or metaphor that puts you in relation to your dominant sensation. For example, working from the sensation, "confused—new campus and people," one writer portrayed herself as:

a jackrabbit
frozen in the dark
in the center of a two-lane highway
headlights approaching from both directions

If you have a hard time starting the metaphor, begin with "I feel like" and then describe yourself in terms of something nonhuman.

Third, after writing your metaphor, take another sheet and label it "Centering—So?" Then freewrite about the brainstorm and the metaphor with the aim of becoming more aware of what you have been feeling lately and how it is affecting you. Can you explain the source of your sensations in a two- or three-sentence generalization? Do you want or need to do anything as a result of what you have learned in this exercise?

Finally, staple these three sheets of paper together and place them first in the section of the Learning Log you are using for your PDJ. You will need them for further reference.

An Example

If the procedure for **Centering** seems complicated and difficult to you, look at the example of a **Centering** exercise that follows. But before reading the example, try the exercise. The example may make you believe that there is a "right" response to a **Centering** exercise. While there is an established procedure for **Centering,** there is no correct response. Each writer's **Centering** will be unique. What will come through is you—here and now.

Here's a **Centering** exercise by Susan Miller, a freshman away from home for the first time, beginning her first semester at college. Watch her as she discovers some soothing thoughts about the seeming irrelevance of much of what we all must do each day.

Sept. 10, 1987
12:00 P.M.
Home

Centering: Brainstorm

pushed - cramming everything into very little time
broke - everything costs money
homesick - every day things get worse My dad isn't
here to help me work things out.
sore - marching makes my feet hurt so bad. It hurts
just standing up.

relaxed—when I know I've done everything I should
    have done.
thankful—I learned how to write a memo.
excited—tomorrow I get an interview for a job I
    really want bad.
computerized—I'm taking everything in and remem-
    bering it until the time comes when I'll
    really use this information.
hungry—I wish I was on the meal plan for week-
    ends. I'm not disciplined enough to fend for myself.
small—everything around me is so big, educated,
    and intellectual.
dirty—the practices get so long and hard. I feel like
    a sweaty pig when it's all over.
head-ache—from trying to do too much
tired—from staying-up late and waking very
    early. Not getting much sleep in between.

Metaphor

A bottle of wine in a dark and creepy cellar.
Hidden from view by crates and crates of bottles
filled with the same thing. This bottle will
hold its flavor, its color, and its scent until
someone decides it's time to put it to use.
Then someone will enjoy its fruitfulness and
realize just how wonderful it really is.

———

Centering- So?

*Everything will have a use. Everything I'm
learning will one day be of real importance.
Right now a formula for lines on a graph
might not seem too important, but maybe
someday three years from now I'll need it.
That is when I'll be glad I learned it and
I'll realize how important it really is.*

In addition to seeing how this exercise can serve as an example for you, you might notice how nicely Susan's metaphor comes from her brainstorm, and how sensibly and positively she draws from all the pressure, confusion, and anxiety of her everyday life a sense of worth and purposefulness.

Her use of "computerized" in the brainstorm rightly expresses much of what we must do in school—receive information and be ready to call it up from our memories for use in appropriate situations. The sense of storing for use in the future counters the feeling of impatience that can cause us to overlook important information sometimes. Susan may be temporarily confused by the avalanche of physical and emotional sensations and overwhelmed by all the new information and experience, but this **Centering** exercise has helped her gain a sense of her context and purpose. In the end, she has her marching boots set firmly on the ground, ready for the band to begin its next tune.

Susan's is only one example of what can come through a **Centering** exercise. Yours may or may not resemble hers in its outcome because not all of us are likely to have the happy resolve she has. Not all of her **Centering** exercises were as positive. You may feel some anger while **Centering.** Anger generally signals a need for change. Make the resolve to change. Sometimes you will find you are completely satisfied. That's great! The point is that the **Centering** exercises provide an opportunity for you to probe your now and use it as an access point for the future. Take the opportunity.

You will follow this same procedure, except, of course, for changing the numbering and labeling of the paper, five times in the 14-day PDJ cycle. You will write **Centering** exercises on Days One, Four, Seven, Ten, and Thirteen. In addition, you will use a **Centering** exercise to begin the **Reflections** exercise.

DAY TWO—REMINISCENCE: PLACE

The **Reminiscence** exercises ask you to write about your past. Writing about the past systematically is a good way to learn the origins of your current values and beliefs. Values and beliefs form the code, the unstated rules, that guide your behavior, that help you determine whether something is important or not, good or bad, to be celebrated or avoided. Remember, whether you are conscious of your values and beliefs or not, they cause you to act the way you do. Being consciously aware of your values and beliefs can help you understand why you feel a certain way about something and why you do certain things. Such awareness permits change, which is a hallmark of growth and learning.

This first **Reminiscence** exercise asks you mentally to visit an important place from your past. The exercise has three parts.

First, return to your quiet writing place, take a sheet of loose-leaf paper, label it with the date, time, and place of the writing, and title it "Reminiscence: Place." Then, as you did for the **Centering** exercise, relax and clear your mind of its everyday clutter. Then begin to think about places in your past. Think until one place becomes very clear and vivid in your mind's eye. Try to remember as many sensations as possible: aromas, sounds, tastes, textures—everything. Once you have this place in mind, write about it. Describe it with you in it. Make the place come alive on paper. When you are done, separate this section from the next by drawing a line across the paper.

Second, after having brought the place back to life through your description, begin to consider the what and why of the place. If it is a favorite place, why? If not, how do you feel about it? Does the place remind you of specific incidents or adventures you had with your family and friends? Are you alone and perhaps enjoying the solace of a protected place? Freewrite about the significance of the place.

Third, after freewriting to discover the significance of the place, draw another line across the page. Review your freewriting, and condense—or abstract—the significance of the place into a two- or three-sentence statement. Writing the abstract requires you to compress a large idea into a short, coherent statement. Your abstract will generally reveal some value or belief important to you. The place you have recreated through the reverie gives you access to your beliefs.

For example, one writer completing this exercise described a river that ran through a park close to his house. He visited the river frequently because there he was free from family conflicts that came from having an older and a younger brother and a mother who had in the three of them as much as any human could handle. In his abstract, he wrote, "The river was not just a river but a constant friend, a friend who would leave me alone to do whatever I wanted."

He continued, "Even today I cherish places where I can be alone and undisturbed. I know that I like to work by myself rather than with others. But I must learn to work with others since cooperation is the key to success." There is an important insight in this abstract. Note that the writer crystallized this insight about himself through reminiscing about a place from his past.

You may discover similar insights when you complete the **Reminiscence** exercises. Try it. When completed, include **Reminiscence: Place** in your binder.

An Example

The first two steps in completing the **Reminiscence: Place** are common writing activities. Freewriting and describing a place are probably familiar tasks you have completed many times. The third step, writing the abstract, however, is a little more complicated. An example may help you make sure you are on the right track. Remember, use the examples to understand the procedure. Do not consider them "correct answers."

The following **Reminiscence: Place** was completed by Lisa Rodrigo, a freshman, whose love for the rural New Mexico ranch of her childhood radiates through the selection, warming us as the bright sun warmed her beloved valley.

Sept 6, 1987
8:36 am
State Fair Dorm

Reminiscence: Place
Sophia Valley from the Ranch House

The land stretches forever, it seems, broken only occasionally by a house until it runs up against the mountains that surround the valley. I have always loved our ranch being out in the open prairie with the blue skies and fresh air. The sun shines bright in the middle of the day.

Freewriting
This is my favorite place because of the beauty of the land. I love its openness. Fresh air is always there, not like in town. It is a clean and open place where I can think. It reminds me of my family because of the warmth. It holds a special quality, making me feel I am part of the land. When you work with the land it becomes part of you.

Abstract

The land holds a special quality that very few realize. Having worked with the land, you feel a part of it. The beauty of the open land can't be compared with the "man made" beauty that so many people find pleasant to look at. The land is best, most beautiful.

In addition to providing a model of the movement from description to free-writing to writing the abstract, Lisa's **Reminiscence** is interesting because it focuses on her sense of identity with the land on which she grew up. How she loves her family's Sophia Valley ranch, a site of so much work, warmth, and joy. Remembering this love was especially important to her when she wrote her PDJ because she had left that home to get an education. Many people who leave the land to gain an education end up leaving the land permanently. She is concerned that she has broken the ties, that some of the magic may have disappeared.

She is also confident, however, that she has done the correct thing, that the land will always be there for her. It is a comforting thought, one that will help her through the initial trials of leaving for school. A respite in the storm, a peaceful shelter where quiet reflection can happen, this is how Lisa is using her PDJ. You can find the same peace and calm for yourself in yours.

DAY THREE—CINEMA: MILESTONE

Cinema exercises invite you to write about your future. They allow you to fantasize and construct dreams, so you can write about your ideal future. They are an opportunity to play, to shape your life as you might like to live it. Writing about the future can help you make discoveries about yourself. After close consideration, you may discover that what on the surface seems attractive is really not attractive or appropriate. Or you may find something completely unexpected lurking just beneath your conscious thoughts. This something may change your direction entirely. These exercises give you a chance to venture deep in the realms of your dreams and fantasies. **Cinema** exercises can help you set goals and make plans for a future that may someday become your reality.

In the **Cinema** exercises you will be using a skill called imaging. Because it is helpful in achieving goals or solving problems in diverse areas, psychologists often train people in its use. Bankers, engineers, social workers, and others report positive results from imaging. Athletes use the skill often. The golfer learns to concentrate on a putt, to imagine the ball rolling across the green and dropping into the cup—to actually see this mentally—before putting.

In the PDJ you will use imaging to create vivid scenes of yourself acting in the future. You will record these scenes and then assess them to determine whether and how you can make them become real. In the **Cinema** exercises, you will be creating an imaginary script of your future.

This first **Cinema** exercise asks you to write an extended, imaginative obituary for yourself. The form for this exercise is loosely derived from the "Milestones" column in *Time* magazine. If you want, refer to several back issues of *Time* to get a sense of what you will be writing. Imagine yourself a *Time* magazine reporter who must write a "Milestone" for a very noteworthy person who has recently died—you!

The "Milestone" is more than the local paper's spare listing of the mundane facts of someone's life. Rather, it takes a large view and discusses the central themes, accomplishments, and contributions of someone's life. And remember, this is life as you would like it. As Rocky Balboa might say, "Go for it!"

The "Milestone" exercise has three parts. *First*, return to your quiet writing place, take a sheet of loose-leaf paper, write the date, time, and place heading as usual, and label it "Cinema—Milestone." Relax and close your eyes; clear your mind of all its clutter. Once you've relaxed, imagine yourself as you would like to be in your fondest dreams. Perhaps you want to be a famous person of great accomplishment. Start brainstorming the most important incidents and accomplishments of your imagined life. Do not limit yourself with sensible expectations; make your life as fantastic as you can imagine. If you want to be a politician, write yourself into the U.S. Senate. Perhaps your dreams are more modest, and you want to be a fine parent or upstanding citizen. That's okay. Put yourself where you would like to be and make it become real.

The brainstorm should include personality characteristics by which you would like to be remembered and perhaps a few short and telling comments or quotes from your friends or your speeches and writings. If you set any records in your lifetime, note them. Brainstorm a substantial list of information based on the image of yourself you create on your mind's movie screen.

Second, change roles and become the *Time* reporter charged with writing the obituary. Review the brainstorm as if it were notes from research including an extended interview with the now-deceased personality. The brainstorm is a fact sheet you will now use to compose the "Milestone." The "Milestone" should be three or four paragraphs long. Copy your obituary onto a separate sheet of loose-leaf paper labeled "Milestone."

Third, on another sheet of loose-leaf paper labeled "Milestone—Assessment," spend several minutes freewriting about the "Milestone" exercise. Did you surprise yourself with what you imagined? Did you write what you would really like to be remembered for? Is it realistic? Can you start doing something now that might help you realize your ambitions? Staple this assessment to the other sheets in the "Milestone" exercise and place them together with the other exercises in your PDJ.

An Example

The following "Milestone" will give you a sense of the general form for a "Milestone." Paul Barrisford is a writing teacher who completed this "Milestone" during a workshop. Note his playful spirit, a key element in making this a successful exercise.

10:30 p.m.
October 28, 1980
631 Woodland, Absecon, NJ - Study

MILESTONE

DIED. Paul Avery, "the Bear," Banisford, 46, prize-winning poet, renowned university teacher, and the pride of the Philadelphia Phillies, of undetermined causes, while yachting off Newport, R.I.

Banisford's early success in academe culminated in his appointment as Professor of Wisdom at Montana's Valhalla State University in 1987. In 1988, he won the Nobel Prize for Literature for his collection of poems — Trails and Trials, meditations and reflections from thousands of miles running while avoiding near-blind, reckless 4 × 4 drivers, ill-tempered dogs, and occasional avalanches.

At 38, Banisford quit everything to devote all his time to his first love - baseball. In his resignation from the university, he wrote, "It's time I finally graduated and got back to the baseball diamond like a normal kid." He earned a spot on the Phillies' roster at rookie camp when he hit 16 ~~consecutive~~ consecutive pitches out of the ball park. Eventually known more for his pitching, his bearded, round-shouldered appearance and the frightful grunt that accompanied each pitch earned him the nickname, "the Bear." Banisford led the Phillies to six consecutive World Series Championships.

Rumors of his impending retirement from baseball sparked speculation that his health was failing or that he had political ambitions. His death was unexpected.

His life long friend, Steve Griffey, owner of the Phillies, summarized Barisford's ~~multi-~~ faceted life: "He was torn between the ~~silence~~ silence of the library, the warmth and fellowship of the classroom, the isolation of the running trail, and the roars of appreciative fans. His dream was to become the Babe Ruth of poetry and the Robert Frost of baseball. He died satisfied."

According to his wishes, Barisford's ashes were sprinkled over Philadelphia's Veteran's Stadium.

Paul's "Milestone" picks up most of the information he wrote in his brain-storm, but he combined the various pieces in a way the brainstorm would never suggest. This is important to note. The brainstorms provide raw materials for these exercises, but they do not provide the final form of the writing. If you are merely changing the brainstorm from a list into sentences, you are not doing enough.

In his assessment, Paul focused on certain ironies and incongruities in the "Milestone." While his fantasies are not realistic, he believes they are healthy.

MILESTONE - Assessment

I enjoyed writing this MILESTONE for several reasons. I enjoyed writing about my death with humor. We can sometimes get too serious about death. It is an eventuality we all have to consider. Maybe it is not a bad idea to think of it with a chuckle. I also enjoyed turning my physical peculiarities into advantages. My body has always been a problem. Arthritis has prevented me from ever doing any sport really well. But I could hit a baseball! I also enjoyed inverting my priorities since I place much more importance on my writing and teaching than I do on ~~any~~ anything ~~or~~ else. But I don't know if this is good. In a sense, the MILESTONE is a message to me to evaluate my priorities, to make sure I am doing enough of what I need to do — running, playing ball, sailing — to enrich my writing and teaching. The MILESTONE made me think about the balance of my life.

DAY FOUR—CENTERING TWO

Follow exactly the same procedure established in the **Centering One** exercise. Relax. Brainstorm. Metaphor. Centering—So? When you have finished, place it with the other exercises in your PDJ.

An Example

Here is an interesting **Centering** exercise. The writer, Ruth Lytle, goes to school in addition to working full-time and keeping a household. Watch how she is able to make being alone, something she does not like, okay. And more, look how she uses the writing as a way to express her general satisfaction with life.

Sept. 19, 1987
11:00 a.m.
Trailer table

Centering Two
Brainstorm

alone
tired -- worked last nite
anticipation -- looked forward to concert
homesick -- tired of housesitting
want to go riding.

tired of self-examination
happy - just am
annoyed -- had to take stupid cat out
tired -- no stereo
apprehensive -- job at work going to change
tomorrow will be a busy day.

Metaphor

I am the dog, chained up for
a day, restless but not
unhappy, for I'm secure in the
knowledge I'm in but a
temporary situation.

Centering -- So?

Wow. Just realized how much
time passed while I wrote
this. All continues to go
well. Got a real sense of
well-being today, and I'm
going to bed after I write
this. And although I
usually hate to be alone,
right now it is not bothering
me in the slightest. In fact,
I'm relishing it. I don't think
it's insecurity that causes me
to hate being alone; I just
like people and prefer to
have them around.

DAY FIVE—REMINISCENCE: PERSON

The next exercise in the cycle, **Reminiscence: Person,** very closely resembles **Reminiscence: Place.** The three-step procedure is the same, but you will focus on a person rather than a place. Relax, bring someone from the past to mind, and brainstorm that person to life. Then write about the significance of the person, about all that person means to you. Finally, write an abstract.

The person can be living or dead. The important point is that the person must have meant a lot to you and must have been a source of influence. Put the completed exercise with the others.

An Example

Not as a model for you to follow but as an example of the potential of the **Reminiscence** section to explore the depths of vital matters in an individual's life, consider the **Reminiscence: Person** written by Tony Bower, a freshman in his mid-twenties, coming back to school after selling hardware and lumber for several years. He had never written in a journal before.

Sept. 4, 1987
9:00 p.m.
Kitchen Table

REMINISCENCE: PERSON

Brainstorm

wheelchair   Athlete
proud   war injury
big heart   love and respect
good father   mean child - me
state champs

Freewrite

My father has always played an important role in my life. But unlike most other fathers, my dad was injured in Vietnam while flying a reconnaissance mission. When I was four years old, my father was paralyzed and left in a coma for six months. I was too young to realize what was happening, but I knew something was wrong because my mom was always crying.

Anyway, as I grew up, I started to do things more for myself and took on the responsibilities of being the man of the house. My father was now back at home but confined to wheelchair. I think back and see how mean I sometimes treated him because he wasn't able to get out of his wheelchair and hit me. I don't know how many times I've apologized for being mean to him during my early years of growing up.

When I entered high school, it struck me that my father was never going to walk or run again in my lifetime or his. I would sit in my room and cry because I couldn't imagine how somebody who used to be active in all kinds of sports could live without being able to participate in any of them. I decided to make my father proud of me, so I joined many teams in school. I wrestled and played football for Eldorado High. I guess it was because my father couldn't run that I got into jogging every day. I just felt that it was wrong to be able to do things and then not do them because of being lazy.

I wasn't until my junior year that I was happy with my own accomplishments. That year Eldorado went 13-0 in varsity football, and we won the state championship over Clovis. I started each game as the place kicker. All through the season I sat my father on the sidelines, so that he could watch the games.

I'll never forget the feeling I got when those last seconds ran off the clock in the championship game. I ran straight over to my father, yelling, "We did it." He was so happy and proud that right then I realized that I had accomplished one of my goals. Why I was playing was for him, and we had won

Now my goals are set on college and learning as much as I can, so I can show my father that I can be successful in life. I want him to know that he did one of the best jobs of raising me that a father could do. Even if my father is still in a wheelchair, I would stack him up against any father in the world.

Abstract

Because of my father I set high goals for myself. I know that he has always supported me 100%, and there is nothing that he wouldn't do for me. Now I want to return the things he's given to me. I want him to look at my accomplishments and tell his friends "Yah, that's my boy!" So it's very important to me that I reach my goals.

I thank God that I have the father I do because he helped me realize all the neat things there are in life to enjoy. I now try to live each day to the fullest, and I will do so until the day I die.

Tony wrote about what is for many of us an important concern. As we grow older, we become aware of the sacrifices our parents made for us. We want to repay them by proving that their efforts were not wasted. We may use personal accomplishments in sports, in music, in academics, in business—wherever. But our wish is much like Tony's that our parents will proudly say, "Yah, that's my boy!"

Of course, Tony's is a very special case. His father is a disabled Vietnam war veteran. Living in a wheelchair, he is unable to raise his child as other fathers would. Tony is aware of this concern in his father.

Early on Tony takes advantage of his father's plight. Now he realizes what a mean child he was, and he has apologized. As Tony grows, so does his awareness of his father. And his love. He tries to give his father pleasure through athletic successes. Note that Tony's first thought after winning the state championship is about his father.

Now Tony is working hard to shift from athletics to academics in order to continue to make his dad proud. He wants badly to let his life become proof of the quality of his dad's performance as a father.

In this journal entry, Tony is working things out. He is addressing the fundamental problem caused by his father's injury. He accepts it and turns it to his advantage. He confesses his childhood shortcomings and expresses his adult desire to embody his love in his actions. He describes the sometimes strained relationship he has with his father with an intensity characteristic of the best use of the PDJ. He is getting things off his chest but at the same time discovering what is really important about his past—how it shapes his present actions.

DAY SIX—CINEMA: NOONLIGHT

Cinema: Noonlight asks you to imagine yourself basking in the warmth of success and contentment, enjoying the next phase of your life. Relax and clear your mind, then bring to mind images of how you would like to be and what you would like to be doing when you have finished school and you are settled into the next stage of your life. Build a solid mental image, then brainstorm. Record sensations, images, and facts. You will be using this brainstorm as a fact sheet to recreate the scene in the PDJ. Label this sheet as you have all the others and title it "Cinema: Noonlight—Brainstorm."

Next, take another sheet of paper, label it "Cinema: Noonlight—A Day in the Life," and use the brainstorm you have just completed to describe a typical day in your life. Write an account that records your various activities. Try to create a verbal videotape of the day. Be as complete as possible. Focus on activities and personal interactions that account for your contentment and success. The entrepreneur is aggressive and seeing an opportunity takes advantage of it. The parent finds great joy in sharing some time with the children. Write yourself being that entrepreneur or that parent—whatever you like. Remember, **Cinema** exercises give you an opportunity to make ideal and fantastic movies of yourself acting in the future.

Finally, on another sheet labeled "Cinema: Noonlight—Assessment," evaluate what you have discovered through this writing. You have been thinking and writing about your life in its next phase. Do you have the personal characteristics required to become the person you have imagined? What can you do to develop or enhance needed traits? In retrospect, is what you imagined what you really want? When you have completed the exercise, staple all the sheets together and place them with the other exercises.

An Example

Alex Tanner, a freshman keeping a journal for the first time, completed the following **Cinema: Noonlight.**

February 3, 1987
9:15 p.m.
Dorm Bed

Cinema: Noonlight
Brainstorm

I'll be the youngest judge ever to be appointed to the Colorado State Supreme Court.
I'll have a pleasant home in the suburbs of Denver and a cabin at Vallecito Lake where I'll spend lots of time.

Although I'm not yet married, I'm seriously involved with a beautiful green-eyed attorney.

In my spare time, I'll throw darts and review books and stories for the Denver Post and the Southwest Literary Messenger.

I'll be working on my first novel. I'm ~~frus~~ frustrated, but I'm beginning to work it out.

Cinema: Noonlight
A Day In The Life

I'm awake early this morning and lie in bed letting my mind wander where it will. Suddenly, I get a great insight and inspiration -- a new direction for my novel. Carefully, so as not to wake Jessica, I get out of bed, shower, then set myself to my typewriter to put it to paper. I am quite pleased and satisfied. For the first time I see hope for the book.

I'm due in my chambers at 11:00, so I gather my things, drive into town, and arrive at the courthouse 15 minutes early. In my spacious office, which is like a library with its floor-to-ceiling bookcases, I sit at my desk, shut my eyes, and consider the upcoming case. It is a very delicate case and may end up going to the U.S Supreme Court. But we've been instructed to try and deal with it here.

Donning my robes, I meet the other two justices, and we enter the courtroom. After hours of debate, we retire and discuss the issues. We are unanimous, and I am chosen to write the decision for the court. It's not an easy task. I'll have to finish it at the cabin over the weekend.

Back at home, working on notes for the decision, I'm waiting for Jessica to get home, so we can head up to the cabin. Can't wait to go fishing tomorrow. I know there is a trout waiting just for me.

Cinema: Noonlight
Assessment

It seems that every time I think about being a judge or writing a novel, especially after I've put it into words in this journal, I feel disappointingly far away from these goals.

To be a judge you ~~first~~ have to first know yourself and be confident in yourself. Only then ~~can~~ you can be responsible and fair, and give true justice to others. No way am I to that point yet. I still have to come to grips with myself. I have too little confidence in myself yet to ever judge others.

A writer must have some experiences, must have a chance -- a long chance -- to observe the world, people, and himself. I don't feel that I could write anything of value yet.

But I'm not discouraged by the long path before me. I have faith in me.

Alex's "A Day In The Life" exemplifies how productive journal writing can be. In the brainstorm and the narrative, he fantasizes about his two life goals, being a judge and a writer. He imagines a high-responsibility situation. But he seems to be tugged in many directions at the same time. He wakes early to write. He brings work home from his day in court. He wants to get away to go fishing. He imagines an ideal situation, but there is too much that needs to get done.

In the assessment he begins to come to grips with some of the tensions set up in the narrative. He is frustrated on two levels: by choosing two goals that demand so much commitment and responsibility, and by being young and far away from achieving either of the goals.

Through the **Cinema: Noonlight** exercise Alex has encountered some of the problems his ambition will create. He has identified problems he can work on solving: developing the wisdom and confidence that will make him a good judge and gaining the experience and vision through observation that will make him a good writer. He has uncovered frustration, but he also remains firm in his commitment. He has faith in himself.

Cinema: Noonlight allowed Alex an opportunity to explore his fantasies. His exploration reminds him there will be challenges, frustrations, perhaps some disappointments. But with his mention of "faith" at the end, he establishes a sense of direction, and, more importantly, a sense of confidence. Here is the positive power of the PDJ to discover and raise to awareness the essential self. His awareness, coupled with resolve and very hard work, can make him, or anyone, raise his potential for success. Someday we may be reading his novels.

DAY SEVEN—CENTERING THREE

Same procedure as before. Brainstorm. Metaphor. Centering—So?

An Example

Peter Adams, an older student who has returned to school after several years of working, wrote the following **Centering** exercise at a time in his life when he felt threatened by change. In it, he confronts the problem of change and focuses on the promise that accompanies its threat.

June 3, 1987
9:30 a.m.
Writing Class

Centering Three
Brainstorm

tired — don't sleep well away from home
worried — sense a distance from K.
pleased — classes are going well
anxious — visit to Florida could be a disaster
judgmental — too sensitive to comments from K. like
     "you don't like them," when she knows I do.
fat — belly sloshes when I exercise
mind — pinched — distracted by roommate noises,
     what a pig!
empty — nerves shot by roller-coaster living
inspired — good sermon last Sunday
anxious — something is about to happen

Metaphor

"anxious — something about to happen"

I am a barnacled crab skirting along the edges of
its territory, waving fierce claws at whatever tries to

invade, but ready to quickly withdraw beneath the rock ledges' protection. I am fearful of confrontation, the life/death struggle.

———————

Centering - SO?

The crab image is rich. The most important point it makes for me — I'll interpret this in a positive light — the crab has to shed its carapace yearly — has to get out of itself and leave its shell behind. That's growth, the chance to form a new and better shell. Also a time of danger and vulnerability.

DAY EIGHT—REMINISCENCE: DIALOG

Remember, the **Reminiscence** exercises help you examine your past to discover the values and beliefs that consciously or unconsciously guide your behavior. Becoming aware of these influences allows you to make conscious choices either to continue to act as your past has prepared you to or to connect new insights and experience and allow them to guide your behavior. Some psychologists, in fact, define maturity as the ability to adjust existing patterns of behavior to fit the demands of new experience. The **Reminiscence** exercises give you an opportunity to consider your past and its relation to your present.

Reminiscence: Dialog asks you to write about a person from your past whom you believe has had a major impact on your life. This person can be a relative— for example, a parent, brother, sister, aunt, uncle, grandparent—or a friend, teacher, or mentor. Choose someone who has clearly affected your life and has influenced the way you think and act.

First, return to your writing place, take a sheet of paper, put the customary heading on it, and label it "Reminiscence—Brainstorm." Use the relaxation technique to clear your mind; then focus on a memorable person. Once someone comes clearly to your mind, write that person's name on the paper, and begin brainstorming about that person and what you remember about him or her. What you remember will often be how that person influenced you. For example, one writer, discussing his grandmother, remembered in the brainstorm how patient she was and how this made her seem to be a very calm and loving person. This is how he would like to be. Most of the brainstorm captured images of her calmness.

Second, after you have completed a substantial brainstorm, take another sheet of paper, and label it "Reminiscence—(NAME): Dialog." Take a few minutes to think, and then engage the person you are remembering in a conversation about you and what you are doing with your life. Make sure to go beyond the superficial. Discuss matters of importance. Consider whether the person would approve or disapprove of what you are thinking and doing. Work hard to put yourself in that other person's mind; say what he or she would really say. Go deep; let the person assume his or her own identity. If you must, defend your behavior; at least explain yourself. There need not necessarily be disagreement.

Many writers discover, after some false starts and rethinking, that what they are doing is exactly what they believe their dialog partner would have them do. And further, they discover that their behavior is clearly based on some belief or value that was communicated to them, directly or indirectly, by that person in the past. There is the breakthrough. Do not set up superficial arguments you can easily win; have hard discussions and make discoveries. When you write your dialog, make it seem like the transcript of a recorded conversation, or write it like a dialog in a play or short story.

Third, after you have completed the dialog, rest awhile, and read it over. Then take another sheet of paper, label it "Reminiscence: Dialog—Assessment," and freewrite for a period, considering what you discovered from doing the exercise. Often this is the most fruitful part of the exercise, the time when you make connections and uncover the degree to which the past is affecting your behavior in the present. When you've completed the exercise, staple all the sheets together, and place them in your PDJ.

An Example

In the following excerpt, watch how Tom Mendoza works his way through some especially disturbing feelings by engaging an old friend in an imaginary dialog. A veteran of the Navy, Tom has left loved ones behind in order to come to school for an education. He discovers the value of a "close" friend, a friend who can listen and sympathize, but who can also provide the needed kick in the pants to snap him out of his depression. Even when that friend is far away.

September 14, 1987
8:20 p.m.
In Flight From San Diego

Reminiscence – Mikey Kaiser: Dialog

Me: Hi, Mikey, how are you doing? I can't believe you came all the way to Las Cruces to visit me!
Mikey: I can't either, but me and Steph needed

a vacation from the East after being in Norfolk for so long, and we decided to visit you.

Me: Mikey, I really am glad you came to visit because I have so much to talk to you about.

Mikey: Like what?

Me: Well, you know all the stuff I talked to you about before I left the ship to come here?

Mikey: Yeah.

Me: Well, things have gotten to the point of me almost giving everything up.

Mikey: Why?

Me: I just don't feel right about me being in at college with Brenda C. still back at home. I feel so selfish.

Mikey: Listen, Tom, we've talked about this before and realized that you two were just not made for each other.

Me: Yeah, I know, but I still feel so selfish. My daughter. I feel I should be there.

Mikey: Tom, just because you're there won't mean you'll love her mom any more than you did before. And besides, how are you going to make her happy if you're not happy?

Me: Mike, I know we've talked about this so many times before, and every time we finish talking I feel better. But time makes me feel so guilty.

Mikey: Tom, you're like a brother to me, and it hurts me to see you this way. You won't help things by worrying so much. Just take care of you, then you can start taking care of someone else.

Me: That's what I should do, I know, but

you know me, Mike. I'm so stupid sometimes.

Mikey: Listen, Tom, you might be a lot of things, but you're not stupid. You've got to make a decision and stick by it no matter what.

Me: That's so easy for you to say because you're you. But I'm me. I wish I were you, Mike, you've got it all.

Mikey: Tom, you've just got to believe in yourself and live your life as good as you can, and the rest will come after you've given it your best.

Me: I don't know what I would have done if you hadn't shown up. I was feeling pretty low. When do you take off?

Mikey: Me and Steph don't have to leave for another couple of days, so you won't have any excuses for not working out. And, by the way Tom, you're looking too skinny. When's the last time you worked out?

Me: It's been too long, Mike. I signed up for a weight lifting class, and should get back into it this fall. Hey, Mike, let's stop talking for now and go out for dinner. Maybe later we can take Steph out for a night on the town.

Mikey: Sounds great. Remember all those great stories you told me about the food here? Well, I'm ready to find out for myself.

By the way, Tom, don't forget you've got a friend forever, and that I care no matter how far away I am

Reminiscence Dialog – Assessment

All through my life, I've had only two people who I could call close friends. One of them died in a car accident. Her name was Geni, and her death really hurt me for a long time. The other is Mikey Kaiser. He's a guy that I admire for his determination and his friendship for me.

I met him on board the USS Ticonderoga CG47. He really helped me get going in the right direction by listening when I needed someone to listen. And he gave me the confidence to better myself. I realized in this exercise that he really has been an important part of my life. He still is.

I really was mixed up with my emotions, not knowing how to feel or what to do about Brenda and the baby, unsure of myself and ready to give it up. Then he came into my life and let me know how important I was to him and everyone else. A lot of times I wish I had a friend here in Las Cruces who I could talk to in times of despair. This journal is like me having my friend here now because I can hear him listening.

DAY NINE—CINEMA: ACCEPTANCE SPEECH

Cinema exercises ask you to imagine your ideal future through writing in the PDJ. Writing about the future will help you discover your personal objectives, so you can make plans and set goals to help that future become a reality.

Today's **Cinema** exercise asks you to write an acceptance speech. You are to picture yourself at the climax of your ideal career. *First,* return to your writing place with plenty of paper and the tools you need to write. Take one sheet, put the normal heading on it, and label it "Cinema: Acceptance Speech—the Scene." Then breathe deeply, close your eyes, relax, and free your mind to wander and imagine great things. Today is a special day for you, so prepare yourself for it.

Once you have relaxed, imagine a scene in which you are receiving the award that signals public recognition of valuable accomplishments in your field. If you want to be a journalist, you are receiving the Pulitzer Prize. If you plan on working in the sciences, picture yourself receiving a Nobel Prize. A public servant can receive the "Citizen of the Year Citation" from the local chamber of commerce or community church. Parents can earn the Mother/Father of the Year Award from the PTA. Give yourself the award that best fits what you want to do with your life. If your goals are modest and you want only to live a good and comfortable life, give yourself the "Best at Being ME Award," and write a speech explaining how your life, though unremarkable, has been personally satisfying.

After you have the award and the scene set clearly in your mind, begin to brainstorm. Work hard to capture your feelings and the essence of the occasion. As usual, this brainstorm will become source material for the next part of the exercise, so make it rich with detail.

Second, take another sheet of paper, label it "Cinema: Acceptance Speech," and compose the speech you will give when you accept the award you just imagined winning. This speech should pay special attention to establishing the significance of the award as well as making sure, in a modest way, that you deserve it and appreciate the recognition. The speech should also recognize and thank those who helped you earn the award.

You are familiar with this kind of speech from watching award ceremonies on television. If you would like an example of a formal acceptance speech worth noting both for its form and its message, read the following example—William Faulkner's "Address upon Receiving the Nobel Prize for Literature." Faulkner's speech considers the nature of the modern world and the responsibility of the writer in such a world. The writer he is talking about is, of course, himself.

ADDRESS UPON RECEIVING THE NOBEL PRIZE FOR LITERATURE

Stockholm, December 10, 1950

I feel that this award was not made to me as a man, but to my work—a life's work in the agony and sweat of the human spirit, not for glory and least of all for profit, but to create out of the materials of the human spirit something which did not exist before. So this award is only mine in trust. It will not be difficult to find a dedication for the money part of it commensurate with the purpose and significance of its origin. But I would like to do the same with the acclaim too, by using this moment as a pinnacle from which I might be listened to by the young men and women already dedicated to the same anguish and travail, among whom is already that one who will some day stand here where I am standing.

Our tragedy today is a general and universal physical fear so long sustained by now that we can even bear it. There are no longer problems of the spirit. There is only the question: When will I be blown up? Because of this, the young man or woman writing today has forgotten the problems of the human heart in conflict with itself which alone can make good writing because only that is worth writing about, worth the agony and the sweat.

He must learn them again. He must teach himself that the basest of all things is to be afraid; and, teaching himself that, forget it forever, leaving no room in his workshop for anything but the old verities and truths of the heart, the old universal truths lacking which any story is ephemeral and doomed—love and honor and pity and pride and compassion and sacrifice. Until he does so, he labors under a curse. He writes not of love but of lust, of defeats in which nobody loses anything of value, of victories without hope and, worst of all, without pity or compassion. His griefs grieve on no universal bones, leaving no scars. He writes not of the heart but of the glands.

Until he relearns these things, he will write as though he stood among and watched the end of man. I decline to accept the end of man. It is easy enough to say that man is immortal simply because he will endure: that when the last ding-dong of doom has clanged and faded from the last worthless rock hanging tideless in the last red and dying evening, that even then there will still be one more sound: that of his puny inexhaustible voice, still talking. I refuse to accept this. I believe that man will not merely endure: he will prevail. He is immortal, not because he alone among creatures has an inexhaustible voice, but because he has a soul, a spirit capable of compassion and sacrifice and endurance. The poet's, the writer's, duty is to write about these things. It is his privilege to help man endure by lifting his heart, by reminding him of the courage and honor and hope and pride and compassion and pity and sacrifice which have been the glory of his past. The poet's voice need not merely be the record of man, it can be one of the props, the pillars to help him endure and prevail.

Source: *The Portable Faulkner*, Malcolm Cowley, ed. New York: Viking Press, 1974.

While the speech you compose may not be as polished as Faulkner's, you should nevertheless aim higher than the typical incoherence exhibited during the Academy Awards.

Third, after completing your speech, consider again the award you received, the reason you received it, and the significance you attributed to it in your speech.

Then, take another sheet of paper, label it "Cinema: Acceptance Speech—Assessment," and freewrite about what you discovered about yourself. Consider your purpose in life, especially as it is reflected in your speech. Move through the outward trappings like motivation for money, fame, glamour, security, and so forth to examine the significance of what you have imagined yourself rewarded for doing with your life. Upon reflection, do you find the award and the career for which it is earned worthwhile and appropriate for you? If not, why? If so, what can you start doing now to begin the journey toward that award? When you have completed the exercise, staple all the sheets together and place them with the other exercises.

An Example

Cathleen McLane, a freshman and science fiction enthusiast, created for herself the "Pan-Galactic Writers' Prize," which is awarded to the individual who has done the most to break down barriers between governments, cultures, and solitary souls. These are her comments upon receiving the award.

Cinema: Acceptance Speech

I look out among you and see faces. Faces not of men and women, divided by their ideals and allegiances, but of men and women united in their commitment to the preservation of a frail and endangered species — the human soul. The award given here tonight is not a tribute to the dedication of any one writer, but to every writer who has ever taken or will ever take pen and paper in hand in defense of the soul.

The human soul I speak of, that elusive essence, that driving force that makes us endure as a species, has faced and, no doubt, will again face many attacks whose aim is to destroy its will to survive. Attempts to control and restrict the human soul are doomed to failure. Indeed, the soul emerges from these trials wiser.

To find the reasons for the perseverance of the soul, we must turn our thoughts inward and examine our very nature. Socrates, among other ancients, asserted the immortality of the soul. Given this, are there some lessons we can learn by attempting to uncover its past, lessons that will enable us to become better masters of it? And if the assertion is false, then how may we find some frame of reference or hand hold that permits us to become better acquainted with our souls?

As a part of our commitment to the preservation of the soul, we are obliged to seek out and pursue answers. Without this common objective, all we can hope to produce is page after page of worthless text: words without substance, without meaning, without relevance.

We must, therefore, firmly entrench ourselves in the channels of thought that search for those answers.

In a world where the ultimate answer to every question posed in the past has been violence, and in a world which can no longer survive this violence, we must strive to turn the tide. We must, when and wherever possible in our work, address the questions that will give the human soul back the peace and strength of will it has lost. For no longer can the soul be subjected to the abuse and torment of the past and hope to survive even partially intact. Our efforts must be, in some part, directed towards the renewal of the soul— a renewal that will bring the soul out of the centuries of neglect and inactivity that have resulted in its depleted condition.

When taking on this great task of rejuvenating the soul, we must not cast off the memories of ancient neglect, nor must we dwell on them. It is our goal rather to strike a balance between the two—a balance that would allow the soul to replenish itself, while at the same time to evaluate both past and present before time progresses.

Until we can reach this goal, we are failures: the human soul will be forced to plod blindly on the path to self-destruction. Our efforts, coupled with those others who would not see the soul destroyed, will combine to not only prevent the soul's destruction but also to reverse the effects witnessed thus far in human history.

Cathleen has met the assignment head on. She has met the challenge to discover what it is she would like to contribute to the world and in doing so has uncovered a noble undertaking for herself. She has broken through appearances, the wealth and fame we associate with being a successful writer, and focused on the real role she sees for writers—shepherds of the human soul. Hers is a giant task, but this speech makes me believe she is preparing for it.

DAY TEN—CENTERING FOUR

Use the same procedure as for all **Centering** exercises: Brainstorm. Metaphor. Centering—So?

An Example

Watch Julia Acosta, homesick, unsure of what she wants to study, worried about worrying so much.

September 14, 1987
Dorm Room
5:48 P.M.

Centering Four Brainstorm

lonely — I haven't seen my parents for a month
alone — nobody understands
sick — cold and fever
upset — bad grades in chemistry
hurt — sprained ankle
worried — because I worry too much
confused — don't know which direction to go

Metaphor

A deer, running scared. One leg half-eaten by a coyote. All the other deer know which way to go; I can't see where they went. I'm confused, running, trying to look for a safe place, an escape.

Centering — So?

My main feeling is homesickness. I think about my parents and hope they are okay even though I call them once a week. The other feeling is that everyone I talk to knows what they want to study, while here I am so confused. My worrying is getting to be too much, so I have to learn not to worry so much.

Recognizing and understanding a problem, in this case Julia's excessive worry, often is the first step to a solution. And once Julia looks a little closer, she will realize that she is not the only unsure one. She is the one honest enough to admit she is unsure.

DAY ELEVEN—REMINISCENCE: MYTH

The past is not dead. It lives in us, in our memories, and in all we do each day. **Reminiscence** exercises encourage you to discover more about yourself by investigating the past and how it has influenced you. **Reminiscence: Myth** asks you to write about the past in a special way. You are to write a myth about one of your ancestors.

Myths are stories that explain natural phenomena or establish laws and principles of behavior. Everyday, ordinary things and people assume great significance. Myths establish essential truths and help us understand and accept our place in the world. Because myths are created by humans for other humans, and because they date to our earliest history, myths tell the human story.

Myths teach lessons, but they do so indirectly, by weaving the lesson into a story. You are familiar with all kinds of examples. Some seem silly. When the angels bowl, there is thunder and lightning. That story explains weather in a way that comforts a child and makes the surprise of the rumble of thunder and the flash of lightning a little less frightening. Many of the fables and fairy tales we heard as children have this same mythic purpose; they teach lessons important to our well-being. Little Red Riding Hood learns not to trust strangers because they may be mean "wolves" out to do no good.

Stories about national heroes work the same way. The tall tales about Daniel Boone and Davy Crockett emphasize their strength, steadfastness, and frontier wiles. Davy Crockett's fight with the bear not only entertains, it also illustrates in an exaggerated manner a personal characteristic Americans generally value. In the end, these stories establish models for us to follow. In all instances, despite their fabulous or humorous veneers, myths explain or establish something of religious, national, or cultural importance. They help us understand the way things are.

Your task today is to write a myth about your family. Make a particular ancestor the hero or villain of the myth. Explain what heroic or memorable acts brought your family where it is. Do not hesitate to stretch the truth a bit because exaggeration is one of the characteristics of myth. For example, my family is French-Canadian. We come from a long line of fur-trappers and sailors. Myths about my family always emphasize how strong my ancestors were. To survive, they had to kill wild animals, brave terrible blizzards, and weather fierce North Atlantic storms.

But there is no way they could really have been as strong as the myths portray them. Uncle Nate may have been big, ugly, and mean, but could he really have frightened away a hungry wolf by looking at it cross-eyed? The exaggeration makes the point about the severe demands of forest and frontier life. The influence of trapper ancestors has made my family strong. Their influence is physical (that is, part of our genetic make-up) and, because we value their physical prowess, psychological. The **Reminiscence: Myth** will allow you to explore similar characteristics in your family.

First, return to your writing place, put the normal heading on a sheet of paper, and label it "Reminiscence: Myth—Brainstorm." Then complete the relaxation procedure. Concentrate. Allow your regular, deep breathing to chase everyday distractions from your mind. Then begin brainstorming material you can use for your myth. Write about the "characters" in your family. Sketch the story about your crazy cousin that gets told every holiday when the family gathers at the dinner table. Use the brainstorm to capture the essence of these memories. Do not quit until you have plenty of material to make your myth.

Second, take another sheet of paper, label it "Reminiscence: Myth," and begin writing your narrative. If you are stuck, start with a stock line like "Once upon a time. . ." or "In the beginning. . . ." Write the story of some important character or incident in your family's history and write it in a way that shows how that important part of the past still influences your present. Write your story with a beginning, middle, and end.

Third, take another sheet of paper, label it "Reminiscence: Myth—Assessment" and spend some time freewriting about the experience of writing a myth about your family. How did you choose the characteristic that you ultimately exaggerated? How does this characteristic influence you? Write so as to turn the making of the myth into a lesson about you as an individual. When you've completed the exercise, staple all the sheets together and place them in your PDJ.

An Example

Tina Santos, a freshman from the legendary mountain country around Pecos, New Mexico, wrote a particularly rich myth encapsulating the entire life of her great-great grandfather. This is her myth and some of the significance she discovered in it.

Reminiscence : Myth

Alejandrino Vigil was the biggest and strongest mountain man who ever lived in the Sangre de Cristo Mountains. He was also my great-great grandfather.

He was an only child, born under an evergreen in the middle of winter in 1817. His mother died shortly after giving birth to him. He was raised by his father.

When I say he was the biggest mountain man, I really mean the biggest. Born with an abnormal pituitary gland, he grew to a tremendous height of 8 and 1/2 feet.

When my great-great grandfather was ten years old, he was left alone. A case of scarlet fever took the life of his father, an intrepid mountain man who had given his best efforts to teach his only son how to survive in the untamed wilderness.

My great-great grandfather never forgot any of his father's teachings. At the age of twelve he was already a skilled hunter. He hunted mainly for food but learned to make use of almost every part of any animal he killed. Some of the clothes he made from skins still exist.

My great-great grandfather had a great respect for all living things and, therefore, was respected by the other mountain men who came to know him through the years. Then again, who wouldn't respect a man who was 8 and 1/2 feet tall and all muscle?

His size contributed greatly to the abilities he was known for. He was once attacked by a very large and very angry black bear. He wrestled with the animal for hours before finally killing it by breaking its neck. He sustained several severe wounds in the struggle. One covered his back entirely and left the imprint of the bear's whole paw. He kept one of the bear's claws, made it into a necklace, and wore it all his life. The scar and the necklace earned him the nickname, "Bear Claw."

Bear Claw never left his mountain home but was nevertheless well known by the townspeople. Stories of his size and strength were widespread. These stories were started by other mountain men he had helped. One in particular,

"Honey Boy" Adams, couldn't tell enough about him. My great-great grandfather had saved his life by stopping his "runaway" wagon from going over a cliff.

When Bear Claw was close to the age of thirty, he married the daughter of one of the older mountain men, one of his own father's best friends. My great-great grandmother was five-foot nothin'. What a pair they made. They spent the rest of their lives in their mountain home, never going into town. They had twelve children, all of whom had that same love for the wilderness and respect for its wild-life.

The same holds true for my father's family. They are all hard workers too. The men and some of the women are physically and mentally strong. They have endured many hardships growing up in the wilderness, then having to adjust to life in various towns and cities.

Alejandrina "Bear Claw" Vigil lived a life filled with hardships. Most of these he had to endure alone, relying on his instincts and memories of his father's teachings. He survived the coldest winters and the hottest and driest ~~of~~

summers. He fought the most severe of blizzards and the most threatening of forest fires.

My great-great grandfather died at the age of 96. He was buried near his home, under the same tree where he was born.

Reminiscence : Myth — Assessment

Physical strength and strong will are two things I have always admired in my father's family. I remember having to look up at my father and uncles. They have always been big men with what sometimes seemed like unlimited physical abilities. More importantly, they are strong-willed. They have often overcome hardships when it would have been so easy to give up. Their sense of responsibility always carried them through. This is true of the women as well.

I often wonder how some people can carry on so faithfully when the situation is dim. Especially when it so often means sacrificing a great deal. I don't feel I have this characteristic in me. I'm working on it.

DAY TWELVE—CINEMA: TWILIGHT

In the **Cinema** exercises, your aim is to write an ideal future for yourself. You previously completed the **Day Six—Cinema: Noonlight** exercise in which you imagined exactly what a day in your life would be like. You brainstormed, then created a verbal videotape—"A Day in the Life"—and then assessed its worth and determined what you could do to begin to realize that dream. **Cinema: Twilight** follows roughly the same procedure. But rather than being wrapped up in a career and making your way in the world, you will imagine yourself as an elder, someone whose major accomplishments are complete and who is enjoying the fruits of that previous labor, as someone enjoying the sights and shadows of the twilight. Follow the pattern used earlier. Relax. Brainstorm. Describe "A Day In The Life." Complete the assessment. When you have finished, staple the sheets together together and place them in your PDJ.

An Example

Gene Lenardi is a business major who is preparing himself for law school. In the following **Cinema: Twilight,** watch how he prepares himself for the hard work ahead of him by focusing on the many rewards it will bring. Note the realism in his assessment. He expects a lot out of life, but he does not count on anyone handing it to him on a silver platter. He's ready to earn his security.

SEPTEMBER 20, 1987

6:30 A.M.

CHAPTER ROOM

CINEMA: TWILIGHT

A DAY IN THE LIFE

SITTING IN THE MASTER BEDROOM, LOOKING AT A PHOTO ALBUM. READING OVER SOME NEWSPAPER CLIPPINGS FROM MY BEST CASES. I THINK TO MYSELF THAT I HAD GUTS TO TAKE CHANCES LIKE I DID. I THINK BACK TO THESE CASES AND REMEMBER HOW BRILLIANT MY DEFENSES WERE. THERE IS A PICTURE OF ME RECEIVING THE LAWYER OF THE YEAR AWARD FROM THE PRESIDENT. I WAS SO PROUD ON THAT DAY.

THERE I AM IN THE LOBBY OF THE HOSPITAL WAITING FOR GENE JR. TO BE BORN. I WAS AT THE HOSPITAL IN THE SAME ROOM IN THE SAME CONDITION TWO MORE TIMES. I WAS NEVER SO PROUD AS WHEN GENE, MIKE, AND DIONE WERE GROWING UP. I HAD SO MUCH FUN WITH THEM. I KNEW MY HARD WORK WOULD KEEP THEM ALWAYS HAPPY.

HERE IS A PICTURE OF MY LAST OFFICIAL DAY AT WORK. I HAND THE FIRM OVER TO GENE JR. KNOWING HE CAN DO THE JOB. BUT I WILL ALWAYS MAKE SURE TO KNOW WHAT IS GOING ON IN THE FIRM. WITH MIKE AND

DIONE IN LAW SCHOOL, IT WILL NOT BE LONG UNTIL THEY ARE IN THE FIRM TOO.

HERE IS A PICTURE OF ME ON MY WEDDING DAY. THE HAPPIEST YEARS OF MY LIFE I HAVE SPENT WITH MARIA. THEY CONTINUE.

I LOOK SO HAPPY IN THIS PICTURE OF ME, GENE, AND HIS WIFE, FELICIA, ON THEIR WEDDING DAY. GENE HAS HAD MY ONLY TWO GRAND-CHILDREN SO FAR, AND THEY ARE A GREAT FAMILY. HERE ARE PICTURES OF MY TWO GRANDCHILDREN, LITTLE GENE AND ANTHONY, WHO ARE SIX AND FOUR. I ALWAYS HAVE FUN WITH THOSE TWO CHARACTERS.

I HAVE HAD A GREAT LIFE.

CINEMA : TWILIGHT — ASSESSMENT

I HOPE THAT WHEN IT IS TIME TO START LOOKING BACK ON MY LIFE, I SEE A LIFE OF SUCCESS AND HARD WORK. I WANT TO BE VERY SECURE, THE SECURITY COMING AS A REWARD FOR HARD WORK. I WANT TO BE VERY SUCCESSFUL, TO BE PROUD OF WHAT I ACCOMPLISHED AND HOW I DID IT.

DAY THIRTEEN—CENTERING FIVE

What kind of day has it been? What has struck you? Where are you right NOW? This is the last **Centering** exercise. Brainstorm. Metaphor. Centering—So?

An Example

Dave Walker, an agricultural economics major, is having a particularly fine day.

Sept. 14, 1987
Library
1:30 p.m.

Centering Five
Brainstorm

Exteme happiness - everything going great
Excitement — Nothing wrong

Accomplishment - got my work done
Anxiety - too many things to Look forw.
Hyper - Lots of energy

METAPHOR

I am a coke that has been shaken up. First I was fine, just a few bubbles. Then someone, something, shook me up - for the good, of course. Now I'm just waiting to explode on someone.

Centering - So?

This one was gREAt. I guess it is because I'm in such a good mood. Things are so good, not a care, no homework. I can do anything I please. Today it seems there will never be a poor day.

DAY FOURTEEN—REFLECTIONS

The final exercise in the PDJ sequence asks you to assess all that you have written and to establish new directions in your life or to rededicate yourself to your present goals. Think of this program as an extended research project. What you have been investigating is your self, and what you will finally produce is a confident and aware self well-equipped to direct your unfolding life. **Reflections** causes you to RE-search all that you've discovered about your past and RE-view all that you've projected about your future. We look back again so we can look more confidently into the future. Now is the time to put all the thinking and writing you have done for the PDJ to work for you.

Reflections has three parts. *First*, return to your writing place with plenty of paper, take one sheet, head it in the normal way, and label it "Reflections: Centering." Then relax. Make your mind a clear canvas waiting for new and beautiful shapes and colors to cover it. When your mind is ready, read through and review all your writing in the PDJ. Recapture all you thought and felt while working through the exercises. Then, complete another **Centering** exercise. Remember to complete the process entirely: Brainstorm, Metaphor, Centering—So?

Second, review all the **Centering** exercises, including the one just completed, and select two that you would like to spend more time exploring. These two can be the most contradictory or the most similar ones, the two you enjoyed doing most, or the two you think are the best. But be sure you choose two worthy of further consideration. Having selected two, take another sheet of paper, label it "Reflections: Interaction," and reconstruct the personality who wrote each of the two exercises. Each **Centering** exercise represents a separate aspect or facet of your personality. Each of us is really many personalities working together within one person. Once you have reconstructed the personalities, engage them in some kind of interaction.

What you are doing here is the reverse of the **Centering** process. You are creating a personality from a metaphor rather than distilling a metaphor from the complex personality represented by the brainstorm. As you do this, refer to the brainstorms for specific details.

The interaction between **Centering** exercises can take a variety of forms. Some writers have had one personality offer the other advice about some problem. Others have written letters from one **Centering** to the other. Some of the most interesting interactions have been written as dialogs or debates. Whatever the form, remember the purpose: your aim is to discover agreement and/or conflict within the various parts of yourself as they have found representation in the **Centering** exercises. Raising your awareness of these aspects of personality allows you to sharpen or smooth edges, to put your various characteristics to work in service to the goals and ideals that you have discovered and established throughout the PDJ. Engaging these aspects of yourself in interaction can help you gain awareness and control.

Third, take another sheet of paper, label it "Reflections: Insights," and spend a good amount of time freewriting about your whole experience of writing the PDJ. What did you enjoy most or least? What exercise took you places in your mind that you did not know existed? Get as many different impressions as you can down on paper.

Next, draw a line beneath the freewriting. Search it, and abstract three *major* insights you have had as a result of writing the PDJ. Consider their source and significance. Finally, consider whether these insights challenge or confirm and reinforce the way you think and feel about things. Consider your values and beliefs. Are you more aware of them now and more secure in their worth? Are there changes you would like to make as a result of what you have discovered? As you write about changes, try to be as specific and complete as possible. Make these resolutions you can work with. Write so you can start to act upon your discoveries even today. When you have completed the exercise, staple all the sheets together and place them in your Learning Log together with all the other writings that make up your PDJ.

A Last Example

Reflections is a demanding exercise. It should be; it is the culmination of 14 days of intense thinking and writing about your self. Do not let the complexity of the exercise confuse you. Follow the directions precisely, as Amy Watson does in this example.

Throughout her PDJ, Amy, a twenty-two-year-old who h...
rectly from high school only to do poorly and quit to work and...
been dealing with her confusion at discovering feelings she could...
but could not dismiss. Much of the confusion resulted from her attitu...
the past. She revels in memories but sometimes feels limited by her past an...
it makes her expect of life. Notice that her Centering Metaphor portrays her a...
newly empowered child, for the first time able to make decisions for herself. Then
she has her self's two distinct aspects interact through short letters. By the end
she has developed a healthy respect for her past, but she has also distanced herself
from it. Thus, she can look to the future unencumbered. She ends on this hopeful
note.

September 20, 1987
    9:00 p.m.
    Study

Reflections: Centering

relieved — it helps to write down your
    feelings.

happy — in my mind I have visited
    people I missed

confused — I never really make sense

surprised — some things I've written
    I can't believe I feel. There
    is more to me than I thought.

worried — my handwriting and grammar
    in the journal

scared — I can't finish the story on my
    own death

Metaphor

I am a child who has learned to open
and close doors. I can go into or out of

rooms, as I choose. I can keep or leave anything I want or don't want in my life.

Centering — So?

I have really had a hard time about the future. I realize this comes from the fact that I want something, yet sometimes I don't. I have also learned that I don't always make sense.

I like reminiscing about people and places, because it makes me happy and it also makes me a little surer of what I want and who I really am.

Reflections: Interaction

Centerings one and three show me as two completely different people, one calm, the other crazy.

Dear Calm:
I am so mad. My friend is trying to steal my boyfriend. My boss is unfair. School is alright but some of my classes are boring.

Also, do you know what Helga said? I can't believe it, but she said I was stuck-up. I have a good mind to go over to her house and show her the real meaning of stuck-up!

Life here is great. Ha-ha.

Sarcastically yours,
A. W.

Dear Crazy;

I don't understand why you get so upset. Why are you so worried about what everybody says? Isn't the most important thing in life how you feel about yourself? Relax. See how beautiful everything really is. Who cares if Helga thinks you're stuck-up. She's a turkey. All that really matters is how you and your friends think you are. Start concentrating on yourself.

Confidently yours,

Amy

Reflections: Insights

I really enjoyed parts of the P.J. and I wasn't expecting to. Some (especially the Milestone) were too hard for me to write down on paper. I'm afraid to face some things. Not ready yet.

I enjoyed the reminiscing because I felt as though I was losing touch with parts of the past that I love so much.

Now I realize I can keep it fresh in my mind if I try.

I realize I live too much in the past, trying to be and have what I was then. I also realize it is good to remember, even the bad.

I think that after a while I will be able to release my innerself and write down what I am now afraid to write. I need to. Only in the reminiscences and in Centering Three did I really let it all out. It felt good.

Conclusion

Now you have finished the 14-day Personal Development Journal cycle. How great a sense of accomplishment you must feel. You have examined your self, your past, and your present, and you have imagined your future. And you have done all this with an intensity few people have ever experienced. You should feel a sense of control that not many others know.

But most of all, you have begun a process of awareness building through keeping a personal journal. You can depend on it always. Many write in their personal journals frequently, sometimes daily. Learning what you have about both the benefits and the techniques of keeping a personal journal, now you must decide how you will continue. You can use any one of the PDJ exercises to create a single daily journal entry. Knowing the general pattern—brainstorm, structure, assess—and the places to explore—past, present, future—enables you to conceive your own variations. You are limited only by your own imagination.

Now you know what a personal journal can do for your self-development. Now you know how to keep one. It's your responsibility to determine how to use what you have learned to your best advantage.

PART TWO

WRITING FOR THE OUTSIDE

CHAPTER 3

Writing a Personal Narrative Essay

INTRODUCTION

When WRITING FOR THE OUTSIDE, our job is not complete until something gets done in the world. We accomplish this by using our writing for *informing*, *arguing*, and *persuading*. We inform readers so they can do what we can already do—that is, how to complete a job application, how to make a computer run a program, how to design a scientific experiment. We present arguments to readers in order to explain and defend our position on issues—that is, why a character acted a particular way in a novel or movie, why second-hand smoke harms a work environment, why Congress should raise taxes to reduce the budget deficit. We persuade readers to do work we want or need done—that is, to buy the refrigerator we are trying to sell, to volunteer to teach in the local adult reading program, to vote for the candidate we support.

The concern for having an effect on a particular audience is the major difference between WRITING FOR THE INSIDE and WRITING FOR THE OUTSIDE. It is what you will be learning to do in this and the following chapters in Part Two. You will learn to use specific activities during the writing process to help you discover, structure, evaluate, and communicate ideas for audiences beyond yourself. You will learn several essay forms that you can use to structure ideas so they can have an impact on public audiences. All this will prepare you for the WRITING FOR THE OUTSIDE you will be required to do in school and beyond.

LOG EXERCISE: A Personal and a Public Letter

To prepare for our discussion of WRITING FOR THE OUTSIDE, you will first write two letters and then examine the process you used to complete them. You need to choose a controversial subject about which you have strong feelings. Choose a subject you already know something about so you can write your letter without having to complete extensive background reading or research. Possible issues include nuclear policy, school prayer, women's rights, and so on. If you cannot settle on an issue immediately, page through a newspaper or weekly newsmagazine, or watch the evening news to sample a range of issues, then select one that is interesting and familiar to you.

Once you have selected a topic, spend time writing in your Log to discover your position on the issue. Answer these questions: What do you know about the issue? Why do you feel as you do? What do you feel you ought to learn about the issue to feel more confident in your position? This writing resembles what you have already been doing in your journal writing.

When you have finished writing in your Log, draft two letters. Address the first one to someone you know and who knows you. This is a personal, informal letter. Let your reader know how you feel about the issue, how strongly you feel, and why.

Having completed that letter, write another. But this time write to someone who holds an influential position in an organization involved with the issue and who does not know you. Write to a government official, such as a member of Congress or the local legislature, or a leader of one of the organizations involved. Choose someone who determines policy and who might be influenced by your opinion and arguments. To find addresses, check your local newspaper or phone book, or ask a reference librarian who can help you with directories and other sources.

When you write to the public official, make your letter more elaborate and formal than the personal letter. Use a college writing handbook to check the format for business letters. Look there also for hints about the structure and organization of formal letters. In addition, pay close attention to your language and the effect it will have on your audience. Consider your purpose also. You are stating and defending your opinion in order to influence another person. Your job is to encourage action. Keep this in mind as you write the letter. How to do this is the challenge confronting you in this assignment.

When you have completed the drafts of the letters, revise them, make photocopies to keep for yourself, and mail the originals. You will probably get some kind of response in a few weeks.

When you have completed and mailed the letters, respond to the questions below in your Log. Be specific with your answers and be prepared to discuss your experiences and findings with your classmates.

1. Which of the two letters was easier to write? Why?

2. Briefly describe how you wrote the letters. How did you prepare to write? What sources and materials—dictionaries, background articles, and so on—did you consult? How did you structure your letters? How much revising did you do? How much time did you spend writing?

3. Compare the writing of the informal letter to the formal one. Can you draw any conclusions about the writing process as a result of comparing the way you wrote these two letters?

4. Compare the language you used in the two letters. Are there differences? Mention one or two specific instances and account for the differences.

5. Consider the difference of purpose in the two letters. How did that difference affect the way you wrote? Be specific.

WRITING FOR THE OUTSIDE

In doing this Log exercise, most writers discover that writing for the distant public audience is more complicated than writing for the close private audience. They discover that all writing involves four basic elements: *preparation, structure, language,* and *purpose*.

First, writers find some important similarities. They find that getting started is about the same for both letters. Discovering their opinions is not difficult; a ten-minute freewriting session like those so frequently used in the PDJ exercises produces a workable position statement. Many supplement the freewriting with other journal writing to find reasons to support their positions. In short, discovering how they feel, what they believe, and why, regardless of the ultimate use of the information, basically comes through the same process, through WRITING FOR THE INSIDE.

Writing to a friend is generally considered the easier of the two tasks. Usually, writers assume their friends believe as they do, and this greatly affects their writing. The letter is written without extensive *preparation*, with the ease and directness of a journal entry. The *structure* of the personal letter is simple and straightforward. Writers explain why they are writing, state and defend their position, and close the letter. The *language* is that of normal conversation—informal and personal. They know the audience, so they trust that such language will be understood. Their *purpose* is as much to discover, confirm, and report their positions as it is to argue; they are not overly concerned with changing minds or inspiring action. Upon reflection, they feel the letter's most important function is clarifying their feelings and establishing contact between friends.

However, writers report great differences in considering the formal letter. Writing for the public audience raises more complicated problems. In terms of *preparation*, they need more ideas and evidence to establish a position and argue it. Thus, after they have used journal writing to determine a position, they frequently discover that they do not know certain basic information that is crucial to their argument, so they must go to the library or consult experts to research the topic. In short, they report doing more because they need more—more information, more arguments—to choose from in order to write effectively for the public audience.

Structure, how the parts—the opening, argument, and closing—fit together, also receives much more detailed attention in the public letter. Formal letters to public officials require attention to conventions and formats, including margins, page design, addresses, titles, salutations, and so forth, which can largely be ignored in the personal letter. More significantly, writers adjust the structure of their arguments to accomplish their goals, changing the minds of readers and inspiring them to action. They create a context—why they are writing—and announce their message—what they want to happen—much more explicitly. They structure the letter more logically, moving from one key point to another, developing all the key points in relation to the major point. The letter is written for one purpose, to lead to the conclusion, a way to think or act. Structure becomes a major concern when WRITING FOR THE OUTSIDE.

Writers find that their *language* changes in the second letter. It becomes public. They can no longer trust any private meanings shared between writer and reader. They select language that anyone reading the letter will understand without difficulty. Even the slightest chance of confusion or ambiguity causes them to search for more precise words, or to add words and clarify more. They want to be understood.

They also change from familiar, conversational language to public, formal language. When preparing the public letter, they use dictionaries and thesauruses extensively. They check the accuracy and precision of words; they want their language to be powerful and impressive. They search for words that will cause readers to identify them among the well-educated and socially powerful. They strive to sound like individuals who ought to be listened to. They are willing to work hard and take risks in order to make their point.

Perhaps the greatest change between writing the two letters involves *purpose*. Rather than merely expressing their position, they are concerned with getting the audience not only to understand but to act in a certain way. Their purpose is not accomplished until they have changed minds and motivated the audience to change or strengthen policy or law. This is the fundamental difference between WRITING FOR INSIDE and WRITING FOR THE OUTSIDE. When writing for a public audience, writers are concerned with making something happen in the world.

So where are we? We must view these contrasts in terms of ultimate outcomes. In the personal letter, the main tasks are discovering a position and recording it for another. In the public letter, in addition to discovering and recording, we must inform and persuade a distant, perhaps hostile, audience. We must explain and defend a position, make readers see its value, and move them to act.

THE COMPOSING PROCESS

As you know from experience, WRITING FOR THE OUTSIDE such as that required in the formal letter can be a costly activity, consuming lots of time and energy. Good writers strive to be efficient. They manage their work by determining the whole job that needs to be done, breaking that task into manageable subtasks, developing routines for completing the subtasks, and integrating the parts into a whole. A set procedure, which can move us step by step through a writing assignment from beginning to end, will help us manage this work efficiently. Developing such a process will be our purpose here.

We will be considering a *model* process for composing essays. As a model it has flaws. Some writers may think the model is like a soup recipe, a guarantee for success. Throw a little of this and that into the pot, bring to boil, simmer for thirty minutes, add some more of this and that, simmer for another forty minutes and *voilà*—soup.

If you know anything about cooking, you know that good cooks make adjustments and personalize recipes. The chef is not a slave to the recipe; using it as a guideline, she or he combines it with other information and previous experience to make a great soup. So, take the suggestions that follow as guidelines, not as an absolute recipe. They reflect what many successful writers report they do. But what is right for them may not be appropriate for you. Ultimately, you must develop your own composing process.

Most experienced writers insist that good writing does not come through a linear, recipe-like process. You probably know what they are talking about. Think back to writing the PDJ exercises. Did you ever change your mind in the middle of an exercise, develop a new tack or angle, or even change your subject entirely? In the **Reminiscence: Place** exercise, for example, many writers will brainstorm about several places and then describe another place altogether. If they stick with the first places that come to mind, they may not discover the place they really need or want to write about.

These types of changes can take place all through the composing process, and they demonstrate an important point about writing. Writing is *recursive*; it does not happen in direct succession, with one procedure following another, one word, one sentence, one paragraph neatly following the one before. While editing and putting what seem to be the finishing touches on an essay, a writer may discover that a major idea is missing or poorly developed. Should the writer then only patch the essay up and not do any significant rewriting because editing is supposed to involve only minor changes coming at the end of the writing process?

In fact, many inexperienced writers may fall victim to a common mistake— making a superficial change when a substantial revision is really needed. Not understanding the writing process, they may fail to evaluate effectively. They may not try to reconceive and revise. They may fail to make connections and discoveries that would make their writing better, would increase their learning, and would improve their essays.

Experienced writers understand that rather than being a straight-line process with a beginning, middle, and end, writing is like a set of irregular loops, a set of cycles—thinking, writing, researching, reading, rethinking, rewriting, writing and so on. It may look more like this:

like a misshapen spiral, weaving itself all together into an intricate design. The point is, do not let the linear presentation of the various tasks and procedures fool you into believing that writing can come from a recipe. Good writing comes from a process.

The rest of this chapter will describe and allow you to practice the basic elements of the "ideal" composing process, so you can adapt them to fit your individual style and purposes. In the end, however, we cannot forget that there is no single composing process; rather, there are composing processes.

For purposes of instruction and practice, we will break the composing process into three distinct phases, which suggest particular tasks needing to get done at different times in the process. We will call the three phases *discovery*, *drafting*, and *revising*. Other names could be used; in fact, you may be familiar with certain alternatives like prewriting, writing, and rewriting, or outlining, writing, and editing. Still others are also possible. But discovery, drafting, and revising best describe the activities we will use while writing a formal essay.

Discovery

In the discovery phase, you prepare to write. The tasks that must get done involve finding a subject and relevant information about it, and conceiving an angle or strategy for developing that subject in writing. In doing this, you must determine exactly what to write—a term paper, an essay exam, a letter to a prospective employer, whatever—and what its purpose is—to collect and record data, to entertain, to inform, or to persuade and move someone to action.

The discovery phase helps you develop the "big picture," an approach to the whole assignment, what and why you are writing. This done, you then can focus on particular details:

What you know about the topic

How you feel about it

How you can learn more about it

Whom your audience is—familiar or unknown, close or distant

What you want your audience to do

What language will accomplish the task best—informal or formal, conversational or specialized

The discovery phase as you might experience it will be something like this: First, some thing or person catches your attention, some problem needs solving, or a teacher or supervisor gives you an assignment. Mulling over the situation, you recall from your experience some particular details that you can connect, at least tentatively, into an idea. Then you examine the idea using several strategies. You write about the idea in your journal. You begin to pin the idea down, to give it some shape. Once it has sufficient shape, you begin to talk about it with friends and colleagues. You test the clarity and potential of the idea through these informal discussions.

Often the discussions reveal that you need to consult an authority, something or someone with more knowledge about the subject or the idea than you have. Having conceived the idea for an essay, and having written in a journal and talked about it, you read to gather more information about the idea. You read to find models to imitate and to discover what problems you have not anticipated and how others have solved those problems. You consult experts or you complete some library research early in the process to see if the idea is worth your further attention and commitment.

Writers cycle and recycle through this process until an idea is formed well enough to deserve *commitment*. This sense of commitment is very important; it provides the motivation necessary to complete the later phases of the composing process. Commitment is the sense that the idea has value, that it can accomplish your purpose for writing.

Though you are now convinced the idea is worthwhile, you are not yet finished with the discovery phase. The next step involves giving some concrete shape to the idea. You return to your journal to write more and determine what you want to do with the idea. You think and research some more, perhaps consulting additional authorities and gathering more information in the library. Armed with more data, you talk some more.

Finally, you review all you have thought and written, and distill it into two or three sentences that succinctly state your topic, what you want to write about the topic, and what your goals and purposes are. This two- or three-sentence distillation is your preliminary thesis statement; it includes the subject and the central point you are going to make about it in your essay. Once you have a tentative thesis, then you develop an idea outline, a page or so of topics and subtopics you will have to consider, ordered as you suspect they will have to be considered.

The discovery phase follows this general pattern. First comes the stimulus to write, either an assignment or an idea you choose to develop by yourself. Then you proceed to pay attention to what is happening around you so you can bring all your experience and knowledge to bear on the assignment. Then you begin the process of thinking, connecting, journal writing, talking, researching, distilling, and outlining.

ESSAY #1: WRITING A PERSONAL NARRATIVE ESSAY

The first essay assignment will be writing a personal narrative. This will help you bridge the gap between WRITING FOR THE INSIDE and WRITING FOR THE OUTSIDE. Writing this essay will also introduce you to a model composing process formulated from the experience and insights of professional writers.

In writing your personal narrative essay, you will select an experience from your past and recreate it in a story. You will take an incident that had an impact on you, an incident from the **Reminiscence** section of the PDJ, and "compose" it so that it becomes meaningful not only to you, the private audience of your PDJ, but also to a public audience. You will explain the experience in terms of its significance—the impact it had on your life. You will be the narrator who tells the story.

We will work through this and subsequent essays in a sequence of "Assignments" accompanied by explanations, analyses, and step-by-step procedures designed to help you manage the choices of composing to your advantage. Follow the procedures as they are presented. Do not jump ahead or skip steps because later exercises will depend on your having worked through the whole process.

ESSAY #1: PERSONAL NARRATIVE—DISCOVERY

ASSIGNMENT: FROM PERSONAL DEVELOPMENT JOURNAL TO IDEA OUTLINE

Now we will start to work writing your personal narrative. Specifically, we will consider selecting and developing your subject, the narrative incident. We will read and analyze a sample personal narrative to determine how best to organize and structure the essay. In addition, we will develop criteria for evaluating personal narratives that will guide us through the next phase of the composing process—drafting.

Structure and Purpose

Writers generally begin a personal narrative by establishing a frame for the story. Basic details—the who, what, when, and where of the incident—prepare readers for what is to come. Then, the story is told in chronological order; that is, it is organized by a time sequence. Transitions words such as "first," "in the beginning," "while," "then," "next," "after," and others are used to signal time shifts and developments in the sequence of events.

Personal narratives are effective if they are interesting and entertaining. Often they involve incidents of common experience retold in an uncommon way. The writer will share a reminiscence from early school days or recount a dark and frightening experience, recreating the scene through the use of carefully selected details that make the scene come alive for readers. Appealing to the senses and emotions, these details cause readers to become involved with the story.

Personal narratives are effective if they clearly suggest their significance. The writer must show how the incident has significance beyond the writer's experience. It is not sufficient for the writer merely to tell a tale. The narrative must demonstrate how the incident caused the writer to assume a new direction in life or taught the writer a lesson about an important aspect of life. For example, a reminiscence of a traffic accident in which the writer, as a child, first witnessed the horror of serious injury and death, and the effect this had on the narrator, would be a good subject for a personal narrative. However, the narrative need not recount an extraordinary experience; many effective personal narratives relate common occurrences that connect with the normal experiences of readers to make an important point about life and its meaning.

But the most important characteristic of a good personal narrative is that the writer is obviously involved with the subject. The writer must sense the significance within the story. Only then can the writer communicate the sense and significance of the incident to an audience. Only after reconstructing the incident in all its details, selecting what is important and ordering the events so they make personal sense, only then can the writer begin the act of composing—shaping the story—for others so the narrative can make sense to them. This shaping for an audience beyond the self is the essence of WRITING FOR THE OUTSIDE.

500 words

A Student Sample with Analysis

Journal writing such as that you did in the **Reminiscence** exercises of the Personal Development Journal is an excellent discovery technique when writing a personal narrative. Such writing will provide you with the subject and the general chronological sequence of the incident you will develop in your essay. Because you first wrote about your subject in the PDJ, it also has the prerequisite significance that will motivate the commitment you'll need to create an effective essay for a public audience.

However, studying the personal narratives of other writers, especially how they solved problems of structure, will provide additional useful insights. To help you prepare to write your personal narrative, read the following example. Consider it carefully, and answer in your Log the questions for analysis that follow it. Remember to read purposefully. You are looking for solutions to problems you will soon confront. The following personal narrative was written by an older student returning to school to earn a teaching certificate. He also wanted to study journalism. He had just completed the PDJ. The source for the essay was **Reminiscence: Place.** As you read the essay, evaluate its effectiveness using the elements important to the success of personal narratives. These include

Clear organization through chronological order
Vivid details
A sense of life-changing significance
The writer's obvious involvement with the topic

Bread and Butter
by
Albert Johnson

I don't remember the first times I played at writing, but my mother told me I caused quite a bit of wear on walls as layer after layer of paint was washed off with the crayon wax I'd used while ''writing.'' But my first real memories of writing come from my early years in school. One in particular returns to me frequently.

I am in second grade. The room has a very high ceiling and feels more like a cavern than a classroom. The sliding doors of coat closets make the back wall. One side wall seems entirely made of windows reaching all the way to the high ceiling from just above the steam heat registers and the shelf made by their tops which are covered with potted plants and a globe of the earth. Next to the globe is the pencil sharpener.

Through the windows are the playground and then the railroad tracks. Venetian blinds, adjusted to allow as much light and air through the windows as possible, bang and whistle with the fall breeze. The only other sound I remember is the hum of the fluorescent lights, a ''monitor'' hum since whenever it was time to change an activity we had to settle into a silence quiet enough to make the light noise seem to roar in our ears. Along with the wind and Venetian-blind whistle, I could hear the lights hum. We were about to start an activity.

All I can remember of the other two walls are the chalkboards covering the walls from corner to corner broken only by the doors that let us in and out of the classroom. On this day they are filled with neatly written words and phrases. They fell into columns as we had called them out to our teacher, Miss Kelly. She had asked us to think of descriptive words, words of color and texture and size. As a student would offer a word, she would offer praise, talk about the word and what it meant, and copy it neatly in its place. Soon all the chalkboards were covered with words. The walls were alive with words.

We didn't know why we were covering the walls with words, but we knew that we were spending so much time coming up with them and Miss Kelly was being so careful and neat that something was about to happen. We left school that afternoon with a question we were to think about and answer by talking with our families: Who were we? Where did we and our families come from? What did we want to be when we grew up? We were going to spend the next days writing our autobiographies.

I remember the rest of that week clearly. Each day we would come in and the chalkboards would look at us with those same words. Miss Kelly had a portable chalkboard near her desk where she could write what she needed during

these days without disturbing the walls which had become
our word bank. We wrote several hours each day that
week. I can remember beginning to work through a
sentence, getting stuck, looking to the board, and finding
exactly the right word to get me started again. I can
remember writing whole sentences just to use words I found
interesting.

How fine I felt each day while writing that second-
grade autobiography. One section dealt with my
family. How hard I worked to write how much I loved my
grandmother, how special she was to me. ''My grandmother
smells like bread and butter'' found its way onto my page.

Near the end of each day Miss Kelly would visit with
each of us to see how we were doing. I was a bit nervous
when she came by on ''grandmother'' day because I wasn't
sure where the bread and butter idea came from. It didn't
come from the board. It came from a more important place,
from inside of me.

Miss Kelly came by and I gave her my paper. She read
it and smiled and said ''My Nana smells like Sugar
Daddies. Every time I see her, even now, she gives me a
Sugar Daddy.'' Then she showed me how to explain the
smell. When grandmother was visiting my family, she would
make me bread and butter as a snack when I got home.
That's why she smelled like bread and butter. The smell
was part of what I loved about her and why I loved her.
Bread and butter made complete sense to me after Miss
Kelly showed me how to explain it in my autobiography.

When Friday came and it was time to finish the
autobiography, recopy it, and decorate it with crayon
drawings and other second-grade art, I was not happy. I
didn't want to draw and copy over, I wanted to write
more. I didn't want to learn how to make a fancy cover
page and tie the pages together with a ribbon. I wanted
to write more.

Late that Friday, as we were packing up our books and
supplies and straightening our desks for the weekend, Miss
Kelly took the eraser and cleared the board of all those

words. How strange it seemed. The room felt empty.

One reason I remember so much about that autobiography is that through some quirk of fate, my Aunt Evie still has the now-grayed booklet. I had given the autobiography to my grandmother as a present. After my grandmother died, Evie found the little book among grandmother's things and kept it for herself. Even now, almost thirty years later, whenever I talk with Aunt Evie the autobiography comes up. She talks about how my grandmother loved that book and how even now when Evie makes some bread and butter she thinks about her mother, my grandmother.

Three things strike me about writing the autobiography and explain why I remember it so vividly. First, I remember the vocabulary boards and ''bread and butter'' because for that week writing became real to me and I became real through writing. I was able to put words together to create something important. Through the process of writing, I was discovering myself. ''Bread and butter'' helped me understand my world and the sensations and experiences that made it. This made me better able to live in it, to understand it and enjoy it more.

Second, other people—Miss Kelly, my family, and especially my grandmother and my aunt—made the writing seem important and meaningful. I wonder whether I would remember the incident at all if I did not receive praise from my teacher and later from my family for the autobiography. I gained from their response to my writing a sense of how writing can have an impact on people, on readers. I learned, as well as a second grader can learn, that writing could make me an influence on other people.

Finally, I learned then what a wonderful power resided in being a teacher like Miss Kelly, a teacher who could make the world a place of wonder and joy for young people. Now I understand why I am back in school and why I will not be truly happy until I have the opportunity to help children as Miss Kelly and the autobiography helped me.

LOG EXERCISE: Questions for Analysis

Consider "Bread and Butter" and answer the following questions in your Learning Log, giving specific examples from the essay in your responses:

1. Organization: Use of Order and Transition

How does the writer establish the framework for the narrative? Does the writer organize the essay effectively? Does he make use of chronological order? What other kinds of order does he use—spatial (organized by the relation of one thing to another in a place), logical (organized by showing how one conclusion follows from another, causes another, exemplifies another, or is a part of another), climactic (building to a climax, from least to most important or dramatic)? Does he combine different kinds of orders? What are some of the specific transition words he uses, and how do they contribute to the organization of the essay? How does he move from one incident to the next?

2. Subject Matter: Use of Specific Detail

What is the writer's subject matter and how does he approach it? Is it a common experience recreated in an uncommon way? Is it an extraordinary experience? Does the writer's use of detail contribute to the effectiveness of the narrative? List three details you remember and briefly explain the effect they had on you.

3. Significance

Why did the writer tell this story? What was its significance? What significance could it have for readers? Summarize the significance in two sentences. What suggestions would you give the writer to make the essay more understandable to you and other readers? Formulate at least one specific suggestion.

4. Writer's Involvement

Do you believe the writer's statements about the incident? Why or why not? Explain your answer in two or three sentences, making specific references to the essay.

Be prepared to share your analysis with other members of your class. Keep in mind that you are still preparing to write your own personal narrative and that these questions can help you evaluate your own essay.

Choosing and Developing a Subject

You have familiarized yourself with the general structure of a personal narrative through analyzing Albert Johnson's essay. Now it is time to start working in earnest on your own. To complete the rest of the discovery phase of this assignment, you must find and shape a subject of your own and develop a plan for turning it into an essay for a public audience.

First, you must choose and develop your subject, in this case, the story you will build your personal narrative around. To do this, review your PDJ and select an incident from a **Reminiscence** exercise to serve as the subject. Because you have already spent considerable time on this exercise, you will have plenty of ideas and details to work with, as well as having already found the incident worth examining and being committed to it.

After you have selected your subject, however, you will want to complete some of the other discovery activities suggested earlier. For example, try some more journal writing. Try talking to a friend or a classmate in order to test your readiness to write. Research your **Reminiscence** by consulting participants in the incident if they are available. Because you are working from personal experience and memory, formal library research will probably not be needed. Work hard on formulating your statement, on making sure you have remembered all that is important in the incident so you can narrate it completely. Gain the sense of mastery of facts and significance needed to write an effective personal narrative for a public audience.

Writing an Idea Outline

Having completed this early phase of the composing process, you need now to create an idea outline to guide you through the next phase of writing the personal narrative. Remember your purpose in this early phase of composing: pay attention to the movement from the inside out, from personal and private significance to public meaningfulness.

Idea outlines are informal lists of the topics and ideas you plan on developing in your first draft. The list can be a catalog of details, a sentence or two that previews the whole essay, or a bunch of short phrases that will each become a major episode in the essay.

Idea outlines resemble the brainstorms you did during the journal-writing exercises. Their purpose is to give you data to work with. Often the idea outline suggests the organization of the draft by listing ideas in the order they will be developed in the essay. Remember, the idea outline is tentative, so you do not have to use all that appears on the list, nor are you limited to only what is on the list. Some of your best ideas will come to you as you write.

Take a look at the idea outline Albert Johnson created for "Bread and Butter." Although the list of details is sparse, most of the major ideas as well as the organization of the essay are suggested in the idea outline. Do you see any details in the idea outline that have been left out in the final version? Can you determine why these details and the episodes surrounding them were eliminated? Has anything else been changed?

```
          The Making of a Writer


      Why I want to write and teach.
First writing--writing on the walls.  Mom's stories.
2nd grade autobiography
     The Scene--inside/outside sounds, the coal train
```

```
            --WALLS ARE ALIVE WITH WORDS
            --portable chalkboard for arithmetic
   The Week--Nana and the smell of bread and butter
            Tony M. gets in trouble for giggling
   The Result--Nana's illness and death; Evie and the
   fond memories: power in writing
               --making myself through writing
               --wanting to share the power and good
                  feeling, wanting to write more and to
                  teach.
```

Assignment Summary

By now you should have completed three pieces of writing to help you through the discovery phase of the composing process.

1. The **Reminiscence** exercise
2. Additional journal work to adapt your entry to the requirements of the personal narrative
3. The idea outline

Having completed the idea outline, you are ready to move from discovery to the drafting phase. Read the next section on drafting before completing any more work on your personal narrative. It will provide you more instructions and exercises.

Drafting

"Writing" is the term many use to describe the activities in the middle phase of the composing process. However, we are using the term drafting. Writing, as we have learned, is part of every phase. We mean drafting here in the sense of trying out a plan for a paper. The writer's task during this phase is like that of the architect of a building. The architect starts with an idea and then plays with it, sketching and reconsidering and resketching, checking the original plan against what will work given the particular materials to be used, what the building will be used for, and what the customer wants. This phase ends with the construction of an experimental model essay that can be examined closely and tested.

As we draft an essay, we impose shape and structure upon the ideas conceived during the discovery phase. We consider what knowledge we have about the subject, what we want to say, what language we have to use, what our audience needs and will respond to, and more. As we connect all these elements we create a minor miracle, the draft. The draft, with its cross-outs, with arrows moving one idea from here to there, with notes in the margins, with sections of one page cut out and taped onto another page, is the victory won by the writer who meets the challenge of drafting.

How exactly do writers work through this process? Again, procedures vary from writer to writer. Many write informal notes in journals or on odd scraps of paper. They review these notes and, following the general plan contained in the idea outline, write the paragraphs and clusters of paragraphs that become the draft when they are all spliced together. These notes either develop new ideas or address problems in the original idea outline. Often writers are blocked because they do not know where a new idea may fit in the outline. Through informal note taking, writers can develop the new idea enough to determine how it relates to others in the idea outline.

After taking notes, writers create the first draft. They start without knowing exactly where they are headed. Although they have been mulling over the topic for quite some time, have the idea outline produced during the discovery phase, and now have notes to help map the essay's way, they sit to write and find that the draft can take its own direction. They write quickly, paying little attention to grammar and mechanics, concentrating on getting ideas out and down on paper. They take great pleasure in watching ideas they believed they had under control get away to make new and unsuspected connections. Often they write until they run out of physical energy. Rarely do they run out of ideas. These sessions can run for hours and generate many pages of material that can be subsequently examined, evaluated, reworked, or ignored.

Once writers have completed a first draft, they begin the hard work of reading and evaluating what they have produced with the goal of producing a finished draft. Often this involves transferring the handwritten first draft into typescript or onto a word processor. As they move from one format to another, they revise lightly, adding information when a point is not clear, eliminating ideas that do not contribute to the essay as a whole, or changing sentences to make them read better. They solve problems they encounter in the first draft.

In short, they are revising, though slightly, even during the drafting phase. Their goal is to create as clean and complete a version of the essay as quickly as possible, a "finished draft," which they can then submit to friends or editors for response.

ESSAY #1: PERSONAL NARRATIVE—DRAFTING

ASSIGNMENT: WRITE THE FIRST AND FINISHED DRAFTS

Your job now is to take the idea outline created in the discovery phase of this assignment and turn it into a finished draft. Try the suggestions noted above—informal note taking, writing the first draft, and recopying with slight revisions—in order to create a draft you will be able to give to others for response and critiquing. Whenever you are drafting, make sure you leave yourself plenty of space to write notes and make changes. If you are using looseleaf sheets, write only on one side of the paper, skip lines, and leave wide margins. If typewriting, triple space with wide margins. The extra space will come in handy during the revising phase.

Since you have spent so much time working on this topic already, the first draft should come easily to you. However, do not work through so quickly that you miss opportunities for surprises and new ideas that can come while drafting. In addition, make sure to use the lessons you learned earlier about structuring the narrative, using details, establishing significance, and demonstrating your involvement with the subject.

Finally, revise lightly as you copy over the first draft to make the strongest finished draft possible. Because you will be sharing your finished draft with peers who will give you responses you can use during the revising phase, it should be easily readable and free of incomplete ideas and obvious errors. The extra care you take now will help you later.

Assignment Summary

By now you should have completed three pieces of writing to help you through the drafting phase of the composing process:

1. The informal note taking, journal entries, and paragraph clusters expanding the idea outline
2. The first draft
3. The recopied, slightly revised, finished draft that you will be sharing with your peers

Revising

We have compared writing an essay to designing and constructing a building. Much work must be completed before the tenants move in. Earlier we considered drafting in terms of an architect using the original idea and rough plan to create a working model, the finished draft. Once the architect has the idea in the concrete form of a working model, the engineer takes over to bring the project to completion. The engineer checks the model's workings against those originally conceived and against what will work in the world. This is the same task a writer faces when revising. When the engineer begins to erect the building and discovers that the architect did not include room for stairways to get from one floor to another when the elevator is out of service, then the engineer goes back to the drawing board to solve the problem. Similarly when a writer discovers that the experimental model designed at the "drafting" board is not working as originally planned, then the writer must revise.

To revise is to "re-see" the idea and the model, to discover problems and fix them. For a writer the problem is not nearly so concrete as the problem of the engineer and the missing stairways. Either the building has or does not have them.

But what about an essay? How does a writer gain a sense of whether it is working or not? Often solving the problem involves finding readers who can respond to the draft and provide the writer with some specific feedback. The writer must then use this feedback while revising.

How do we manage the many aspects of effective revision? The best way is to break the revising process into two major tasks, *assessment* and *reformulation*. Assessment involves evaluating the finished draft of an essay to determine whether it is working as well as it should. First we get peer critiques, then we complete a self-evaluation to assess our peers' responses. Reformulation involves revising—making the changes mandated by the assessment, then editing to polish our style, and finally proofreading to ensure grammatical and mechanical correctness.

Assessment through Peer Critiquing

Most of us cannot distance ourselves sufficiently from our writing to evaluate it effectively. In the heat of composing, when everything is going well, we are so enamored of our own work, so impressed with its cohesiveness and clarity, that we assume it is just as clear and effective for everybody. We believe that we are making complete sense. But, when WRITING FOR THE OUTSIDE, we are not the only readers of our writing. In fact, if we do not consider other readers we will not fulfill the purpose of our writing.

What we must do is to break free from the charm of our own writing. The best way to break its spell is to get other people to read the essay. By giving the "finished draft" to another reader, a colleague or friend, we can get responses beyond our own. Using these responses, we can anticipate the reactions of a much larger audience and shape our ideas and essays to their expectations and needs. Getting these external responses, we can make sure that we are not fooling ourselves, that we are indeed accomplishing our purpose for writing.

Moreover, our peers confront the same problem, but together we can succeed. We can find ways to help each other when revising. What we need is a procedure for soliciting and collecting peer responses. Providing peers with our finished drafts and a set of questions for them to consider allows us to get detailed and specific responses that will help us revise. These questions should reflect the nature of the writing assignment and address issues of organization and purpose.

The following exercise explains the purpose and procedure for peer critiquing, and it provides specific questions for use with the personal narrative essay. Note how the system works, especially in terms of directing the response of peers to particular features of the essay.

Your instructor will also provide certain information about organizing a peer critiquing session. Groups can range in size from two to five. You may be given class time to complete the exercise, or you may meet your peers outside of class. Sometimes you may be required to provide your peers with copies of your finished draft that they will mark on and return to you. Sometimes they will listen while you read out loud. Specific arrangements will vary with essay assignments, instructor preference, and your needs as a writer. Complete the exercise to help you with the assessment aspect of revising your personal narrative.

ESSAY #1: PERSONAL NARRATIVE—REVISING

ASSIGNMENT: PEER CRITIQUING

Assessment through peer critiquing offers writers the opportunity to try their writing out on an audience of their peers. Writers then can use the peers' responses and reactions as they revise. These responses are most helpful when they are truthful, straightforward, and detailed. However, writers themselves will ultimately determine which responses—all, some, or none—will receive attention during revision.

Your peers have a responsibility to you to read or listen closely, respond honestly, and provide specific information that can be helpful to you during revision. It is not enough to say, "I liked it." Peers must explain why: "I liked it because the vivid details helped me *see* your point." Even better would be, "Your use of 'reddish' to describe the color of the just-disked farmer's field reminded me of the red dirt on the farm where I grew up." Peers are not responsible for revising, evaluating, or correcting your writing; they are responsible for providing helpful information for you to do these things for yourself.

General Procedure

Conduct the peer critiquing session for the personal narrative essay in the following manner. Follow the procedure closely to ensure the best use of your and your peers' time and energy.

1. The writer reads the finished draft of the essay aloud **twice.**

2. Peers listen carefully, taking notes only during the second reading.

3. After the second reading, peers may ask for a rereading of a particular part of the essay. (The writer should take note of such requests because they often signal rough spots that will need attention during revision.)

4. After rereading for clarification, peers quickly write responses to the peer critique questions. Responses should not evaluate or correct the paper, unless the questions specifically ask them to. Peers then share their written responses with the writer.

5. The writer reviews the responses and, when needed, asks for clarification and elaboration. The writer must not haggle but should study what the responses say about the essay. Haggling comes later, in the privacy of revision, when the writer determines which responses deserve attention and which should be ignored.

PEER CRITIQUE QUESTIONS

Answer the following questions when providing peer responses to the personal narrative essay:

1. What word, phrase, or sentence do you most remember from the essay? Why did it impress you?
2. What color or emotion best expresses how the essay made you feel? Describe why the writing made you feel that way.
3. Considering the organization of the essay, does the writer use chronological order effectively? List some of the transitions used to smooth the movement from one episode to another. Does the writer use any other kind of order? Which ones and what specific transitional devices did you notice?
4. Are there any places in the essay where you get lost and need more information to bring you back into the essay? List the sentences where you got lost and suggest ways the writer might solve the problem.
5. What is the point of the paper? Summarize the significance of the personal narrative in two sentences.
6. Do you believe the writer? Why or why not?

When you respond to these questions, provide honest and usable information. Remember, you also will read your paper in a critiquing session. Work hard to provide helpful responses, trusting that your peers will do the same for you.

You may be wondering why none of these questions consider the nuts-and-bolts problems of grammar and mechanics. The answer is simple. It is too early to start paying attention to those problems. Peer critiquing helps writers collect general information to be used in revision. We ignore specific problems in grammar and mechanics now because we are paying attention to the quality, completeness, and order of ideas. For now, we are concerned with general problems of organization and meaning. Later, when we edit and proofread, we will consider the details of style, mechanical and grammatical correctness, and manuscript appearance. Remember to consider your purpose in each phase of the writing process and limit your concerns to that purpose. Ultimately, we will pay attention to every aspect of writing an essay.

Assignment Summary

Now you should have completed the assessment through peer critiquing and should have several sets of peer responses to work with in the revising phase of the composing process.

Assessment through Self-evaluation

Writers confront two major problems when revising. We can solve the first, gaining distance and perspective, by getting peer responses to drafts of our writing. This external assessment of the strengths and weaknesses of a draft gives us concrete information to use when we reformulate. The second problem involves self-evaluation. In order to use peer responses effectively, we must determine for ourselves the strengths and weaknesses of our written drafts. We must remember what we were trying to do and evaluate our drafts in that light.

When we get peer responses back that ask us to reconsider basic elements of our essays, we need to determine whether the suggestions are:

1. Not valid responses, ones that we need to deal with seriously
2. A valid objection or disagreement that will probably also disturb other readers and that we must somehow answer or correct
3. A substantial flaw in the essay that may force us to return to the discovery phase, or even to scrap the whole idea.

As writers, we need a way to get ourselves back into our own writing, so we can deal with peer response in a healthy manner. The self-evaluation procedure serves this purpose.

ESSAY #1: PERSONAL NARRATIVE—REVISING

ASSIGNMENT: SELF-EVALUATION

The Draft Self-evaluation is one way you can regain control of your essay. It is a series of questions that direct you to consider the strengths and weaknesses in your finished draft. It includes questions related to purpose, organization, audience, and invention, and it requires you to develop specific strategies for revision.

Use the following procedure with the finished draft of your personal narrative essay. When possible, complete the Draft Self-evaluation after taking a few days' vacation from the essay. The vacation helps you "forget" the essay for a while. This step is a natural and healthy way to get past the blind enthusiasm many writers have for their own words.

Also, carefully review the responses made by your peers. Keep an open mind. Try not to become defensive. If your peers offer criticism, don't take it personally. Just try to understand it. Once you are confident you understand the responses, carefully reread your finished draft with the following self-evaluation questions in mind. Completing the self-evaluation is the last step previous to reworking the draft.

DRAFT SELF-EVALUATION QUESTIONS

1. What is the greatest strength in your paper in its present form?
2. What is the greatest weakness in your paper in its present form?
3. What is your purpose in this paper? How does the paper accomplish that purpose? Consider the method of organization, the selection of details, even the choice of words and sentence structure. How do these help you accomplish your purpose in the paper?
4. Who is your audience for this paper? How does the paper address this audience?
5. How did you find the information used in the paper? Did you use a formal heuristic procedure or an informal one? How will you find more information, if needed, while revising?
6. When you are revising, what elements of the essay are you going to pay the most attention to? Introductory, development, closing, detail and argument, organization, clarifying purpose, addressing audience, voice, style—others?

Assignment Summary

Now you have both the peer critique responses and your self-evaluation of the finished draft to help you continue through the revising phase of the composing process.

Reformulation: Putting Assessment to Work

We have broken revising into two tasks, assessment and reformulation. Having collected peer responses and completed the Draft Self-evaluation, you are ready to begin to reformulate, to rework the essay with revisions based on the commentary you have received and to edit and proofread the essay before submitting it to your instructor for evaluation.

What specific changes will you make during reformulation? Because you have surveyed the responses of your peers and reconsidered your own attitude toward the draft through the self-evaluation, you probably have some specific ideas for revising. But what you are actually going to do will not be certain until you start doing it. Later we are going to look closely at how certain writers revised specific essays and analyze what they did, but now we will mention only a few kinds of revisions.

The most radical kind of revision is scrapping the draft and starting over from scratch. However, if you have completed the various activities recommended for discovery and drafting, you will have a strong draft that revising will make even stronger. In fact, almost any draft can be salvaged through revision.

Basically, there are three kinds of revisions:

1. *Elaborations*—which occur when you discover that what you have written is not completely clear and you must provide more information or illustration.
2. *Additions*—which occur when you discover that you have ommitted an important point and you must add information. Often this involves clarifying context or qualifying arguments and conclusions.
3. *Deletions*—which occur when you realize that you have moved away from your central point and included an irrelevancy that distracts readers. In such instances, you must eliminate the irrelevancy.

You are now ready to complete the revising process and end up with a finished personal narrative essay.

ESSAY #1: PERSONAL NARRATIVE—REVISING

ASSIGNMENT: REVISE, EDIT, AND PROOFREAD

Knowing the basic kinds of revision helps you put the peer responses and self-evaluation to work while reformulating your personal narrative. To solve problems you or your peers discovered in the finished draft, you may have to cycle through additional discovery procedures or complete additional peer response and self-evaluation sequences. Your goal is to produce the most effective essay possible.

Review each revision you make. As you are writing, examine the specific changes and categorize them according to the three types of revisions—elaboration, addition, and deletion. Evaluate the problem you are trying to solve, and consider how your specific revision has addressed it.

Once specific revisions have helped you improve the whole piece, you need to edit. Go back through the draft paying particular attention to individual sentences and words. Revise sentences aggressively. If you find a sentence that is very long and does not make clear sense, cut it into parts and make each part its own sentence. If you find some short, choppy sentences, combine them, cutting extra words and phrases. Check parallelism, subordination, and coordination. Pay particular attention to verbs; make them as forceful as possible. Try to avoid repetitive phrasing unless the redundancy helps your meaning. Use a thesaurus and dictionary to find the "exact" word. The appendix to this text, "The Writer's Resources," provides specific instructions and exercises to help you write effective sentences. Working through it now may be helpful. Use what you learn there while revising.

Finally, you must proofread. Attend to minute apects of grammar and mechanics, striving for correctness and perfection. Search out and eliminate all errors. Beware of sentence fragments and run-ons. Check the agreement of subjects and verbs, verify the agreement of pronouns with their antecedents, check usage and punctuation. Check everything! If you have questions, consult a grammar and usage handbook, a classmate who knows grammar and mechanics better than you do, or a tutor in the writing lab or learning center, if one is available. Strive not to let any imperfections through. Be sure to learn and follow your instructor's specifications for creating the final copy to be submitted for evaluation.

Here's one final suggestion. Before you submit your essay to your instructor, have one or two of your classmates read it over closely to find any errors or problems you may have overlooked. Do the same for them. Mark any problems lightly in pencil, so the writer can fix them neatly. Do not fix the errors; writers must themselves learn how to detect and correct problems, so they will not repeat them. Leave the final corrections to the writer.

When you get your essay back, review the marks made by your proofreaders. Check to make sure you agree that what they marked really are mistakes. If they are, fix them as neatly as possible. If you disagree, check a handbook or trusted friend or tutor to make sure you are correct. If you are correct, erase the marks made by your proofreaders. Finally, photocopy your essay or keep a copy of the file on a computer diskette. It is always a good idea to keep a copy for your records.

Assignment Summary

Now that you have revised, edited, and proofread, you have completed the personal narrative. If you followed all the suggestions, you will have created a solid essay in which you can take pride. Give it to your instructor satisfied that you have done the best you can. But expect criticism. After all, practice and criticism help you improve your writing; that is why you are taking this course. Be open to any suggestions your instructor may make when responding to and evaluating your essay.

Conclusion

Because this is only the first of several essays you will write for this class, you should follow this same model composing process, adding any personal variations that particularly help you. The following chart summarizes all the steps and strategies you have practiced while working the personal narrative through the model composing process. When writing other essays, use it as a checklist to guide your progress through a writing assignment.

THE COMPOSING PROCESS
DISCOVERY

Purposes
     Finding and shaping a topic
     Establishing a tentative thesis statement
     Developing a writing plan

Procedures
     Assignment stimulus
     Awareness building
     Journal writing
     Talking with colleagues
     Researching and consulting experts
     Completing the formal invention exercises
     Distilling the problem
     Forming a thesis statement
     Developing the idea outline

DRAFTING

Purposes
     Structuring and developing the idea
     Designing a model

Procedures
     Informal note taking
     Writing a first draft
     Revising lightly to create a finished draft

REVISING

Purposes
     Assessment
     Reformulation
     Producing a clean final copy

Procedures
     Peer responses
     Self-evaluation
     Revising and redrafting
     Editing the final draft
     Proofreading

Writing a Descriptive Essay

INTRODUCTION: "THE COLLEGE PAPER" AND BEYOND

Writing the personal narrative gave you practice developing WRITING FOR THE INSIDE into WRITING FOR THE OUTSIDE. You turned a Personal Development Journal entry rich in private meaning into a narrative whose meaning was clear to a general audience. In addition, writing the personal narrative introduced you to the composing process, allowing you to explore all three of its phases—discovery, drafting, and revising. You are now prepared to write essays in the various forms and for the various purposes you will encounter in school and at work. This chapter and the rest of the book will give you practice writing these specific kinds of essays.

In high school, many of you learned how to write using the five-paragraph-theme format. In that type of essay, an introduction ends with a thesis statement, the body of the essay includes three paragraphs to defend or develop the thesis, and a conclusion restates the thesis. The form is simple and straightforward; it provides a starting point to allow inexperienced writers to say something that readers can understand. You learned this format because it is supposed to represent "the college paper."

This is true on one level but not true on another. Indeed, the five-paragraph-theme format encourages a writer to say something and prove it. And because it stresses the importance of making and defending a point, it has value for training writers. However, the five-paragraph theme is not the only kind of writing required in college. In different courses you will confront various writing assignments, from lab reports in science, to personal interpretations in the humanities, to field-work reports in the social sciences.

Moreover, various disciplines and professions have developed their own highly specialized writing forms. For example, when submitting a brief to a court, an attorney follows a very specific format designed to structure information and argument to a particular end. The attorney's brief hardly resembles a five-paragraph theme. Knowing only the five-paragraph-theme format can finally become a liability because it does not require all the thinking and composing skills other writing forms require. By itself, it is inadequate preparation.

As a consequence, through the rest of this course you will be asked to write a variety of essays, each with its own form and purpose. These essays will teach you virtually all the thinking and writing skills needed to become a successful writer in school and at work. Writing these essays will teach you to use structure to accomplish specific writing purposes, such as communicating information or persuading your audience to do something.

Specifically, you will write an objective description and an impressionistic description in this chapter, and, in following chapters, a personal significance essay in which you analyze and interpret the effects on your life of a particular incident, two argumentative essays in which you make statements and prove them through logical development, and a persuasive essay in which you convince your audience to act or believe as you do. This broad spectrum of essays will give you practice using the wide variety of thinking and writing skills required for WRITING FOR THE OUTSIDE.

Each of the essays will be presented as assignments for you to complete using the model composing process we discussed in Chapter 3. Instructions will focus on particular aspects of the composing process or on specific problems related to an essay's form or purpose in order to lead you through the essays in stages. In addition, we will analyze sample essays to evaluate how well they meet the specific requirements of the essay form.

Most of the samples are not professional writing. Like those you have already seen from the PDJ and from academic journals, the samples were written by students like you. In the samples, you may detect certain flaws that could be eliminated with some additional work. However, each sample represents a student's best effort. Like the journal selections, the writing is impressive in its quality and depth. Some of the samples will be presented in several successive versions so you can see how a particular writer revised to solve a particular problem and produce good writing. Remember, you are also capable of similar levels of performance. Success in writing is largely a question of dedication and effort, a question of personal choice.

Writing to Inform

WRITING FOR THE OUTSIDE is successful only inasmuch as it gets its job done, whatever that job may be. Informative writing is that kind of public writing whose specific purpose, or job, is providing its audience with the information the writer has been directed to communicate or the information the writer has decided the audience needs to know to accomplish something or to understand something.

In order to produce effective informative writing, then, a writer must:

1. Understand the *subject* well enough to permit a sensible, truthful, and credible treatment
2. Understand the *purpose* of the writing, whether to communicate the information without embellishment so the audience can put the information to use, or to include direct or indirect commentary so the audience will see the information in a particular light and act upon it in a particular way
3. Understand the *audience* well enough to use appropriate language, organization, and development to meet its needs and expectations.

DESCRIPTION

Objective and Impressionistic Description

Description is the most common type of informative writing. We can analyze description most effectively by viewing it along a continuum ranging from *objective* to *impressionistic description.*

Objective description requires that the writer know the subject and present it as a distinct object or event. The writer must know and be able to communicate the basic facts about it. The purpose is to organize and express those facts in as clear and understandable a manner as possible to any reader. The writer must not intrude; the writer's responsibility is to serve as a mirror reflecting exactly what the subject is. The goal is objectivity. The writer's job is to communicate the facts so they can be put to immediate use by an audience.

Impressionistic description is a slightly more complex form of description in which the writer's attitudes and opinions play a central role in the writing. In impressionistic description, the writer selects, organizes, and communicates details so that an audience views the subject from the writer's perspective. The writer both provides information about the subject in question and educates and influences readers' feelings. The writer's job is to create an impression, by using details to suggest the subject's value and implications.

Placing these two types of description on opposite ends of a continuum, we can further subdivide them into three kinds of activities—recording, reporting, and recreating. Graphically, these activities would appear like this:

OBJECTIVE————————————————————————IMPRESSIONISTIC

RECORD   REPORT   RECREATE

Recording is more objective, while recreating is more impressionistic. Reporting falls about in the middle, having some elements of both.

On the objective end of the continuum, writers engage in recording and in some kinds of reporting. The writer remains at a distance from the subject and reports the facts only. These activities are especially important when writers must provide directions or report findings so they can be replicated, as is the case with writing done in the sciences. Journalism and a great deal of business writing also depend upon recording and reporting. Good journalism requires credibility, which comes only from the faithful and objective observing and reporting of facts. Business depends on extensive record keeping and objective analysis of information.

Recording

To illustrate objective description of the kind represented by recording, consider the following paragraph from the *Kaypro II User's Guide*, part of the documentation that comes with the computer. The purpose of the documentation is to help users make the computer work. In this paragraph, the writer's job is to describe the keyboard by *recording* basic facts about it such as its physical characteristics and the ways it can be used. As you read, pay attention to how the writer organizes the material.

> *The keyboard* is a detachable unit connected to the computer via a coiled telephone-style cord. The main keyboard consists of 62 keys (including four arrow keys that control the cursor movement). To the right of the main keyboard are 14 keys in a numeric, calculator-style layout. With the exception of a few control keys like CTRL, ESC, and RETURN, all of the keys have an automatic repeat function, including the cursor arrow keys. Both the numeric pad and the cursor control keys are user-programmable, using the CONFIG program on your CP/M S-BASIC diskette.

Note the use of spatial organization in this example. First the keyboard is separated from the computer by noting that it is connected to the computer by a cord. Then each of the subparts is described by its spatial relation to the main keyboard. The main keyboard serves as the central reference point, so the number pad is described as being to the right of the main board. The use of a reference point and verbal signals, or transitions (to the left or right, in the middle—terms showing relation to the reference point in space), are fundamental in spatial organization. It is often used in objective description.

The computer documentation example also illustrates how purpose and the writer's relationship to an audience are important in informative writing, especially recording. The writer need not worry about describing the physical appearance of the keyboard. The writer assumes that the readers know that the main keyboard has black-based keys, that the number pad is blue, that the metal plate supporting the keyboard is gray with a blue border, and so forth. Because the readers have these things in plain view, this information can be overlooked. It is not essential to the task at hand.

In fact, the writer assumes that readers have direct access to the keyboard while reading the documentation. They must have the keyboard at hand and have only one purpose—to learn how to use it. Otherwise, this description would not be effective. The writer works with this purpose in mind; it determines what needs to be explained and what can be overlooked.

Note also that the description is somewhat spare. There is little elaboration and explanation of the parts. The largest part of the paragraph deals with the potential uses of the several features described. The specific audience for the description includes Kaypro II users who want to learn to use the computer; the writer's only concern is utility. The description will be effective only if the users are able to use the keyboard.

Recording-Reporting

Another example of objective description, but not nearly as spare, is the following paragraph from Rachel Carson's *The Sea Around Us*. The book explains the origin, development, and movements of the seas that cover the earth. As Carson explains the history and science of the seas, she frequently uses descriptions both to record and to report phenomena. The reports depend upon her organizing her observations and expressing them skillfully to give readers a sense of the magnitude of the seas and their activity. She does not only record what happens; in the process, she also makes us first-hand witnesses, standing with her and watching with awe.

> As the waves roll in toward Lands End on the westernmost tip of England they bring the feel of the distant places of the Atlantic. Moving shoreward above the steeply rising floor of the deep sea, from dark blue water into troubled green, they pass the edge of "soundings" and roll up over the continental shelf in confused ripplings and turbulence. Over the shoaling bottom they sweep landward, breaking on the Seven Stones of the channel between the Scilly Isles and Lands End, coming in over the sunken ledges and the rocks that roll out their glistening backs at low water. As they approach the rocky tip of Lands End, they pass over a strange instrument lying on the sea bottom. By the fluctuating pressure of their rise and fall they tell this instrument many things of the distant Atlantic waters from which they have come, and their messages are translated by its mechanisms into symbols understandable to the human mind.

Reading this paragraph gives us a sense of the activity of the waves as they begin far out in the deep seas, forming and shaping themselves as they journey towards the coast, bouncing against islands and currents, ultimately breaking upon the beach. Note again the use of spatial organization—from far out to close up.

But note also how Carson augments this organization by describing the process of the waves first forming out in the sea to ultimately breaking on the shore. Such organization is called chronological because it organizes an event in a time sequence, from beginning to end. Augmenting spatial organization with chronological organization and selecting and organizing specific details as Carson does creates a depth and texture to the writing that moves it beyond recording to reporting.

Style—how the sentences are structured using the details selected—contributes to the impact of Carson's report. Her sentences build and roll and crest and break like the waves she is describing. She selects precise and suggestive details as modifiers such as "steeply rising," "dark blue," "troubled green," and "shoaling."

Note also that Carson creates a sense of drama by having the details build to an end. Her description of the rising and falling of the waves supplies the connection she will use to help her tell the story of the seas. This building toward an end exemplifies climactic order, another important tool for writers. In Carson all these elements contribute to the power and effectiveness of the writing.

Through both the organization and style of the writing, Carson establishes a relationship with her audience. She illustrates her deep understanding of her subject, the sea. She does more than communicate the facts; she invites, almost impels, readers to become participants. Unlike the writer of the computer documentation, Carson cannot suppose that her audience is at Land's End watching the sea and reading that paragraph. She must bring the scene to wherever the readers are. Her purpose is to inform readers and make them share her wonder and awe through her writing.

Carson's paragraph is objective description; what she describes is real and taking place—even now. It is a report in which she filters, selects, and organizes information to leave readers with an impression of the awesomeness of the sea. Though other writers describing the same scene could communicate the same information, no one but Rachel Carson would adopt the same vantage point, select the same facts, and organize them as she does. It is her writing and her sea.

Reporting-Influencing

The presence of the author in his or her writing—brought about by the selecting, organizing, and embellishing of facts and details—differentiates the report from the record. Carson subtly makes her presence felt in the paragraph from *The Sea Around Us*. However, a more striking example of a writer's presence occurs in the following excerpt from William Least Heat Moon's *Blue Highways*. In his description of a contemporary American fast-food restaurant, a hamburger factory, we see objectivity tempered if not entirely discarded, so Least Heat Moon can criticize some of our American behaviors and institutions.

> I stood with the other ambulatory digestive tubes reading the wallmounted, internally lighted menu showing full-color photographic representations of hamburgers and French fries twelve times life size. A slice of potato big enough to lay steel track over did not look appealing. All prices ended in nine. I ordered, and the cash register hummed, spun its mechanism, glared a red number, and an agent pushed me my texturized substitute in its polystyrene sarcophagus. I joined the other diners, some of whose gizzards had already begun wrestling hamburgers named for their weight.

Least Heat Moon's purpose in this description is not to communicate information. Obviously, he is describing a scene familiar to most of us. His purpose is to select details and combine them in a unique way, so we see the familiar in a new and striking way and become conscious of our own excess and artificiality. He depends on our familiarity with the subject. He also depends on the special relationship he develops with his audience through the whole book, a three-hundred-page chronicle of a journey through America.

His description depends on indirectness for its success. Least Heat Moon causes readers to anticipate something out of the ordinary from the first sentence. He waits in line not with other people, but with other "ambulatory digestive tubes." Exaggeration, called hyberbole, is one of his critical tools. He selects and distorts details to make his point. The advertisement for French fries makes a single French fry seem large enough to be a tie on a railroad bed. Machines hum and human automatons smile in a restaurant that is in essence a food factory. We are reduced to cogs in a frenzied roadside eating machine rather than savorers of the tastes and aromas of food and participants in pleasant conversation over hot coffee. For many who read this paragraph, Big Macs never again taste as good as they once did. Least Heat Moon has influenced them; he has done his job.

Recreating

Moving further along the continuum from objective to impressionistic description, we find the presence of the writer playing a larger and larger role. The writer was absent from the computer documentation. Rachel Carson selected details but did not intrude. Least Heat Moon makes his impression the real point of the paragraph. In these instances, the writers are using their presence and their relationship with readers to help fulfill the purposes of their writing.

When describing to recreate, writers work hard to make readers see, feel, smell, hear, and sense the scene or action, to bring them into the picture. In the following excerpt from "The Masque of the Red Death," note how Edgar Allan Poe creates the impression of horror and impending doom by carefully balancing one detail with another. Colors and shapes and sensations combine to create an eerie, frightening atmosphere. Few writers can match Poe's impressionistic powers.

As you read, take notes upon the kinds of order—spatial, chronological, climactic—Poe uses. List the various transitions he uses to signal order and help the audience through the scene. Pay special attention to how each detail contributes to the overall mood.

It was a voluptuous scene, that masquerade. But first let me tell of the rooms in which it was held. There were seven—an imperial suite. In many palaces, however, such suites form a long and straight vista, while the folding doors slide back nearly to the walls on either hand, so that the view of the whole extent is scarcely impeded. Here the case was very different; as might have been expected from the duke's love of the *bizarre*. The apartments were so irregularly disposed that the vision embraced but little more than one at a time. There was a sharp turn at every twenty or thirty yards, and at each turn a novel effect. To the right and left, in the middle of each wall, a tall and narrow Gothic window looked out upon a closed corridor which pursued the windings of the suite. These windows were of stained glass whose color varied in accordance with the prevailing hue of the decorations of the chamber into which it opened. That at the eastern extremity was hung, for example, in blue—and vividly blue were its windows. The second chamber was purple in its ornaments and tapestries, and here the panes were purple. The third was green throughout, and so were the casements. The fourth was furnished and lighted with orange—the fifth with white—the sixth with violet. The seventh apartment was closely shrouded in black velvet tapestries that hung all over the ceiling and down the walls, falling in heavy folds upon a carpet of the same material and hue. But in this chamber only, the color of the windows failed to correspond with the decorations. The panes here were scarlet—a deep blood color. Now in no one of the seven apartments was there any lamp or candelabrum, amid the profusion of golden ornaments that lay scattered to and fro or depended from the roof. There was no light of any kind emanating from lamp or candle within the suite of chambers. But in the corridors that followed the suite, there stood, opposite to each window a heavy tripod, bearing a brazier of fire, that projected its rays through the tinted glass and so glaringly illumined the room. And thus were produced a multitude of gaudy and fantastic appearances. But in the western or black chamber the effect of the fire-light that streamed upon the dark hangings through the blood-tinted panes, was ghastly in the extreme, and produced so wild a look upon the countenances of those who entered, that there were few of the company bold enough to set foot within its precincts at all.

A final example of impressionistic description will illustrate how the selection and organization of details can recreate a scene and communicate emotions with power unavailable in direct, literal, objective description. In the following excerpt from Kevin McIlvoy's A Waltz, notice how the organization of detail and chronology combine to bring the reader into the room to witness the desperation of an old woman locked away from her family and friends, warehoused in the nursing home like forgotten furniture, waiting powerlessly for something to happen to make her feel alive. Note especially how the last sentence contrasts with the literalness and directness of the rest of the paragraph. This contrast resounds as the reader watches Sara's breath of life become the dustball that she herself daily gathers and throws into the trashcan.

Sara opened her tight grip on the broomhandle and, leaning it against her, pushed brittle wisps of hair from her face. The perspiration that had gathered in her hands smelled now, in her hair, like dust. Metal carts shelved full of lunch trays rattled back and forth past the small room. White shoes. White hands. Antiseptic sounds. Though she had swept the room once already, Sara continued her work on the smoky gray tiles and was delighted when she discovered a dustball under Ruby's high steel institutional bed. She carried the broom delicately to the trashcan to shake it clean, but the dustball would not fall from the bristles; and so she upended the broom and picked it off. For the moment she held it she felt it must be alive, as if her breath condensed on the window that morning had become this gray substance and fallen from the cold pane of glass to the floor.

WRITING DESCRIPTIONS

We have spent some time reading and analyzing descriptions to learn strategies we can use to create effective ones. Now it is your turn to write. To develop your skills, you will write *two separate descriptive essays*, one objective and one impressionistic. Follow the instructions provided in the assignments.

As you complete these assignments, recall your work on the composing process in Chapter 3. First choose the subject, the objects or incidents, you want to describe. Make sure you know enough about your subject to avoid the first trap of bad writing—not knowing enough about your subject. The PDJ or other journal writings are good sources for finding subjects you are interested in and know about.

Once you have determined your subject, talk to someone about it, especially in terms of the purpose of the assignment. As you talk, you will discover whether your topic is appropriate for the kind of description—objective or impressionistic—you are attempting. By talking about it, you will also discover your strengths and weaknesses and whether you need to search for more information.

Use whatever discovery strategies you deem necessary. Formal invention procedures, like the ones included in the Appendix as well as other research and consultation strategies, will help you gain control of your subject. While drafting your descriptions, keep your purpose in mind. Make sure you understand the distinctions between recording, reporting, and recreating discussed earlier. The assignments will include student samples with analyses to help clarify the differences between objective and impressionistic descriptions and give you insights about how best to complete your own. Throughout the composing process, concentrate on your purpose: to inform through description.

During the revising phase make sure to complete the peer response activities and draft self-evaluations. The peer critique questions are specifically designed to help you with revising your description. Work hard to put the insights you gain from your peers to work for you. Edit and proofread your essay to make it reflect your expertise as a thinker and writer.

ESSAY #2: WRITING AN OBJECTIVE DESCRIPTION ESSAY

ASSIGNMENT

Write an objective description of a person, place, or thing. Your subject can be static—that is, at rest, like the Kaypro keyboard—or dynamic—that is, in process or motion, like Carson's sea. Choose your own subject and make sure it is complex enough to require two or three typewritten pages, about 600 words for a complete description. The class is your audience. Write to inform.

Before beginning to write, read the student sample with analyses that follows. It will give you some ideas about organization. In addition, the analysis will give you some suggestions about using peer responses while revising.

Follow the general procedure for writing an essay established earlier. Use the checklist provided at the end of "Writing a Personal Narrative" (page 104) to mark your progress through the essay. When you submit a finished draft to your peers for critiquing, use the peer critique questions that follow.

PEER CRITIQUE QUESTIONS

Answer the following questions providing peer responses to the objective description essay.

1. What word, phrase, or sentence do you most remember from the essay? Why did it impress you?

2. What color or emotion best expresses how the paper made you feel? Describe why the writing made you feel that way.

3. What is the point of the essay? Summarize the description in two sentences. Respond not only by telling what was described but also what was said about it.

4. Considering the writer's use of organization, what kinds of order—spatial, chronological, or climactic, or combinations of these—did the writer use? What transitions did the writer use to signal the use of these orders?

5. What single specific suggestion can you give the writer for improving the description during revision? The suggestion may concern topic, organization, use of particular details, style, whatever. Be sure it is a specific and helpful suggestion.

A Student Sample with Analysis

The following essay by Marie Turner is a good sample for us to consider. It exemplifies effective WRITING FOR THE OUTSIDE. She describes a significant subject, a young man lying in a coma in an intensive care unit as a result of a motorcycle accident. She knows that her readers, at one time or another, will have to deal with a similar situation in which a friend or relative is gravely ill and confronting death. Her purpose is to inform us of the horror of severe injury and the tragedy of premature death. She wants to inform her readers, and she wants to educate them. She makes an appeal, indirect but effective, for us all to appreciate life while we can. As such, the essay falls somewhere between Carson's recording-reporting and Least Heat Moon's reporting-influencing.

Marie uses language effectively to communicate the horror of the scene. Her eye for clinical detail combines with concrete language to make this effective description. The language is striking at times; for example, blood draining from a head wound becomes the color of "cherry Kool-Aid." Marie is not naive; the technology that makes it possible to maintain life through heroic efforts—but sometimes to no good end—is symbolized in the plastic bags that collect the life fluids of the injured man.

There is more wrong here than the man's injuries. Marie is a nurse in an intensive care unit; she is writing within her experience. She sees this horror every day,
yet she has not become numb to it. In fact, she is aware enough to capture the
scene and bring us there.

Marie Turner
Essay #2: Objective Description
            You Meet the Nicest People on a Honda

He lay in the bed, or rather, half lay/half sat;
neither opening his eyes when spoken to, nor following any
of the simple requests made. His head was pillowed by its
dressings, a Swami turban of fluffy white gauze, its jewel
a small plastic bulb filled with cherry Kool Aid drainage
and connected by plastic tubing to his head. When his
eyes were opened, the pupils constricted in response to
light, but his eyes did not focus, nor was he able to hold
his eyes open spontaneously.

Beside the plastic tubing that disappeared somewhere
under the dressing on his head, he had yards and yards of
other plastic tubes, fluid pathways between him and
assorted bags and bottles. Hanging above the bed from
poles were plastic bags of fluids, nutrients which
travelled through the tubing into needles in his
veins. The needles were plastic too.

A tube, stained green by its contents, entered his
stomach through his nose; it was connected to a suction
apparatus which kept his stomach emptied. Another tube,
draining into a bag hanging beneath the bed, kept his
bladder free of fluids. As the bags above the bed
emptied, the bags below the bed filled.

A plastic tube entered his windpipe through a small
hole at the front of his neck. This tube connected him by
two lengths of corrugated plastic tubing to a ventilator
which moved oxygen-enriched air to him through one tubing
and carried exhaled air away through the other. The
system functioned as an efficient, closed-circuit, life

sustaining mechanism; the tubings, man's answer to the umbilical cord.

Suspended from an aluminum Tinker Toy frame attached to the bed, his right leg hung above the mattress by a series of pins, ropes, and pulleys. All were held in balance by twenty pounds of lead weights, swinging slightly at the foot of the bed.

Various pillows and rolls supported his arms and head to keep him straight, a rag doll with good posture, in the bed.

The background noises, air being pushed by ventilator bellows, the clicking of the suction machine cycling on and off, the soft computerized ticking of the apparatus controlling the flow, all these were dulled by the sound of Willie Nelson singing from the bedside radio ''On the road again. . . .'' Now and again alarms sound, signalling shallow breathing or an empty fluid bag. But these alarms are few in a patient whose drive to breathe and ability to move are overpowered by drugs given for that purpose.

The educated ear will hear smaller, more subtle noises. The sound of air and fluid will issue from the intestines if they are working. No intestine noises yet; the trauma is too recent. But the chest proves to be a mother lode of noises: air moves through the upper airways with the sound of the wind blowing, changing pitch and becoming softer as it travels deeper into the lungs. Even softer, now and then air squeaks on exhalation, when it has a hard time moving through mucus plugged passages. Over on the right side just below the nipple line are the unmistakable sounds of broken ribs grinding and crunching together with each breath. The heart has a comfortable-sounding slow and steady rhythm with nothing remarkable about its even, lub–dub beat.

He feels warm, not hot, but just about right, and no longer sweaty as he has been on and off. In order to keep him free of fever and visible for observation, very little covers him.

The extent of his injuries goes beyond the fractures. His entire right side is badly bruised and has many crusted over scrapes and cuts. He fairly shines with the antibacterial ointment used to cover these less serious wounds. He has a surgical incision running the length of his abdomen; a row of stainless steel staples gives the appearance of a zipper in the middle of his trunk, with an almost whimsical little jog to the left as the zipper goes around his belly button.

Marie's description is an impressive piece of writing. She uses a sophisticated form of spatial organization to structure the paper. She begins by setting the scene with a large view of the patient lying in a coma in the hospital bed. Then she shifts the focus, closing in first on the head, then on the internal organs, then the lungs, and finally on his legs. It is not by accident that the shifts in focus trace the injuries from the most severe and life-threatening to the least. She is using a variation of climactic order—from most to least dangerous injury—as well as spatial organization. Marie uses her skill as writer and her knowledge as a nurse to structure the essay to make her point.

Each focal point receives sufficient attention to reinforce the primary message: the man's condition is grave. Though we may be disgusted or repulsed by the graphic details, as readers we are still forced to look. Marie makes the transition from one focal point to the next by following the plastic tubing from a machine to the body. Always the shift is accomplished by reference to one of the machines that is keeping the man alive. The image of the bag hung above the man emptying through him into the bag hung below the bed is particularly suggestive; medical technology can rob us of our humanity while maintaining our lives.

Notice also how the second part of the essay is not organized by space but by sounds. Again we move from distant to close focus, from Willie Nelson's "On the Road Again" coming from the radio, to the very internal and private sounds only a nurse can hear, the grinding of broken ribs, the rattling of the lungs, and the drug-imposed regularity of the heartbeat. These details bring the audience closer to the scene. Marie uses her special knowledge effectively; she puts her life experience to work for her as a writer. The sadness she feels while ministering to this wasted life need not be directly stated; the scene makes that point by itself.

When they first read this essay, some of Marie's peers did not know how to respond to the final paragraph. With its image of the zipper and its "whimsical little jog," the final sentence seems to violate the predominant tone of the essay. Except for the comparison of draining blood to cherry Kool-Aid in the introductory paragraph, Marie's tone is direct and literal. The contrast confused some readers; they did not know how to respond.

Reading closely a second time, these readers began to sense a correctness rooted in the strangeness of the zipper image. It culminates a series of images in the essay that combine to become a theme. Plastic tubing, sophisticated life-sustaining machines, and advanced technology in general become instruments of dehumanization. Through this theme Marie makes the indirect but undeniable point that what is in the bed is no longer a human life. This body is a zipped-up bag of skin with a lot of "stuff" inside.

Images such as this one move Marie beyond recording into the realm of reporting and criticizing. She chooses details and structures them purposefully to have an effect on her audience. She has not stepped beyond the bounds of informative writing, however, because she is allowing a faithful though perhaps embellished rendition of the facts to make her point. She wants to inform her audience, to privilege us to her information and her point of view. She is working much as Rachel Carson did in the example provided earlier.

Using Peer Responses: Revising for Audience and Purpose

Deciding to move from recording to reporting while still writing objective description is Marie's great accomplishment. Examining the revisions she made as a result of peer critiquing shows how her peers helped her understand the potential of her draft, potential which was unrealized in her original "professional" objective description. Responding to her peers' commentary, she decided to move away from purely objective description and wrote a more effective essay. This is the finished draft she submitted to her peers for critiquing:

Marie Turner
Objective Description
Finished Draft

The patient is a young, adult male, lying supine in bed with the head of the bed elevated thirty degrees. He does not open his eyes spontaneously or in response to calling his name. He is breathing easily through a tracheostomy tube with a Bear ventilator. Having no spontaneous respirations of his own, his respiratory rate is that set on the ventilator. His color is adequate; the mucous membranes are pink. He has adequate peripheral pulse volumes, and a normal cardiac rate and rhythm are noted on the monitor. His lungs sound clear bilaterally with good exchange of air noted down to the bases. Breath sounds are somewhat obscured on the right by the sound of moving rib fragments in the area of the fractures. The heart sounds are within normal limits.

The abdomen is soft and flat and non-distended. No bowel sounds are heard. There is a naso-gastric tube in his nose draining a moderate volume of clear brown fluid. A midline incision is noted to be clean and dry with staples intact. There is no inflammation, and the wound edges are well approximated. A catheter is in place in the bladder draining an adequate volume of clear yellow urine.

Bulky head dressings are in place and noted to be clean, dry, and intact. Two drains protrude from under the dressings, labelled #1 and #2. They are noted to contain approximately 15cc and 20cc, respectively, in their reservoirs. Drainage is bright red. The pupils are equal at 4mm and react briskly to light. Corneal reflexes are absent. He does not grasp with either hand or follow any other command. There is no response noted to pain in the right upper extremity. A very weak abnormal extensor response is noted in the left upper extremity in response to nail bed pressure applied to the left hand. No response is noted to painful stimulus applied to the lower extremities.

The right leg is noted to be suspended in 20# balanced skeletal traction with good alignment of the femur fragments, and with traction weights swinging freely. Circulation to feet is noted to be adequate, with (3+/4) dorsalis pedis and posterior tibialis pulses noted bilaterally.

Large contusions are noted over the anterior and lateral aspects of the right upper leg, and the right lateral chest wall, and the right shoulder. Abrasions are noted in various places on both lower legs and knees, the right lateral lower chest wall, and over the right clavicle. Abrasions are open to air and covered with antibacterial ointment.

Patient was medicated with Pavulon and Morphine prior to suctioning of the tracheostomy tube. Suctioning yielded a moderate amount of thin white secretions. The patient was repositioned on his left side with pillows for support and with attention to alignment of the right femur.

———————————————

How would you evaluate the success of this draft as objective description? It is a faithful record of the scene, told in clinical terms, employing specialized language that would present no difficulty to an audience of medically trained people. In fact, from one perspective this draft is more precise, more objective, than the final essay.

There is a strong sense of organization. The observations have been structured so an audience can follow the report. The draft uses spatial organization with several focal points used to permit needed elaboration.

But there is a serious problem for an audience of nonspecialists: they cannot understand the scene. And there is a problem with the identity of the writer. In this draft, Marie is writing solely as a professional. She is machine-like, almost as mechanical and impersonal as the respirator that keeps the young man alive. Reread the last paragraph of the draft if you doubt this.

The specialized language and relation of the writer to subject and audience struck Marie's peer respondents. All of them noted the precision and power of the details, but some could not decipher exactly what was happening. The details were not accessible, not understandable, to the lay reader. When asked for the one-word summary reaction, one peer first wrote, "Sympathy—the guy's in bad shape." Then she wrote in reference to herself, "Overwhelmed by medical terms—I had to listen closely to digest the terms." In the two-sentence summary, this same respondent wrote, ". . . seems like a nurse's progress report."

Indeed, this critique cuts to the heart of the problem in the draft. Marie is not connecting with her audience, which, in this case, is her writing class. The specialized language, or jargon, and the professional stance, which are entirely appropriate for the records Marie must keep as a nurse, excluded her classmates. Because the description was so limited in its audience, it was not effective WRITING FOR THE OUTSIDE. The language and stance of the draft needed revision.

Honest and direct peer response helped Marie solve the major problem in her essay. Note how the response is not critical. The peers do not tear down the essay or criticize the writer. Their responses are descriptive. In fact, another respondent blamed herself for not understanding the technical terms and saw the jargon as an "attention getter." In this she was allowing herself to be bullied by the overly "professional" stance Marie had assumed.

Marie, however, realized the problem for the audience and addressed it in the draft self-assessment completed after the peer responses. Concerning the problem of audience, Marie writes: "The greatest weakness is the approach to the audience. *This assignment must address a nonmedical audience.*"

The peer responses have made her aware of both the problem with language and audience and with her relation to the subject. This essay is not supposed to be a nurse's progress report. It is to be a description for a writing class. Addressing the problem of purpose in her assessment, she writes: "The purpose is to describe a victim of multiple traumas through documentation of what was observed in performing a physical assessment. The organization, selection of details, and choice of words accomplish the purpose in a specific situation; that is, in a professional situation. They need revision to accomplish a similar goal for a different audience." She must revise to fit her audience. She must change her style, which includes her specialized language and professional stance, and she must reorganize the paper.

Reread her final essay. It attests the wisdom of the changes she made. She does her job for her audience. What you as a fellow writer need to understand as a result of this analysis of the revision is the role peer responses can play in composing. The peers' responsibility is to be honest and to provide information the writer can use while revising. The writer's job is to consider this information seriously and use it or reject it after careful consideration.

Learn to use peer responses and draft self-evaluation as effectively as Marie did. Use them to help you revise and edit your essay. Finally, proofread closely before submitting the objective description to your instructor for evaluation.

ESSAY #3: WRITING AN IMPRESSIONISTIC DESCRIPTION ESSAY

ASSIGNMENT

Write an impressionistic description. Again, choose your own subject, but make it complex enough to require you to write about 600 words. The description will probably be structured as a character sketch, journalistic report, or short narrative.

Consult your PDJ for places, people, and events that lend themselves to impressionistic description. Refer to the composing process checklist (page 104) to mark your progress through the essay. Use the peer critique questions (page 114) supplied for the objective description when getting peer responses. Consider the following sample and analysis while you are working on the impressionistic description.

A Student Sample with Analysis

Karen Evans' "My First Funeral" illustrates that it does not take professional training and extraordinary experience to write strong essays. Good writers make the most of what they have. The only special training required involves using the powers of close observation and personal awareness that your work with journals and the composing process has already provided you. What you need now is practice.

Read Karen's essay and note how she takes a personal experience and recreates it dramatically. Karen, a college freshman, recounts an incident from her senior year in high school, thereby preserving it for herself and for her audience. In the process she raises some questions we all must confront and may never answer. In this she accomplishes all that we can ask of good writing.

Karen Evans
Essay #3
Impressionistic Description

My First Funeral

The day dawned painfully clear, giving us a good excuse
to wear our sunglasses. I know I was hiding behind mine
as we approached the cemetery.

Nick and I were among the first to arrive. We got
there before the hearse; unfortunately, so did Gwen, the
deceased's best friend.

I had to give Gwen a hug when she arrived, she looked
so pale, so ravaged by grief. She cried on my shoulder
for a minute while her parents looked on, then we helped
her walk to the grave site. When the hearse pulled up,
Gwen let out something between a scream and a moan and
started to cry again, so earnestly that her parents had to
lead her back to the car to try to calm her down.

Nick and I looked on, in horror, as they unloaded the
coffin bearing the body of our friend, Emily. I felt
sorry for her as I watched. She had no formal
pallbearers, just a few strong men the little man from the
funeral home had recruited.

I backed away as they passed with the casket, my high
heels sinking into the soft earth in the cemetery, giving
me the creeping horrors. I glanced around to see whose
grave I had been standing on and was relieved to find
nobody was buried in the spot I had just vacated. Nick
saw me shiver and put his arm around me.

The ghoulish man from the funeral home passed by with a
little white book. It looked awfully familiar, and I
whispered to Nick, ''If that's a guest book, I think I'll
scream.'' Then the poor, misshapen fellow returned and
stopped to talk to our group. I tried not to stare at his
nose, which looked as if it had been eaten away by some
cancer. He looked appropriate for his job.

''The guest register is right over there if you'd care to sign it.'' He pointed to a little stand a few feet away. Nick's grip tightened on my hand.

''Don't scream, Karen,'' he hissed in my ear. I nodded, trying to ignore my churning stomach. The last time I had seen a guest book was at a wedding; something Emily would never see again. I felt myself losing control, and fought the tears that welled up from my chest and overflowed through my eyes. Nick led me to the register, so I could sign.

There was quite a crowd around the grave now. I looked at the sea of faces and realized that of the hundreds of people there, only about thirty were older than twenty-five. It looked as if the entire high school had turned out to mourn Emily's passing.

Most of us could not believe that Emily, who often seemed to be the most alive of any of us, had taken her own life. Laughing, fun-loving Emily was found locked in the garage with a running car Saturday, ending any possibility of her fulfilling the great promise she had shown in her life.

My reverie was interrupted by the cries of Emily's mother as she threw herself on her ex-husband and half screamed, half sobbed, ''Our baby. Oh, our baby!'' I felt the tears returning to my eyes as I watched this woman's pain. I knew that many of the students at the high school thought she had driven Emily to do what she did, and I felt sorry for her. I could not begin to imagine the private hell she must have been going through.

The Rabbi started to speak, and I turned my attention to him, even though he was speaking in Hebrew. Then he began to speak in English:

''The Lord is my shepherd, I shall not want.'' My lip started to quiver as he spoke these familiar words. It was so final.

''He makes me lie down in green pastures; He leads me beside quiet waters.'' I was glad my sunglasses hid my eyes so well, they were starting to overflow again.

''He restores my soul; He guides me in the paths of righteousness for His name's sake.'' I fumbled in my purse for a tissue, then dabbed at my eyes with it, still wearing my sunglasses.

''Even though I walk through the valley of the shadow of death, I fear no evil; for Thou art with me: Thy rod and Thy staff, they comfort me.'' I was too busy crying to pay attention to the rest, until he said, ''And I will dwell in the house of the Lord for ever.''

My sunglasses were off; my eyes were covered with Kleenex to catch the tears. I half-listened to the rest of the ceremony; mostly I studied the faces of my fellow mourners.

I stood there until the end, my tears finally under control. Then the horrid man from the funeral home walked by, telling us the ceremony was over and we were free to leave. I wondered what caused him to do that; did he think that we were so grief stricken we couldn't think, or that we were retarded teenagers who didn't know the social amenities like when it is proper to leave a funeral? We waited until our dead friend's casket was lowered into the earth.

''Ashes to ashes, dust to dust,'' I murmured. I wondered why the Rabbi had not said that, thinking that perhaps I had missed it. I didn't realize that because Emily was buried as a suicide she was not permitted to have the traditional ceremony and would not be allowed a gravestone. And she was buried facing west, away from Jerusalem. I thought that was a cold thing to do, for didn't she need more guidance from above than those who waited passively for their end?

The other day, I asked Nick, ''Who has more guts: Emily for facing the unknown of death, or the rest of us for facing life?'' He looked at me for a minute, I could see him seriously thinking over his reply.

''I don't know, Karen. I don't think we ever will.''

Karen's essay took as long a journey through the revising phase as Marie's did. The draft she read to her peers was more like a journal entry than an essay. It was an extended account of the day's activities that included far too much extraneous detail. Much of it was irrelevant to the task she was trying to accomplish. There was too little focus on the central problem, on trying to deal with the suicide of a young woman.

Her peer respondents provided two important insights. In responding to the question regarding strengths, they focused on the power inherent in her subject—specifically, the grave site, and the funeral. The peers noted, however, that these played only a minor part in the draft. There were too many digressions taking Karen away from the central episode. The respondents also focused on several powerful images that had a dramatic quality. In her self-evaluation, Karen admitted that what her peers read was something she "banged out" because she needed to get it out of her. During revision, she wanted to develop a tighter, more dramatic structure that could take advantage of the power of the grave-side scene and through that express her emotions. She also wanted to avoid the trap of oversentimentalizing.

The dramatic structure she developed for the version you read solved the problem of the rambling, unconnected details that were her earlier draft. In selecting and structuring the details, she separates the gold from the dross. On the whole, she does a good job avoiding trite scenes and expressions and, thereby, avoids oversentimentalizing. Nevertheless, she could still revise some of the teary-eyed images and tighten her language.

Pay particular attention to the structure Karen uses. Overall, the essay is organized chronologically; the funeral is described as an event taking place in time. She sets the scene and then uses a series of episodes to highlight the horror and ironies of the event. She does not introduce characters haphazardly; she uses them dramatically. First comes the best friend, then the parents, then the Rabbi. These reflect a hierarchy—peers, parents, clergy.

She introduces details that help us understand the wrongness of the incident. The ghoulish man from the funeral home symbolizes ever-present, fearful death. Also, she uses minor details to put herself in the scene. When her heels sink into the mud she feels as if Death were trying to claim her too. Though she resents the presence of the guest register, she resigns herself to signing it, just as she must finally resign herself to this death.

Acceptance does not come easily, nor are all her concerns answered. She raises questions about the suicide and about the relation of the mother and daughter. She is confused. At the height of her confusion, the Rabbi begins to read from Holy Scriptures. Karen finds comfort in these words, allowing them to temporarily resolve the problems. God has his ways. God is merciful. But even this resolution is unsatisfactory in this situation. The ritual is incomplete. Emily is buried as a suicide victim. The conclusion emphasizes the remaining questions for which there are no answers.

Karen's essay demonstrates several key points. First, all of us have experiences that we can develop into impressive descriptive essays if we can exercise sensitivity and awareness, develop an eye for detail, and learn to use structure. Second,

Karen's essay is a very strong example of impressionistic description. Her use of detail, figurative language, and dramatic structure cause us to enter the scene and participate.

Finally, Karen's essay helps us see life in a new light. We raise the same questions that Karen does, and we come up with inadequate answers. Like her, we can only sign the guest register and accept death, the inevitability of our own and the deaths of others we love, when they come. This "reflective" element of Karen's essay illustrates how good writing is often critical of life, how it frequently causes us to confront difficult issues. Good writing makes us stop and take account of our normal behaviors. It takes us close to fundamental human problems and causes us to deal with them as best we can. As writers of impressionistic description, we must make this reflective element our goal.

CHAPTER 5

Writing a Personal Significance Essay

INTERPRETATION: DISCOVERING ORDER AND SIGNIFICANCE

A sixteenth-century French statesman, writer, and philosopher, Montaigne retired from public life at the age of 38 so that, as he writes, he could put his psychic house in order. He describes a strange but exciting process through which he takes his mind's "monsters and chimeras" and tames them to make sense of his life:

> Lately, when I retired to my home, determined so far as possible to bother about nothing except spending the little time I had left in rest and seclusion, it seemed to me I could do my mind no greater favor than to let it entertain itself in full idleness and stay and settle in itself.
>
> [But,] like a runaway horse, [my mind] gives itself a hundred times more trouble than it took for others, and gives birth to so many chimeras and fantastic monsters, one after another, without order or purpose, that in order to contemplate their ineptitude and strangeness at my pleasure, I have begun to put them in writing, hoping in time to make my mind ashamed of itself.
>
> Montaigne, "Of Idleness"

You know the experience he describes. As you worked through the PDJ, especially when brainstorming, ideas crashed around in your head like the runaway horses Montaigne mentions. First they formed vague shadows, then they became the clear insights you recorded while completing the assessment section of each exercise. What Montaigne accomplished through reflective writing, in fact, serves as our model as we search our memories and experiences and assign them meaning.

As Montaigne discusses the process of making meaning from experience, he is describing the act of interpretation. Interpretation is central to the human experience. Our very nature requires us to make sense of our physical and psychological environments; for that reason, we are called Homo sapiens—the knowledgeable ones. Through interpretation we make meaning and fulfill our nature. Through interpretation we penetrate the surface of our experience, come to understand it, and, finally, communicate that understanding to others. Through interpretation we determine significance. Determining significance requires that we discover the underlying structure and order of our experience, how the parts fit together. Interpretation moves us through personal understanding into the arena of public meaning. Interpretation is crucial when WRITING FOR THE OUTSIDE. It is the skill you will practice through writing a personal significance essay.

Generally, we interpret experience by considering causation and consequence. *Causation* involves the specific act or sequence of acts that lead up to an experience and how they cause, shape, or influence that experience. *Consequence* involves what follows from an experience, how the experience shapes subsequent thinking and acting. Either separately or together, causation and consequence help us understand experience by discovering relationships and establishing order.

Montaigne wants to gain control of the monsters and demonstrate that not chaos but order rules human existence. This is the goal of interpretation. In this, Montaigne exemplifies the great human undertaking. Discovering order is central to our experience; understanding order helps us gain control and makes it possible for us to avoid failures and to repeat successes. Montaigne wants to "shame" his mind because it did not perceive an order during the experience, and, thereby, compromised his ability to act. But with proper training, his mind will more easily sense the order. Montaigne withdraws from the world to gain control of his life. He uses reflective writing as a tool for gaining control, discovering order, and establishing significance.

We do not often think about the process of discovering order and establishing significance because it is so much a part of our nature. In fact, interpretation is a common task. The business of science is to discover order in nature. By examining and interpreting nature, science attempts to determine and explain—to interpret—how parts as small as immeasurable subatomic particles behave and contribute to the whole. In turn, this interpretation allows others to test the finding and come to a similar understanding.

But not only science is involved in determining significance through interpretation. Almost all planning, personal or commercial, involves collecting information and interpreting it, putting it into some sort of order, finding significance, minimizing failures and taking advantage of successes. Literature, history, and sociology—the arts, humanities, and social sciences—practice this same process. Though what is examined, the specific methods used to complete the examination, and the types of information considered most important may vary, all disciplines and professions are involved in interpretation.

ESTABLISHING SIGNIFICANCE

In this chapter, you will write a personal significance essay. You will engage in the same searching out of order that Montaigne attempted. You, too, will be interpreting the data offered by your personal experience. You will be using sophisticated thinking skills to connect the details of seemingly unconnected experience and to generalize conclusions that can stand the evaluation of a distant, public audience. This is important. Interpretation requires you to move beyond description. You must not only observe the telling details of an experience, you must also discover the order that creates its significance, and you must articulate this significance to others. Learning interpretation by using your personal experience now will give you practice with skills you can use later in school and beyond.

A Sample with Analysis

Interpretation is the primary purpose of the personal significance essay, and interpretation is something we do every day. Very rarely do we interpret with the rigor and sharp eye Jon Carroll uses in the following essay, "Chair Chat." Watch how Carroll reflects upon his experience at a dinner party, discovers its pattern and underlying order, and interprets from it a conclusion that can help us all live our lives more vitally.

CHAIR CHAT

Jon Carroll

1   Here's the Scene: One of those dinner parties with more strangers than friends around the table. The wine is lovely; the pasta is impeccable. Sitting next to me, on my right, is a young man in a wheelchair. We have already spoken of the wine and pasta; we have already praised the undeniable good taste of the hostess and of the food she has prepared.

2   "So," I say to the guy in the wheelchair, "what happened? Why are you confined to that wheelchair?"

3   "Sssssssssstt." It is the woman to my left. She is hissing at me. I swivel my head.

4   "Huh?" I say, ever the graceful conversationalist.

5   "Don't, you know, mention, the, uh, don't," she says, putting her right hand out at table level, palm down, and moving it rapidly back and forth, mezzo-mezzo style. "You know, I, well . . . ."

6   "Multiple sclerosis," says the guy in the wheelchair. "MS. Started about three years ago."

Source: Jon Carroll, "Chair Chat," *The San Francisco Cronicle*, December 19, 1983.

7   "Oh, God," says the woman.

8   "What?" I ask the woman.

9   "Too late," she says. "Oh, no."

10   The guy in the wheelchair continues his explanation. We discuss symptoms, cures, theories, difficulties. The woman to my left sinks lower and lower in her seat.

11   Why is it, I wondered later, that people think it's somehow in bad taste to talk to a handicapped person about his or her handicap? People in wheelchairs know they're in wheelchairs. They pay a good deal of daily attention to their ambulatory appliance. If you bring up this more-or-less central fact in their lives, they will almost certainly not be surprised.

12   "You mean, well, by God you're right. So I am. Never thought of it that way. Wish you hadn't brought it up. Now I'll be depressed all evening." Won't happen.

13   Suppose you were sitting next to an extremely tall person. Maybe you wouldn't bring up his height right away, but after an exchange of views on other topics of the day, you might ask about the thrills and agonies of unusual tallness. It is a topic on which he has some expertise, and it is a truism of social behavior that one should try to draw people out.

14   If you were sitting next to a known Nobel Prize winner, you might at some point ask her about Stockholm. "A very clean city, I hear. Lovely public parks, according to reports. Enjoy yourself?" You know.

15   And yet a surprisingly large number of people think that it's bad form to talk to handicapped people about their handicap. And, it seems to me, that reinforces the sense of shame and apartness that is one of the most terrible side-effects of physical disability.

16   It's almost superstitious, as though talking about it is somehow going to bring the everyday reality of crippling accident or wasting disease closer to home and hearth. Word magic, booga booga.

17   And if everyone at a dinner party is resolutely pretending that Guest A is not confined to a wheelchair, then Guest A is going to have a harder time believing that being confined to a wheelchair is an OK way to be, and even a hard time introducing various amusing or instructive anecdotes centering around his situation.

18   Worse yet, such over-polite reticence reduces the opportunity for understanding. The more opportunities that those of us who are without visible physical handicaps get to have an immediate and direct report on the nature of the experience of those who are so afflicted, the better we'll be able to understand it cleanly and work through our own fears and fantasies.

19   Meaning only to say: Excessive gentility results in boring and emotionally arid evenings. Stop talking about the weather and ask the questions you want to ask.

Obviously, Carroll interprets the woman's behavior as much more than social courtesy. He uses the specific instance to make a generalization about our society's inability to deal with the out-of-the-ordinary. As a rule, we worship the extraordinarily equipped. But while we make heroes of sports stars and entertainers, we segregate or ignore the less-than-normally equipped, the physically and mentally handicapped.

Carroll concludes that the tendency to ignore the obvious realities of the handicapped in the name of politeness cheapens our lives and reinforces the sense of isolation and alienation many of the handicapped suffer. We cheapen our lives because by ignoring the obvious we never get to know the handicapped. This violates normal human curiosity, cutting us off from knowledge that could increase our understanding and make us better able to live in the world. By acting as if there is nothing noteworthy about the handicapped, we complicate and intensify their plight, adding psychological pain to their physical inconvenience.

Review the essay, paying close attention to Carroll's technique. He observes and constructs the narrative from telling details like the woman's hand motions (paragraph 5). He phrases a question that causes him to begin interpreting the incident (paragraph 11). He uses irony and sarcasm to reflect the anger he senses the handicapped must feel at having insults added to their disabilities (paragraphs 12–14). His observations become generalizations about the negative effects on all who ignore obvious physical disabilities under the guise of social kindness. He articulates consequences not only for the handicapped person but also for "polite" partygoers such as you and I (paragraphs 15–19). He pays close attention to the experience, interprets it , and draws a lesson that will help both him and his readers live more effectively.

LOG EXERCISE: Causation and Consequence

Carroll's essay focuses on the consequences of an incident. Just to make sure you understand that interpretation involves both consequences and causation, write a one-page, "flip side" interpretation of the same incident. Instead of seeing things from Carroll's perspective, imagine yourself as the woman at the party and discuss several reasons why you do not want Carroll to call attention to the handicapped person in the wheelchair. Determine several good reasons that cause people typically to ignore the plight of the handicapped. Obviously, there must be reasons for such behavior since it is so prevalent. Be prepared to share your interpretation with other members of your class. Remember the point of the exercise: interpretation involves both consequence and causation.

ESSAY #4: WRITING A PERSONAL SIGNIFICANCE ESSAY

ASSIGNMENT

To complete this essay, choose an incident important in your life, present it in a narrative, and then discuss its significance. In the interpretation you must explain why the experience was important by examining the causes that combined to shape it or what consequences resulted that have affected your life. In order to do all this, the essay must be longer than two double-spaced typewritten pages, about 500 words.

Organize the essay by using a two-part structure. The first part should be a narrative relating the incident; the second part should analyze and interpret its significance. Tie these parts together with a thesis statement, one or two sentences placed strategically in the essay that introduce the central point and suggest how it will be developed.

Writers often use a thesis statement to help an audience understand an essay, especially one that presents an interpretation, argues a point of view, or attempts to persuade. The position and structure of the thesis statement cause it to serve as an organizational signal that puts the audience on notice that a particular idea will follow. We will spend considerable time working with thesis statements in this and the next chapter.

The next several sections present important information about structuring your essay and creating effective thesis statements. Pay close attention to the sections that explain how to use the peer critique questions and the draft self-evaluation questions while revising. Finally, the assignment summary will review the step-by-step process for writing this essay. Use all this information to create the strongest personal significance essay possible before submitting it for evaluation.

Choosing an Incident and Writing the Narrative

To find an incident for the narrative, review the **Reminiscence** section of your PDJ. As you review the Place, Person, Dialog, and Myth entries, think in terms of finding material that lends itself to story-telling. You need not use any single PDJ entry as the incident. Reviewing the PDJ may lead you to another incident that you remember as significant. Think about it further by working through a PDJ exercise or some other journal writing in order to become adequately prepared to write the narrative.

The first part of the essay should tell the incident as a story. It should not be an exact rendering of the journal entry. Rather, the journal entry will provide you with good raw materials for constructing the story. You know enough about the differences between WRITING FOR THE INSIDE and WRITING FOR THE OUTSIDE to avoid the trap of offering a personal journal entry as a public narrative. You also know how the PDJ and other personal journal writing can provide seeds from which can grow impressive meaning for public audiences. The point is that the **Reminiscence** exercises provide a starting point to begin moving meaning from the inside out.

A good way to find more ideas about the incident, especially to determine its significance, is to complete a systematic analysis of the incident. Consult the ''Invention'' section of the Appendix. Consider using Burke's Pentad (pages 255–259), which asks questions such as: What was the scene? Who were the actors? What were their purposes, motives, and instruments? The Pentad also considers what the relations were among these elements. Answering these questions or others like them will help you gain control of the incident so you can relate it with confidence in the narrative. You will also discover information that will help you understand the significance of the incident and will become important in your analysis and interpretation.

Once you have selected the incident and recreated it in draft form as vividly as possible from your memory, draft the narrative. As you write, remember all that you learned earlier about description. Remember the progression from recording to reporting to recreating, remember the writer's responsibility to select and organize telling details, remember point of view and sequencing, and spatial and chronological order. Consider the different purposes of objective and impressionistic styles of description. Make the first part of your paper an effective narrative of the incident.

Analyzing and Interpreting: Imposing Order

After you have drafted the narrative, you must interpret its significance by explaining why the incident is important. As noted earlier, significance can be discovered either by considering the causes of the incident or its consequences. For example, insights gained through leaving home and living independently can make a young person appreciate the value of family in a new and important way. But these insights depend on acknowledging and understanding the *causes* of the departure—the lack of privacy and personal space, the absence of self-determination, the imposition of seemingly arbitrary rules. Understanding such causes may allow the writer to confront and solve similar problems in the future. The writer must demonstrate the significance of the incident by explaining the lesson learned.

On the other hand, a family breaking up after a death or divorce could result in one of the family members losing trust in people. The victim might become cold and distant and find it hard to love anyone or to be loved. Thus, as a *consequence* of the break-up, the victim's behavior is affected in certain ways. Determining the effect of the incident through analysis and illustrating the consequence by providing examples constitute the interpretation. As Montaigne noted, when we reflect and recreate the incident, we discover and can report the order, the sense, the significance of the incident. Reaching such an understanding helps us gain control of our lives.

Once you have worked through the analysis of the incident and come to some conclusions about its significance, draft your interpretation. Use topic sentences and develop main ideas by using illustrations and examples that will prove your point. If you have come to several conclusions, introduce and develop each one in a separate paragraph. Develop each of the elements of your interpretation logically so that you will convince your readers that your interpretation is correct.

Structuring the Essay: Using Thesis Statements

After drafting the narrative and interpretation, you have two separate elements. The narrative introduction presents details, uses order, and employs transitions appropriate to descriptive writing. The analytic body of the essay uses logical and systematic analysis of causes or consequences, the elaboration of insights through examples and illustrations, and the defense of assertions through argument. How can you join these seemingly contradictory elements into a coherent essay?

To graft them and allow them to grow together, you must include a signal for the reader. The signal, a thesis statement, will let the reader know that you have finished the narrative and are beginning the analysis.

For example, in "Chair Chat," Carroll ends the narrative of the specific details of the dinner-party encounter with the handicapped person by asking a question and answering it with a statement of the obvious: "Why is it, I wondered later, that people think it's somehow in bad taste to talk to a handicapped person about his or her handicap? People in wheelchairs know they're in wheelchairs" (paragraph 11). This is the thesis statement. The asking and answering of the question is a signal to the reader that the narrative has ended and the interpretation has begun. It allows Carroll to draw the conclusions about cheapening the lives of the polite and insulting the handicapped. The thesis statement is the kernel of the analysis, the seed from which the interpretation grows. The thesis statement lets the reader know that the incident was significant and suggests why. The thesis statement is the essay in a nutshell.

Make sure you understand the role of a thesis statement. Like the transitions used in description to guide the reader through the essay, the thesis statement is a signal to the reader. However, the thesis statement is more than a signal; it is also a commitment, a contract, letting the reader know what to expect in the rest of the paper. And, as is the case with a legal contract, if the writer does not deliver what is promised by the thesis statement, the reader has no further obligation, and, in fact, ought to sue the writer for damages in payment for wasted time.

In a personal significance essay, the thesis statement is crucial. It is the spine that supports the head and provides a skeleton for the body. The thesis statement is your point, your purpose in writing. You owe it to yourself and your reader to understand your point, commit yourself to it, and organize your writing to communicate it.

A Student Sample with Analysis

In the following essay, pay particular attention to the use Lynn Hardin makes of her thesis statement. Appearing about halfway through the essay, it distills the significance of the episode related in the narrative, and it explains the reasons for her behavior. At the same time, however, the thesis also serves as the structuring mechanism for the rest of the essay. She says she acts not in search of excitement, "but for solace, an independent, selfish, secretive, noncommittal aloneness." Notice that each one of the elements of her thesis receives attention in a paragraph of elaboration. Note also that these paragraphs follow the order used in the thesis. In addition to exemplifying interpretation of personal experience, the essay illustrates the effective and economical use of a thesis statement.

Lynn Hardin
Essay #4
Personal Significance Essay

                    Saturday Morning Sunshine

    The shop always had that musty, mechanical kind of
smell. It did that morning, too. The small place was
dusky inside, for very little sunlight penetrated. The
only rays were those pouring through the window of the
door, unhindered by the painted letters on the glass.

    I had gone to visit him before the shop opened at his
request. I surprised myself by accepting an invitation
from this inappropriate man, who was, by some standards,
practically a stranger. There I was nonetheless. As he
locked the door behind me, the commitment he wore on his
left hand caught the early morning sunlight and cast a
painful glare into my eyes. I simply looked away.

    What happened that morning should have been set to
music. His advances and my evasions, both verbal and
physical, were almost like dance steps—not a bawdy chase
around the work bench, but rather an intricate, precise
series of movements that almost had the air of being
rehearsed. This feeling of familiarity had begun weeks
earlier, when, with tremulous steps, the dance first
began. On this Saturday morning, we would enjoy a
synchronized togetherness.

    We talked about his wife and my boyfriend—the two
principal reasons why we shouldn't have been there
together. I listened as he discussed his shy high school
days. Overwhelming smoothness had displaced his
adolescent bumbling. To me, it seemed almost a shame that
the unassuming teenager had blossomed into this self-
assured man who showed occasional glimpses of insincerity.

    Underscoring every word of dialogue was a deep-seated,
mutually acknowledged physical attraction. The

conversation was the comfortable aftermath of one brief, impetuous, and decidedly uncomfortable incident. But Platonic intimacy replaced carnal interaction. As the hour passed, we established a friendship.

All of this was shaded, however, by the stark light of my reason for being someplace I should not have been with a man for whom I really did not care that much—then or now. At one point he asked me why I was there; he said I was just looking for excitement. I agreed, at the time. Looking back, though, I can see that I was there not to seek excitement, but solace: an independent, selfish, secretive, noncommital aloneness.

My Saturday morning in that shop came at a time when my life was being directed by everyone but me. Parents and friends were, at least indirectly, making decisions for me. I made no moves without getting their approval; I did not deviate from the norm. That morning was, at its best, a deviation: an escapade I could revel in without baring all to everyone and enduring their reproach. Only he and I knew, no one else.

I actually relished the thought of having some part of my life solely to myself. That where I was and whom I was with was potentially dangerous did not disturb me. I thought only of the fact that this was a moment for me alone. I soaked in the selfishness of it all; moments of self-indulgence such as this were rare.

Ironically, I felt a sense of freedom from knowing that this was something I could never share with anyone close to me. I found relief in the secrecy of the whole event. I could give in to anything he proposed or walk away completely untouched, and no one would ever know that I had even darkened the doorway. I could leave and never lay eyes on him again, and life would go on just as it had before. No need for questions, explanations, or apologies.

Most of all, I savored the knowledge that, come Monday morning, I would have nothing to answer for. In truth, I

had only the possibility of another Saturday morning, and
the potential acquisition of a new ''significant other''
who would be, in the light of my circle of relationships,
significant only to me.

"Saturday Morning Sunshine" deserves attention for more reasons than just
its skillful use of a thesis statement. The narrative is an effective one. The first
paragraph establishes a sense of mystery, inviting the reader further into the story.
In addition, Lynn's language is in itself interesting. She describes her friend's wedding ring as "the commitment he wore on his left hand." Such indirect statement
contributes more than just an interesting turn of phrase to the essay; it emphasizes
the questionable morality, the intrigue, of the episode. She admits that she does
not know her host very well, but she will not admit directly that he is married. She
uses indirection.

Lynn describes the interlude as a "dance," again exemplifying her effective use
of language. A dance, in the sense of ballet or jazz, is a series of stylized movements that combine to create symbolic meaning. And Lynn's behavior in this meeting is primarily symbolic, not physical. Lynn freely admits that the meeting may
have been initiated as a result of some physical attraction, either to the person or
the situation, but she uses the immediate physical attraction to begin a consideration of deeper, more subtle behaviors. In this she recognizes something important
about herself and about humanity in general. This is the moral dilemma that ultimately provides significance to her narrative.

As children, we are taught to follow rules, to be "good little girls and boys."
From early on we are trained to deny our baser instincts. We control them by
ignoring them. As a consequence, some of us ultimately fail moral tests because
we do not think about and deal with problems as they come up. When we are truly
tested, we fail. In this case Lynn is dealing both with her baser instincts and with
following laws, with being a "good girl." She is testing herself.

In fact, meeting the test is the significance she discovers through her interpretation. Her behavior testifies to her good sense; she trusts her intuitions and they
serve her well. No ill comes from the meeting. But the real benefit of the experience comes much later, during the writing of the essay. Lynn's drafts and revisions
make this clear. Through reflection and reconsideration—through interpretation—
she comes to her conclusions. She realizes the consequences of denying herself
and mistrusting her instincts. She knows that if she did not act on her impulse she
could have lost her "self."

In the essay, she articulates this lesson. She uses the episode as a way of
getting into the open the dissatisfaction she felt and may still feel about the lack
of power she has over her own life. In the past she has not led, she has followed.
In this instance, however, she exercised some quiet but vital power over her own
destiny. She is not trying to get away with anything. She is ultimately innocent.
She is, however, coming to an awareness, admitting her dissatisfaction with life,

and opening up the possibilities for acting in other ways in the future. She is growing.

Witnessing Lynn's growth is largely why readers like her essay so much. Surely it is a demonstration of her ability to write narrative, to construct a thesis statement and use it to organize an essay. Surely it is a demonstration of her ability to move from personal to public meaning. But more important, the essay presents an insight that has been recognized, refined, and communicated. She connects with her audience. Having experienced similar impulses and incidents, readers know how she feels. In fact, as a result of Lynn's essay, readers know more about their own feelings and experiences. They have been enriched through Lynn's essay.

Using the Peer Critique Questions

Lynn's essay took quite a journey through the drafting and revising phases. There are numerous changes between her working drafts and the version you read, most of these in the second section's analysis and interpretation. Her success in revision is at least partly attributable to her use of peer responses and the draft self-evaluation.

The peer critique questions directed readers to respond to three specific areas. You will use the same questions when you collect peer responses to your draft. The procedure for peer critiquing continues as it did before; only the questions have changed.

PEER CRITIQUE QUESTIONS

Answer the following questions when providing peer responses to the personal significance essay:
1. What is the point of the essay? Summarize it in two sentences.
2. What phrase or sentence do you most remember from the entire essay? Explain why it is so memorable.
3. What emotion best expresses how the essay made you feel? Explain its origin.

Testing the Thesis Statement

When these peer critique questions are used, the greatest focus is usually on the first question, which asks for a summary of the essay. The summaries serve to test the accuracy and effectiveness of the thesis statement. You will want to use the thesis test in this essay and in others that also use a thesis statement. Here's how it works.

When your peers complete the summary, their job is to try to boil the whole essay down into one or two sentences. Thus, the summary has roughly the same function as your thesis statement does. Before you read the peer summaries, search through the essay and underline your thesis statement. After this, compare your underlined thesis statement to the peer summaries. If your thesis statement is an effective one, the one- or two-sentence summaries should quite closely resemble your underlined thesis statement. If there are significant differences between your thesis statement and the summaries, rethink your essay and revise it to correct the discrepancy between the meaning you intended to communicate and the meaning discovered by your readers.

However, these summaries can be used for more than just revealing discrepancies. Often summaries that differ from your intended thesis statement call attention to a strength in the essay you overlooked and failed to develop. During revision you can take advantage of that strength as well as clarify the main point of your essay. Testing the thesis statement can provide important information to help you when you revise.

Remember that the purpose of peer critiquing is to try out an essay on a real audience before the essay takes its final form. Testing your thesis is one way you can put peer responses to work. Do not feel that you have failed if there are discrepancies between your thesis statement and the peer summaries. Rather, use such discrepancies to make your next version more effective.

The summaries written by Lynn's peers very closely resembled her thesis statement: "Looking back, though, I can see that I was there not to seek excitement, but solace: an independent, selfish, secretive, noncommittal aloneness." Her peers focused on the almost reckless independence of the meeting and on its secretiveness and intrigue. The memorable phrase most frequently remarked was "the commitment he wore on his left hand," Lynn's clear though indirect reference to her friend's wedding ring. The emotion called out by the essay was "fantasy—an aura of semi-reality and intrigue." The responses were quite positive.

Using the Draft Self-evaluation Questions

Because there was general agreement between the thesis statement and the peer summaries and because the peer responses pointed to what Lynn already suspected were the strengths of her essay, namely the narrative and her use of language, they served more to reinforce her than to direct her toward specific revisions. Lynn's revisions came mainly from the analysis of the essay she completed with her draft self-evaluation. Take a close look at Lynn's self-evaluation. Remember that these comments refer to the draft read by her peers, not the one you read.

L. Hardin
Saturday Morning Sunshine

Draft Self-evaluation

1. What is the greatest strength in your paper in its present form?

Now I am happy with about two sentences out of the

entire piece. Another strength is the vast number of
paragraphs which have been killed.

2. What is the greatest weakness in your paper in its
present form?

Its greatest weakness is that I AM NOT HAPPY with the
essay. It doesn't sound right to me. Nothing fits. I
don't think I followed the proper form. I hate all but
two sentences. I chose the wrong event. I made the wrong
type of analysis--need I go on?

3. What is your purpose in this paper? How does the
paper accomplish that purpose? Consider the method of
organization, the selection of details, even the choice of
words and sentence structure. How do these help you
accomplish your purpose in the paper?

My purpose was to explain how I felt at one moment in
time. I used over a page to explain what was contained in
one sigh. Whether I did it effectively or not is the
question.

4. Who is your audience for this paper? How does the
paper address this audience?

My audience is the readers in the class. I think I am
pretty honest and straightforward without--as I stated--
''baring all.''

5. How did you discover the information you used in
the paper? Did you use a formal heuristic procedure or an
informal one? What discovery procedure will you use if
you discover you need more information while revising?

I was there. I didn't use a formal heuristic. During
revision I'll just probably use common sense.

6. When you are revising, what parts of the paper are
you going to pay the most attention to? (Introductory,
development, closing, detail and argument, organization,
clarifying purpose, addressing audience, voice, style--
others?)

In revision I'll try to cut down on my repetition It's
basically a boring piece so there's no need to harp on the
matter.

First, note how wrong Lynn's initial evaluation of her draft is. It is not uncommon for writers to misjudge drafts, especially drafts that take risks and investigate significant personal issues. The responses and reinforcement you get from peers will eventually prevent you from being your own worst enemies and missing the potential in your drafts.

Second, pay attention to Allison's responses to questions 1 (strengths), 3 (purpose and organization), and 4 (audience). Concerning strength, she likes a few sentences, and she has already eliminated many irrelevant paragraphs. This reflects the struggle that went into structuring the thesis statement paragraph. In fact, Lynn has already brought this draft a long way from her PDJ entry. She has worked hard polishing the narrative and developing the interpretation. An important task in completing the self-evaluation is determining how much work has been done and how much still needs to be done.

Lynn's response to question 3 concerning purpose and organization reminds us of the nature of a personal significance essay. Indeed, a sigh may deserve a page or more of analysis; a sigh can change a whole life. However, she answers her own question about effectiveness through the revisions she makes. Note that this sigh does not appear in the version you read; it has been relaced by several paragraphs of logical elaboration in the interpretation.

Her response to question 4 concerning audience gets at the problem of honesty and directness versus artful indirection. She is aware that she has created the sense of intrigue as a means of insulating herself from criticism she might confront if she had been more direct. Throughout the essay, everything remains in the realm of possibility rather than completed action. She is involved in a test, not misbehavior. She is satisfied that, though indirectly, she has gotten to the truth, to the essential significance of the incident, "without baring all."

Also interesting is her response to question 6, which asks about plans for revision. She is vague and unduly critical. She is clearly off base; the essay is not boring. Perhaps she knows how effective the essay is—she received praise from her peers—and is indulging in false modesty. More likely, she needs some reassurance. Writing a personal significance essay is a difficult and challenging assignment. Because it requires intense self-examination, the essay can seem threatening. Sometimes we do not want to consider our shortcomings. Moreover, we rarely feel comfortable revealing those shortcomings in a public essay. Writing truthfully may require us to take some risks. We may be embarrassed or criticized. In addition, some of us believe our lives are not terribly interesting or significant. In truth, however, either we have not looked closely enough or we are not giving ourselves the credit we deserve.

Perhaps her vagueness and negativity betray her sense that there is something lacking in the essay, and she is not sure what it is. She is quietly working on the problem, perhaps becoming aware that the sigh mentioned in question 3 is not sufficient and must be reworked in the interpretation. She becomes aware of the problem through the self-evaluation, but she does not solve it until she actually revises.

Lynn's self-evaluation accomplished two important tasks for her. First, it allowed her to distance herself from the peer responses and to reestablish ownership of her essay. This is important for all writers who have tested their drafts against a real audience of peers. Before you begin to revise, you must remember what *you* wanted the paper to be and not be bullied by the responses and suggestions of your peers. It *is your essay, not theirs*. Second, it illustrates a writer's ability, or inability, to determine the strengths and weaknesses in a draft before revision. The difficulties can be finally worked out only through revising. Take the same opportunity, and beware of the same problems, when you complete the self-evaluation. Reclaim ownership and prepare the way for effective revision.

Assignment Summary

Write a personal significance essay. Include a narrative of an incident from your experience and an analysis presenting your interpretation of the significance of the incident. Use a thesis statement to join the two parts of the essay. Your essay should run longer than two double-spaced typewritten pages, about 500 words.

Review the **Reminiscence** section of your PDJ as a source of potential incidents for the narrative. The PDJ may provide the incident itself or may provide direction for more journal writing during which you can discover and master an incident for the narrative. Analyze your incident formally using a method such as Burke's Pentad in the Appendix (pages 255 to 259) to help you understand the incident more completely and recreate it more effectively. This will provide important information for use in the analysis and interpretation section of the essay.

As you draft your essay, pay attention to the elements of description within the narrative. Use the knowledge you gained from writing the descriptive essays to your advantage here. Review our discussion of the function of a thesis statement in order to make it an effective preview of both the meaning and structure of your essay.

Before you revise, make sure to collect responses from your peers. Use the peer critique questions (page 138). Check the effectiveness of your thesis statement through the summary test. Complete the self-evaluation questions (page 101) in order to reclaim ownership of your essay. Revise thoroughly. Finally, edit and proofread your essay to make it reflect your quality and expertise as a thinker and writer. Submit it for evaluation confident you have done the best you can do.

Take this opportunity to turn an analytical eye toward your own experience. Create a personal significance essay in which both you and your readers learn more about interpreting experience as a means of developing personal awareness and understanding.

Writing an Argumentative Essay

INTRODUCTION: WRITING ARGUMENTATIVE ESSAYS

In the personal significance essay, you told a story and explained its meaning to a public audience. In the process, you learned how to interpret, which is a fundamental skill of writing to inform. To connect the two parts of the personal significance essay, the narrative and the interpretation, you used a thesis statement, a tool writers use to make sense to an audience. It encapsulates the meaning of an essay and suggests a structure for communicating that meaning. Suggesting the structure allows readers to check what is announced in the thesis statement against the rest of the essay. The thesis invites readers to become active participants in the essay.

In this chapter, we will move from narrating an incident and explaining its significance to making an assertion and arguing its credibility. We will learn another form, the argumentative essay. Its structure and pattern of development are designed expressly for making a point and defending it.

As usual, we will write the essay in segments. First, we will discuss the nature of argument and basic argumentative structures. We will examine the function of thesis statements in argumentation and develop several ways to evaluate them. You will draft and revise a thesis statement and two paragraphs defending it. Second, we will discuss introductions and learn how to evaluate them. You will draft and revise an introduction for your thesis statement and two paragraphs of defense. Third, we will discuss conclusions and learn how to evaluate them. You will draft and revise a conclusion, edit and proofread your entire essay, and submit it for evaluation. Finally, you will work through the entire procedure one more time in order to make sure you have mastered the argumentative essay. This is an important essay form to master, for its basic structure is used frequently both in school and out.

Interpretation versus Argument

The essential difference between personal significance essays and argumentative essays is the difference between explaining an interpretation and arguing a point of view. Although both are instances of writing to inform, the strategies used differ greatly.

In the personal significance essay, the writer's job is to make the narrative clear and the interpretation comprehensible. Readers need not necessarily agree that the causes or consequences are exactly as established; rather, they must only agree that the interpretation is reasonable. As readers, we can understand and appreciate Lynn Hardin's frustrations, and we can accept her desire to act independently as a reasonable explanation for her behavior in "Saturday Morning Sunshine" (pages 135–37). However, had Lynn argued that the motivation for her secret meeting was a deep-seated resentment of her mother, or that she was following the commands of voices whispering in her ear, we would dismiss her interpretation as unreasonable.

As we read an interpretation, we monitor; we do not argue or contest. If the writer has done an effective job, we accept the interpretation as one valid way of looking at the experience. In Lynn's case, what makes her essay successful is the use of common, shared experience. Because many of us have had similar experiences and have confronted similar problems, we read Lynn's essay with interest and sympathy, and we accept her interpretation.

An argumentative essay, however, requires more. The writer must state and defend an assertion that may or may not reflect common experience or widely held public opinion. The writer must develop a point of view, accumulate evidence to support that point of view, and structure an argument to convince an audience. The thesis statement announces the central point of the argument; the body of the essay provides specific elaboration and defense so that readers accept it. Success comes when readers accept the facts and argument exactly as presented.

In argument even more than in interpretation, the thesis statement is crucial. It organizes the material and invites readers into the argument. The thesis statement controls the interaction between subject, reader, and writer, resulting in effective WRITING FOR THE OUTSIDE.

Basic Argumentative Essay Structure

It is an oversimplification to believe, as too many writers have been taught, that an effective essay tells readers what it is going to say, then says it, and finally concludes by telling readers again what it said. Such a formula permits only simple meanings and makes for bored writers and readers.

Despite the limitations of this formula, it contains a ke[...] writers need to understand. To construct tight and forceful essa[...] patterned repetition. They state their point and reiterate it, def[...] ways. Thus, meaning accumulates. This repetition is not the c[...] kind of the formula essay noted above, which insults readers an[...] Rather, it is subtle and allows writers to make a point by annou[...]

Basic argumentative essay form uses patterned repetition. A simple and manageable form, it allows writers to make a point clearly without boring or insulting readers. The first paragraph provides an introduction and establishes a context for the essay. It ends with the thesis statement that encapsulates the whole essay. The body of the essay, the next several paragraphs, elaborates and defends the thesis statement. Each section of the body begins with a transition to establish a link to the thesis and previews the upcoming defense. This same pattern—statement with elaboration and restatement with elaboration—is repeated as many times as the complexity of the subject and thesis statement require. Finally, the writer concludes by developing an application or explaining the significance of the thesis.

In sum, argumentative essays use a three-part structure: (1) introduction with thesis statement, (2) body with elaboration and defense, and (3) conclusion with application or significance, as shown graphically, in Figure 6-1 on page 146.

ESSAY #5: WRITING AN ARGUMENTATIVE ESSAY

This essay assignment gives you practice using a simple but widely applicable essay form. You will begin by writing a three-paragraph argumentative essay. By the end of this chapter you will expand the form by adding a one-paragraph conclusion. This simple form can be used for short academic papers, essay exams, or any writing task that requires making and defending a statement. It is a pattern that can be shrunk or expanded, depending on the need.

For now, your essay is to be no longer than three paragraphs. The first paragraph will be comprised of the thesis statement only. It must suggest a structure for the argument. You will write two paragraphs of defense, each dealing with a separate aspect of the thesis statement. Transitions must clearly indicate relations between the paragraphs. Do not write the introduction or conclusion now. You will write them in separate exercises after drafting the thesis statement and defense. The whole essay should eventually run longer than two double-spaced typed pages (600 words).

ASSIGNMENT

Select a Common Subject

What should you write about? Good question. Generally, limiting yourself and the peers you will be working with to a particular subject is a good idea. It will assure that your readers have sufficient information to be participants rather than spectators in the argument. This will allow them to evaluate the success of your argument.

BASIC ARGUMENTATIVE ESSAY FORM

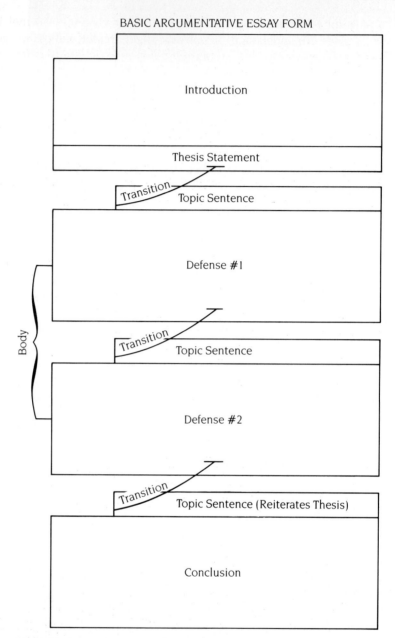

Introduction

Thesis Statement

Transition Topic Sentence

Defense #1

Body

Transition Topic Sentence

Defense #2

Transition Topic Sentence (Reiterates Thesis)

Conclusion

Figure 6-1
THE BASIC ARGUMENTATIVE ESSAY FORM

How should you select the common subject? First, with your peers, brainstorm a long list of possible topics. Books, short stories, poems, films, social issues— whatever. Many different topics can work for this assignment. You may be studying a particular book, story, article, or poem in class that would work.

Once your group has a list, then discuss the possibilities. Eliminate those that are not sufficiently interesting or require too much specialized information to understand. Also, consider the length of this assignment. Choose a topic that can be handled in this form. Do not choose a topic so complex it cannot fit into the few paragraphs you have to work with.

The student examples we will analyze are based on Toni Morrison's *The Bluest Eye*, a short novel dealing with a young black girl's experiences growing up in racially segregated Ohio in the 1930s. The writers are addressing their peers and instructor; they had read and discussed the novel in class. Their job was to convince readers to accept the plausibility of their point of view.

Establish a Tentative Thesis Statement

Once your group has selected a subject to write about, you must limit it for your own purposes, abstract its central point, and argue that it is best understood in the context of that central point. Answer this question for yourself: What is X about and how does it work? The answer becomes your tentative thesis statement.

Then, proceed through the discovery and drafting procedures already discussed for writing essays. Consult the Appendix for appropriate invention strategies. Particularly effective invention strategies for argumentative essays include brainstorming and bubbling to find a center of interest in the subject, supplemented by particle, wave, and field analysis or Pentad analysis to arrive at your thesis statement. The invention exercises will also provide you with the data you need to defend your thesis. Conceive your thesis statement and compose your argument completely before worrying about an introduction or conclusion. You will receive instructions on formulating those later.

THE BASIC STRUCTURE BRIEFLY EXPLAINED

You are writing an argumentative essay based on the diagram in Figure 6-1. The first paragraph must be an introduction, and it must conclude with a thesis statement that announces the point you will make in the paper. The thesis must resemble a statement like "Motorcycles should be outlawed because they are noisy and dangerous." Admittedly, this thesis statement is extremely simple and difficult to argue, but it can serve as an example. Note that it has announced the subject to the audience, it has invited them into the argument because it deals with common knowledge and experience which most people will have an opinion about, and it establishes the structure of the paper. Thus, it could be an effective thesis statement.

In the brief plan that follows, note how the transitions relate the paragraphs in the essay:

PLAN: BAN THOSE OBNOXIOUS MOTORCYCLES

Thesis Statement: Motorcyles should be outlawed because they are noisy and dangerous. (Last sentence of introductory paragraph.)

Transition 1: Motorcycles contribute greatly to the noise pollution that disrupts our environment and should therefore be outlawed. (First sentence of paragraph 2, the first paragraph of defense.)

Transition 2: Not only do motorcycles contribute to the noise that disrupts our environment, they are frequently the cause of serious personal injuries and should be banned for safety reasons. (First sentence of paragraph 3, the second paragraph of defense.)

Peer Critique Questions

After you have constructed an essay following the three-paragraph plan, use the following peer critique questions to direct peer response before you begin revising. Given the nature of argument, rather than only listening to the writer read the draft, respondents will need to have a copy of the draft for reference.

PEER CRITIQUE QUESTIONS

Answer the following questions when providing peer responses to the argumentative essay:

1. What is the point of the essay? Summarize it in one or two sentences.
2. What was the strongest aspect of the essay?
3. What was the weakest aspect of the essay?
4. What two questions raised by the essay do you need to have answered in order to believe the writer?
5. Why do you agree or disagree with the argument the writer makes in the essay? Explain briefly.

Note how these questions require respondents to move beyond remarking memorable elements in the essay; they must evaluate the effectiveness of the argument. Such a change signals a shift from describing an essay to criticizing it. Asking for this criticism allows you to test the effectiveness of your essay.

A Student Sample with Analysis

Before you begin to write, consider the following sample of an argumentative essay based on *The Bluest Eye*. This student draft has both strengths and weaknesses. Read it, respond to the peer critique questions, and compare your responses to those provided in the analysis.

Some background information on *The Bluest Eye* may help you determine whether the argument is clear and the essay is successful. The novel portrays the life of poor blacks in an industrial part of Ohio in the 1930s. Morrison tells the story from the point of view of Claudia, a precocious ten-year-old black girl.

The story centers on Pecola, whose family has dissolved as a result of poverty and racism. Pecola is an ugly young girl, not very smart, who has been impregnated by her father. Her father, Cholly, is not so evil a character as he is a victim of a long series of events which make life tolerable for him only through an alcoholic fog. He is so reduced in his humanity that he can show love only through violence. Cholly rapes Pecola, resulting in her pregnancy.

Pecola's mother, Cholly's wife, is a hard woman who takes better care of the white family she serves as a maid than she does her own family. It seems clear that she loves that family more than her own.

Throughout Morrison's book, whiteness is symbolized by the blue eyes of toy dolls given to black and white children alike. Whiteness is epitomized in Shirley Temple, the cute, child movie star whom many blacks consider the ideal child in the ideal world. The greatest gift is to be like Shirley Temple, to have those cute blue eyes. In the book, blacks idolize whiteness and white ways even though through segregation they have been banned from mainstream culture. Their only recourse is to become white-like, to possess whiteness as it is embodied in the children of the white families that blacks work for. Whiteness—"blue eyes"—becomes the only source of beauty and worth.

At an early age, the narrator, Claudia, becomes aware of the irony of this value system and rejects it. She realizes that in that system she, as a black girl, can never be beautiful. She revolts and makes a world for herself. Her friend Pecola is not so strong nor so lucky. Ultimately, Pecola is driven insane and begins to believe that she has blue eyes—in fact, the "bluest eyes." She believes that she is white and beautiful. She has been destroyed by poverty, racism, and violence. She has lost herself.

Claudia comes to hate whiteness and resent white people because whiteness and white people alienate blacks from themselves by denying them the opportunity to be beautiful. However, she and her family transcend the horror of their situation by developing their own standard of beauty based on human love. The book is well worth reading and writing about. It provides many insights about the saving nature of love and beauty in oppressive social conditions.

Alex Tanner in "Burden of Hate" analyzes *The Bluest Eye* in the context of twentieth-century existentialism. Read his essay, paying particular attention to the way he develops his argument and the way he uses evidence from the novel. Then answer the peer critique questions about his essay.

Alex Tanner
Essay 5
Argumentative Essay

Burden of Hate

For centuries, mankind has clung to the Judeo-Christian justification of human suffering: there are divine reasons beyond our mortal comprehension. Through religion, mankind found reason and will to endure. With the advancement of science and technology, and especially with the passing of two World Wars filled with horror and human misery, twentieth-century man, on the whole, no longer finds God's mysterious ways a satisfactory answer to his suffering. God's will no longer provides sufficient comfort and meaning. In what then, can man place his faith? Why must he suffer? Many modern writers, such as Sartre and MacLeish, have expressed the existential philosophy that man must find meaning within himself, in the way he bears his burden of suffering and accepts his fate. In her novel, The Bluest Eye (NY: Washington Square Press, 1970), Toni Morrison portrays a black society oppressed by extreme racism and grinding poverty and shows how the people in this situation live and react to their suffering. Indeed, the novel not only shows the way to rise above an oppressive environment and endure, but also warns that giving in to despair and hate leads to unhappiness. Thus Morrison illustrates, by contrasting the character Cholly, who turns to hate in his suffering, with the narrator, Claudia, who sees the hate and instead chooses love, that hate leads only to destruction whereas love gives worth and meaning to suffering.

Cholly, rejected by his parents, lost all room for love
in his life and turned to bitterness and hatred. Ever
since Cholly was a child, he built his life on hate. When
two white hunters discover Cholly making love to Darlene
in the bushes and force him to continue in the light of
their lamp and jeers, Cholly immediately turns to hate:
''He hated her. He almost wished he could do it––hard,
long and painful. He hated her so much'' (p. 117).
Here Cholly's hate for Darlene is not reasonable––his
powerlessness is not her fault. Yet that is the only
reaction he allows himself. Hating the hunters would get
him nowhere: ''Never did he once consider directing his
hatred toward the hunters. Such an emotion would have
destroyed him'' (p. 119). Cholly hates his situation.
He hates his own inability to do anything about his
suffering: ''. . . he hated the one who had created his
impotence. The one whom he had not been able to protect,
to spare, to cover from the round moon glow of the
flashlight'' (p. 119). Cholly's hatred leads not only to
his own downfall, but also that of his daughter, Pecola.
When he comes home drunk one afternoon, he pities her
because he knows the suffering she will go through—indeed,
is going through. He sees her life filled with misery and
without hope: Cholly feels, ''His revulsion was a
reaction to her young, helpless, hopeless presence.
Her back hunched that way; her head to one side as though
crouching from a permanent and unrelieved blow. Why did
she look so whipped?'' (p. 127). Again hatred rises up
in Cholly. He feels guilty and impotent; he is torn
between pity and wanting to help Pecola, and hatred of her
because, like Darlene, she ''. . . bore witness to his
failure, his impotence'' (p. 119). Still Cholly feels the
need to reach out to her somehow, to touch her life in
some manner. Thus, Cholly, as ''the tenderness welled up
in him'' (p. 128), forces on Pecola the only thing he has—
—sexual love. Cholly succeeds in reaching her as no one
had before. He not only impregnates her, but also destroys

her sanity. Cholly, in his hate and frustration at the harshness of his existence, alienates himself from his family and destroys the mind and future of his daughter. Thus, Morrison shows that reacting to suffering with hate and despair is a harmful attitude that leads only to hurt and destruction.

Throughout the novel, the narrator, Claudia, quietly observes all the hatred and envy in her environment. She understands—or perhaps just feels—the futility and destruction caused by the hate and bitterness resulting from being black and poor. Claudia and her sister: ''Thought only of this overwhelming hatred for [Pecola's] unborn baby. We remembered the knuckled eyes of the school children under the gaze of Meringue Pie and those same children when they looked at Pecola. Or maybe we didn't remember: we just knew'' (p. 149). Claudia, caring for Pecola and her baby, plants marigold seeds in the hope that through some miracle both the seeds and the baby might flourish. Doing this, she breaks through the barrier of hatred, and reaches a maturity beyond most of the adults. Claudia states: ''I thought about the baby everybody wanted dead, and saw it very clearly . . . . I felt a need for someone to want the black baby to live— just to counteract the universal love of white baby dolls, Shirley Temples and Maureen Peals'' (p. 148). Thus Claudia, seeing the result of hate, chooses instead to turn to love—true and unselfish love. She realizes that only through love is suffering bearable and life worth enduring. Only through love will the marigold seeds thrive and bloom.

Before we pay attention to Alex's essay and how he might go about revising, we need to consider how the peer critique questions work with an argumentative essay. The relevance of the first question should be obvious. Given the function of a thesis statement as the main idea or abstract of the essay, it seems clear that the peer summaries and the thesis statement should resemble one another closely.

They need not be exactly the same because the peer summaries will include not only the main idea but also the method used to prove the argument. Peers also may not focus exactly on the same ideas that the writer or other peers do. The point remains, however, that gross differences between the peer summaries and the thesis statement suggest real problems in the essay. In such cases, what the writer wanted to communicate did not come through clearly to the readers. This is information the writer can use while revising.

In order to clarify the point about agreement between summaries and thesis statements, consider the following summary offered by one of Alex's peer respondents: "The writer contrasts the behaviors of Cholly and Claudia to demonstrate that falling victim to hate can lead only to violence and despair, and that avoiding the trap of hate through awareness encourages tolerance, love, and hope, which can make a hard life bearable."

Now consider Alex's thesis statement which appears as the last sentence of the introductory paragraph: "Thus, Morrison illustrates, by contrasting the character Cholly, who turns to hate in his suffering, with the narrator, Claudia, who sees the hate and instead chooses love, that hate leads only to destruction whereas love gives worth and meaning to suffering."

Comparing Alex's thesis statement to the summary, we find that on the whole they support each other. The basic points—that contrasting characters is the method, that hate leads to violence and despair, and that love and awareness can make a harsh life tolerable—come through clearly in the essay and become part of the summary. If this were the only summary Alex received, he could feel confident that he communicated his point.

How about your summary? Did it resemble the one provided? Did it resemble Alex's thesis statement? If not, why not? Did you read Alex's paper closely enough to be able to summarize it effectively? Note that responding to an argumentative essay requires you to *read* the paper closely and have it there for reference. Hearing it read aloud is not sufficient when responses move from description to evaluation. The reader can no longer be only a witness or spectator; the reader must become an active participant in the argument.

If your summary disagreed substantially from the one provided and also from Alex's thesis statement, read the essay again to see if you might not revise your summary. The point here is that an essay that has as complex an argument as Alex's requires close reading and response.

Becoming a Close Reader

An essay must be complete and coherent in itself. To produce such an essay, a writer must anticipate the close reader, the reader who does not forgive, who does not allow the benefit of the doubt when a writer claims two points are related without showing the relationship. The close reader takes nothing for granted.

Close reading is a valuable skill that you need to develop for yourself. You need to become your own close reader, especially when analyzing thesis statements. Remember, the thesis statement is a contract between you and your reader. You are obligated to fulfill the expectations you establish in your thesis statement.

To prepare to evaluate your own thesis statements, read Alex's thesis state-ment as a close reader would. Your first task is to isolate the *key words and operative terms*. These are the words and phrases that direct the development of the essay. In Alex's thesis statement, the key words are "Cholly," "hate," "suffering," and "de-struction" and "Claudia," "sees hate," "chooses love" and "worth and meaning in suffering."

To make his point for a close reader, Alex must demonstrate that Cholly is vic-timized by hate, that he suffers, and that he causes destruction. On the other side, he must demonstrate that Claudia witnesses hate and recognizes that it can only lead to destruction. Finally, he must show that her realization leads to an aware-ness which allows her to choose love and salvage worth and meaning from suffer-ing. The key words Alex uses in his thesis statement require him to address all this in his argument in order to fulfill the contract he has established with his readers.

In addition to key words, however, a thesis statement must also include *opera-tive terms*. Operative terms suggest how the writer is going to prove the claims. Alex's thesis includes two operative terms—"characters" and "contrasting." "Con-trasting" seems obvious enough. As an operative term it is crucial to an effective thesis statement. The thesis statement must not only announce what it is going to say, but it must also suggest *how* it is going to prove its points. Alex's method is clear; he is going to contrast the two characters and their ways.

Close readers will also pay attention to "characters" as an operative term. In the context of an essay analyzing a book, "characters" carries special meaning. In the first place, it makes readers expect character analysis to be part of the argu-ment. Analysis requires describing actions *and* investigating their motivations. For example, examine how Alex develops the "Cholly" paragraph. He may not be as successful in the "Claudia" paragraph, but more about that later.

The point is simple: close reading causes writers to be thorough. Close readers give no slack; they require each of the elements of the claim made in the thesis statement and its method of argumentation to be clearly announced. Becoming your own close reader forces you to break your thesis statement down into its parts so you understand what you are promising your readers and are better able to deliver on those promises. It is a valuable exercise you should complete before seeking response from your peers.

So, where are we? We have seen that we can test how accurate our thesis statements are by comparing them with the summaries produced during the peer critique exercises. In addition, we have learned that we must become our own close readers, and we have discussed *close reading* techniques. We learned how to analyze thesis statements by considering *key words* and *operative terms* and the expectations these create in readers. We now have several concrete ways to evaluate thesis statements.

Though we have learned to analyze and evaluate our own writing, we must not forget how much peer response contributes to writing effective essays. The strengths and weaknesses questions encourage peers to analyze drafts in terms of what is working or not working. Strengths are what we want to take advantage of during revision; weaknesses are what we need to eliminate or to develop into strengths.

EVALUATING PARAGRAPHS

Assessing Strengths

Alex's paper has several strengths. We have already
uses evidence to develop his argument, especially regardi
long second paragraph serves as a good one to examin
ment. Reread the paragraph and consider it in terms of
definition, diagram, and analysis.

A paragraph is a sequence of sentences developing one main idea. Most paragraphs consist of a topic sentence, generally the first sentence, which introduces
the subject of the paragraph and makes a statement about or qualifies that subject.
The body of the paragraph provides examples or arguments to develop the statement of the topic sentence through a series of episodes, units of one or more
sentences elaborating the main idea. Transitions connect the episodes and show
the relation of the episodes to the topic sentence. Many paragraphs end with a
conclusion or clincher sentence that ties the episodes together and/or recapitulates
the main idea of the paragraph. Represented graphically, a paragraph would look
like Figure 6-2 at the bottom of this page.

Now here is Alex's second paragraph on Cholly:

---

[1]Cholly, rejected by his parents, lost all room for love
in his life and turned to bitterness and hatred. [2]Ever
since Cholly was a child, he built his life on hate. [3]When
two white hunters discover Cholly making love to Darlene
in the bushes and force him to continue in the light of
their lamp and jeers, Cholly immediately turns to

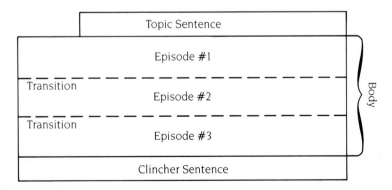

Figure 6-2
THE BASIC PARAGRAPH

''He hated her. He almost wished he could do it--
long and painful. He hated her so much'' (p. 117).
re Cholly's hate for Darlene is not reasonable--his
powerlessness is not her fault. [5]Yet that is the only
reaction he allows himself. [6]Hating the hunters would get
him nowhere: ''Never did he once consider directing his
hatred toward the hunters. Such an emotion would have
destroyed him'' (p. 119). [7]Cholly hates his situation.
[8]He hates his own inability to do anything about his
suffering: ''. . . he hated the one who had created his
impotence. [9]The one whom he had not been able to protect,
to spare, to cover from the round moon glow of the
flashlight'' (p. 119). [10]Cholly's hatred leads not only to
his own downfall, but also that of his daughter, Pecola.
[11]When he comes home drunk one afternoon, he pities her
because he knows the suffering she will go through--
indeed, is going through. [12]He sees her life filled with
misery and without hope: Cholly feels, ''His revulsion
was a reaction to her young, helpless, hopeless presence.
[13]Her back hunched that way; her head to one side as though
crouching from a permanent and unrelieved blow. [14]Why did
she look so whipped?'' (p. 127). [15]Again hatred rises up
in Cholly. [16]He feels guilty and impotent; he is torn
between pity and wanting to help Pecola, and hatred of her
because, like Darlene, she ''. . . bore witness to his
failure, his impotence'' (p. 119). [17]Still Cholly feels
the need to reach out to her somehow, to touch her life in
some manner. [18]Thus, Cholly, as ''the tenderness welled up
in him'' (p.128), gives Pecola the only thing he has--
sexual love. [19]Cholly succeeds in reaching her as no one
had before. [20]He not only impregnates her, but also
destroys her sanity. [21]Cholly, in his hate and frustration
at the harshness of his existence, alienates himself from
his family and destroys the mind and future of his
daughter. [22]Thus, Morrison shows that reacting to
suffering with hate and despair is a harmful attitude that
leads only to hurt and destruction.

Using the elements introduced in the previous paragraph
gram, we can analyze Alex's "Cholly" paragraph like this:

Topic Sentence: Cholly, rejected by his parents, los
instead turned to bitterness and hatred.

Subject: Cholly.

Statement/Qualification: lost love and turned to bitterness and hate.

Episode 1: Sentences 2 through 9.
   Develops: addresses origin of loss of love in dramatic scene in which
   white men interrupt love making.
   Transitions: ever since, when, immediately, here—yet.

Episode 2: Sentences 10 through 20.
   Develops: explains that Cholly's rape of Pecola reflects bitterness and
   hatred.
   Transitions: when, again, still, thus, though.

Clinchers: Sentences 21 and 22.
   Sentence 21 recapitulates the statement made in the paragraph.
   Sentence 22 reestablishes context of the whole essay, ties paragraph
   to proof of thesis statement.

Although Alex includes a reference to his own parents that is not developed in
this paragraph, his first sentence is still a strong topic sentence. It announces all
that will be included in the paragraph. Reading this topic sentence closely, we see
the key words "rejected," "lost love," "bitterness," and "hatred."

Operative terms are important in topic sentences, too. Just as a thesis statement must present the main idea and the method of development, so should a
topic sentence present the subject of the paragraph and the way it will be developed. The operative terms in the topic sentence are the verbs and how they promise to develop the ideas. Alex's verbs are "lost" and "turned." These are operative
in the sense that both imply change: to have lost love requires having once had it;
to have turned to bitterness and hatred requires once having loved. So, the paragraph must deal with this change—how it happened and what resulted from it.

The paragraph addresses those topics effectively. The paragraph moves from
the episodes that caused the loss and the turn—Cholly's humiliation by the white
hunters and the resentment he develops towards black women because he has no
power over white men—to Cholly's abuse and rape of Pecola as his only means of
showing affection for his girl child.

Another strength in this paragraph deserves note. In each stage of the argument, Alex goes to the book for tangible evidence to prove his assertions. Doing
this, he proves that the author has constructed the story in this way. He does not

his argument at the level of opinion or feelings. He argues from the book. In the end, Alex proves his claim; a reader would be hard pressed to dispute this. The use of evidence, especially in the second paragraph, is one of the great strengths of the essay.

Assessing Weaknesses

Knowing how to find and analyze Alex's strengths helps us understand how to use peer responses regarding weaknesses. In fact, the two combined provide concrete direction for revision.

In Alex's case, the strength of the second paragraph indicates the flaws of the others. Responses to the weakness question should call Alex's attention to several problems. The changing role of religion and the influence of existentialism mentioned in the introduction are interesting but undeveloped ideas. That humans must accept their fate and suffering and find meaning within themselves is worth writing about. But Alex abandons this topic to go on to his thesis statement, and he ignores it through the rest of the essay. Mentioning an idea in the introduction and not developing it creates a problem. Violating the contract between writer and reader, Alex has aroused expectations that he has not fulfilled. Ideas need to be either developed or deleted. In this instance, the flaw could be corrected by revising the introduction to focus on the theme of existentialism, weaving that theme through the body of the essay, and returning to it in the concluding paragraph.

If Alex is going to use the existentialism theme, he must revise his essay in two ways. First, the second paragraph must specify that Cholly is the victim of the fate of modern man. He obviously is. He does not endure his plight nobly; he causes injury to others. Doing this, Alex involves Cholly in the existentialism theme. Second, Alex needs to expand his third paragraph to describe Claudia as the transcendent heroine, the heroine who fulfills the existential requirement to accept life, find meaning within herself, and cause no one harm. This is possible in the third paragraph as it stands if Alex would solve a problem near the end of the paragraph.

In your close reading, and in responding to the weakness question, you have probably noticed that there is an imbalance both in the length and depth of argument between paragraphs two and three. Paragraph two deserves all the praise it earlier received for its close argumentation, systematic development, and use of tangible, concrete evidence from the book. Paragraph three is weak by comparison.

Reread Alex's third paragraph:

Throughout the novel, the narrator, Claudia, quietly observes all the hatred and envy in her environment. She understands—or perhaps just feels—the futility and destruction caused by the hate and bitterness resulting from being black and poor. Claudia and her sister:

''Thought only of this overwhelming hatred for [Pecola's] unborn baby. We remembered the knuckled eyes of the school children under the gaze of Meringue Pie and those same children when they looked at Pecola. Or maybe we didn't remember: we just knew'' (p. 149). Claudia, caring for Pecola and her baby, plants marigold seeds in the hope that through some miracle both the seeds and the baby might flourish. Doing this, she breaks through the barrier of hatred, and reaches a maturity beyond most of the adults. Claudia states: ''I thought about the baby everybody wanted dead, and saw it very clearly.... I felt a need for someone to want the black baby to live--just to counteract the universal love of white baby dolls, Shirley Temples and Maureen Peals'' (p. 148). Thus Claudia, seeing the result of hate, chooses instead to turn to love--true and unselfish love. She realizes that only through love is suffering bearable and life worth enduring. Only through love will the marigold seeds thrive and bloom.

Let's analyze the topic sentence of paragraph three as close readers to see if we can find the problem and discover a solution. The key words are "hatred and envy in the environment." The operative terms are "narrator," "observes," and "throughout the novel." As close readers we expect this paragraph to prove with concrete evidence that Claudia observes hatred and envy throughout the novel. The paragraph does not do this, does it? Rather, the paragraph skips to another assertion about Claudia, that she acts as well as observes. Indeed, Claudia goes beyond observation to action; she is the existential heroine Alex claims her to be. But his third paragraph does not show this very well. The problem is that the topic sentence does not provide adequate direction to force him to prove his original assertion. The topic sentence and the argument are incomplete.

This is another, almost fatal, problem in the essay. Paragraph three does not argue its point as effectively as paragraph two does. The last part of the paragraph claims that Claudia has the power of love. This is Alex's claim. Does he prove it? No. He presents no evidence, leaving the claim at the level of an assertion, his own opinion. He leaves an important element of the thesis statement undeveloped.

Alex seems to have run out of gas in his third paragraph. With another revision, he would probably solve the problem. He would need to expand the topic sentence to include the idea that Claudia changes from observer to actor, that she evolves and grows. A suggested revision for the topic sentence would be "Through most of the novel, Claudia quietly observes the hatred and envy of her environment and notes its destructive powers, but ultimately she realizes that through acceptance, love, and mutual support people can weather the worst of circumstances with hope."

The revised paragraph would focus on this evolution and would introduce concrete evidence in support of the claim. The evidence would show Claudia at work loving, rather than feeling the need to love. This evidence is available in the book and could be found through a Pentad analysis of the final chapter. This expansion would also solve the balance problem by making paragraph three about equal to paragraph two both in length and in depth of argument. In addition, such a revision would complete the argument implied in the thesis statement by illustrating that Claudia transcends and becomes an existential heroine.

These revisions would help Alex complete the argument he advertises in his thesis statement and solve many of his problems. Paragraph three would balance paragraph two both in length and depth of argument. He would successfully establish Claudia as an existential heroine, thereby completing the promise of the introduction. Showing that Claudia changes, that she evolves by personal choice, would prove the assertion of the thesis statement. These revisions, which were suggested through analysis of the weaknesses of the essay, would tie all the threads neatly and securely together.

Analysis of the draft essay's strengths and weaknesses generated a specific revision strategy to correct its flaws. In fact, what we have just completed, though indirectly, is the draft self-evaluation that Alex would complete as he worked further through the revising phase.

Alex has understood Morrison's story, and he has discovered the theme of awareness as a means of transcendence which is the key idea of the novel. Knowledgeable readers who have studied *The Bluest Eye* will concur with Alex's argument. They will agree with his point and respond favorably to the final peer critique question.

That leaves only one peer critique question left to consider. Question 4 asks us to write two questions raised by the essay that still must be answered. A large question remaining after we read this draft is this: What role does religion play in *The Bluest Eye*? Alex raised this question by mentioning the failure of religion and the development of existential philosophy. Its source is Alex's wide-ranging introduction and his failure to pick up certain themes in the body of the essay. Some, but not all, of the problem was solved by revising the third paragraph. We will address the rest of the problem when we discuss introductions.

A second major question remaining after we read the draft involves an issue that Alex fails to consider anywhere in his essay. What made Claudia different, able to see the futility, and evolve? This is an important question Alex needs to address because it enters the realm of characterization, an area he must consider to convince his audience he understands how Morrison's novel works. There are several ways to solve the problem. The first would be to produce evidence from the book explaining Claudia's special vision. Is she more intelligent? Does she have a teacher or a model who shows the way and whom she can emulate? Completing an in-depth character analysis of Claudia should answer the question.

Summary

We have analyzed Alex's essay closely for several reasons. By comparing your responses to the peer critique questions with those provided in our discussion, you should have gained some insight about what constitutes an effective peer response. Let these insights inform your peer responses to make them as helpful as they can be.

We also spent quite a bit of time analyzing Alex's paper. In this analysis, you should have learned how to complete a *close reading* of an essay. You should have learned not only how to read other writer's essays closely, but also how to read your own more effectively.

Using close reading strategies, we generated concrete *procedures for evaluating thesis statements and topic sentences* including identifying key words and operative terms. You should use these techniques not only when analyzing the writing of others but when drafting your own essays.

Finally, we spent time developing specific revision strategies based on responses to the peer critique questions. The focus of our work has been completing and putting to effective use the peer response and self-evaluation strategies that are crucial to the revising process.

ASSIGNMENT: WRITE THE THESIS AND DEFENSES

Now that you understand argumentative essay structure, you are ready to draft a preliminary version of your essay. This draft should include only the thesis statement and the paragraphs of defense. We will work on introductions and conclusions shortly. Remember to use close reading techniques to evaluate your thesis statement and your paragraphs of defense. Share these with your peers using the peer critique questions, and use their responses while revising.

INTRODUCTIONS AND CONCLUSIONS

Typically an essay has three parts: an introduction, a body, and a conclusion— a beginning, middle, and an end. We have already worked extensively on the body, which includes the paragraphs defending the thesis statement. In addition, we discovered how writers can use thesis statements to structure and control the argument. However, the thesis statement determines neither the introduction nor the conclusion, the other standard parts of a essay.

Now we will consider the functions of introductions and conclusions and describe and analyze several student samples. Then you will write an introduction and conclusion to the thesis statement and body of the essay you have already written.

Introductions

It may seem odd to discuss introductions after you have written several for previous essays. But those introductions presented little difficulty. The nature of the essay, a description or a narrative, determined your introduction. For example, Marie Turner began her description (pages 115–17) of an injured motorcycle driver with mention of the subject —"he lies in the hospital bed"—followed by a quick focus on a striking detail—the bandaged head. The detail helped Marie accomplish her purpose to catch the attention of the reader.

Essays whose purpose is to argue or persuade generally require more complicated introductions. They use a variety of approaches: the narrative, the historical perspective, the nagging question, or the definition of the problem. You are already familiar with the narrative introduction. The others will receive attention soon.

Regardless of the approach used, introductions have three key functions. The first is *to introduce the subject of the essay*. In doing this, introductions prepare the way for the thesis. The writer's goal is catching the reader's attention and making the subject interesting.

The second function of introductions is to *provide the context of the argument*. Context includes any background information readers need to understand an essay. This can include historical background, definitions, related subjects, and a variety of other considerations. To understand an essay about apartheid in South Africa, for example, readers need to know some history, what the term means, and where to look for more information. Preparing the way for the thesis includes setting the context of the argument the thesis implies.

Third and finally, the introduction *provides the initial connection between the writer and audience*. In the introduction, the writer establishes the voice to be used through the entire essay. Voice—how the writer relates to readers—is a tool we can use to convince readers to believe us.

Kinds of voice cover a wide spectrum, ranging from the expert voice to the amateur, nonspecialist voice. The expert voice uses extensive experience and study, professional training, and an attitude of mastery: "I know this subject better than anyone else because I have studied it so much." The expert makes the reader believe by strength of authority. Of course, a writer using the expert voice needs to demonstrate the value of the analysis and conclusions, or readers will dismiss both the voice and the argument.

Using the expert voice can also cause problems between the writer and readers. Remember the first draft of Marie Turner's description? The expert voice she assumed was inappropriate for her readers. It kept them out of the description instead of inviting them in. She discovered this through peer responses and revised to make the voice more responsive to the needs of her readers.

At the other end is the nonspecialist, the voice of an interested bystander. Using such a voice, a writer depends on common identification and sympathy to convince readers to believe. The writer says to the reader "I'm quite a bit like you are, a regular person, who has spent some time thinking about this subject" or "I have confronted this problem and this is where my thinking has led me." Identification between writer and reader provides a sympathetic connection that can be developed into credibility. This is the stance Albert Johnson develops with success in his personal narrative (pages 88–91).

Of course, there are variations between these two ends of the spectrum. In most instances, writers will mix the expert stance with the "I'm a person just like you" stance in order to create identification and sympathy in the audience. Voice is a key concern when discussing introductions because the introduction establishes the voice to be used through the entire essay.

Evaluating Introductions

Knowing the three common functions of introductions allows us to turn them from descriptions to questions that can be used to evaluate the effectiveness of introductions. Consider the following evaluation questions for introductions:

EVALUATION QUESTIONS: INTRODUCTIONS

1. Does the introduction catch the readers' attention, interest them in the subject and prepare them for the thesis?
2. Does the introduction provide sufficient background so readers will be able to understand the thesis, and establish a context so they can see the value and application of the argument while not introducing distractions?
3. Does the introduction establish a voice that is appropriate to the subject and the writing purpose and that readers can believe? How does it do this? What is the nature of the voice?

Let's use these criteria to evaluate Alex's introduction to "Burden of Hate" and see how successful it is. In terms of catching the audience's attention, the first sentence employs two of the common approaches, historical perspective and the nagging question. Alex establishes a historical perspective by mentioning the failure of traditional religion to provide solace and strength in the modern age. Then he asks the nagging question: why do humans suffer? Both techniques, the *historical perspective* and the *nagging question*, make readers want to read on.

However, as mentioned earlier, the historical perspective is abandoned and the question is not answered. A reader soon begins to suspect the beginning of the introduction paragraph to have been a false start. Indeed it is; it should be recast to enter the real question at hand, the real subject of the essay—modern attitudes toward suffering and the human condition. Note that introductions using the historical perspective often establish false or unmanageable expectations in readers. The historical perspective should be used sparingly, only after rigorous evaluation has proven its contribution to the whole essay.

Alex used two good strategies, but he fell victim to the problem of relevance. The introduction must be interesting, thought provoking, and challenging, but it must also be relevant. Irrelevance in the introduction has damaged the credibility of his thesis statement. Alex must get to his real subject more directly.

In this light, Alex should concentrate on the beginning of the introduction. Here's a revision that might solve the problem:

Revised Introduction

Through the ages, man has asked why he must suffer. War, famine, racism, political corruption—the list could go on, but all result in human suffering. Many modern writers addressing this question have concluded that man does suffer, that there is no escape, that man must accept his fate and endure. Modern writers like Sartre and MacLeish have expressed this existential viewpoint that man must find meaning within himself in the way he bears his burden of suffering and endures his fate.
In fact, they call this resolution heroic. In this vein, Toni Morrison's The Bluest Eye examines how American blacks, oppressed by intense racism and grinding poverty, react to their suffering. Indeed, the novel demonstrates how surrendering to hate and despair leads to unhappiness while choosing love ennobles individuals, allowing them to transcend an oppressive environment. Such transcendence is best exemplified through contrasting the abusive father Cholly, who turns to hate in his suffering, and the daughter/narrator Claudia, who sees hate and instead chooses love.

While the thesis statement remains essentially unchanged, this revised introduction much more efficiently establishes the themes that will be developed through the rest of the paper. As noted in the revision suggestions earlier, Alex would need to weave the question of human suffering and the themes of existentialism and transcendence more thoroughly through the argument and develop a concluding paragraph built on the same ideas.

How about the second criterion, context and background? Most of Alex's energy in the introduction is used to establish the background of The Bluest Eye. Alex concentrates on establishing a particular context. The problem, again mentioned earlier, is that the background becomes more important than The Bluest Eye. The introduction raises all kinds of questions in a reader's mind which require answers. If they are left unanswered, if they remain loose strings, then they weaken the paragraph and the essay. Readers need to know the relation between religion and The Bluest Eye. However, Alex leaves this relation undeveloped. He must eliminate loose strings to get to topics that will receive appropriate attention. He must develop focus as suggested in the revision above.

What voice does Alex use in the introduction? How does he connect with a reader? As readers, we should compliment Alex's ambition. Putting *The Bluest Eye* in the context of all human suffering, considering the function of religion, and mentioning the evolution of existential philosophy suggests that he is widely read and knowledgeable—an expert—in a variety of areas. He places the book in a long tradition. Either he knows what he is talking about, or he is willing to take big risks by making large statements.

We should appreciate the ambition of Alex's introduction. But again we are confronted with the difference in focus between the introduction and the essay itself. Alex never gets around to developing the relationships he establishes. The introduction is too broad and ambitious for the very concentrated focus and format of the three-paragraph argumentative essay. To properly deal with all the elements at work in this introduction, Alex would need to write a much longer essay.

In sum, Alex's introduction is interesting and thought provoking, and it catches the audience's eye. But it sets up expectations that are not and cannot be met in a short essay. We noted earlier, however, that with the deletion of the broad historical context and a quick entry into the real subject, the theme of human suffering could serve as an effective introduction.

A Student Sample with Analysis

Use the criteria and analytic method developed above to evaluate Trina Chamber's "Blue Is Better," another introduction to an argumentative essay on *The Bluest Eye*.

Introduction

Toni Morrison's The Bluest Eye probes the dark depths of the dirty destructor, racism. Effective on both a personal and societal level, her story allows the reader a peek into the lives of those who are the victims of racism. She suggests that the victims themselves must become aware of their plight before anything can be solved. In her tale, she shows the human sacrifice of a small black girl, Pecola, and how it allows the metamorphosis of Claudia.

Since there are potentially as many responses to these evaluation questions as there are readers of the paragraph, do not compare yours directly to the answers provided here. Neither is right or wrong. However, your purpose in this analysis is to assure that you can apply these criteria to your peers' drafts and to your own introductory paragraphs.

Did Trina's introduction catch your attention, make you interested in the subject, and ready to consider her thesis? Most would respond, "yes." The paragraph is economical—direct and to the point. It uses the definition of the problem approach. It reveals the real subject—how victims of racism might escape its ill effects. It does this with interesting language. Racism is described as a "dirty destructor," an awkward but an ear-catching phrase. We are told we will be probing the depths of a real problem. All this makes readers want to read on.

Does she provide sufficient background for readers to understand the thesis and context for her argument without introducing loose strings to distract? Trina earns a mixed evaluation by this criterion. She introduces a problem, a loose string, when she packs the second sentence with the statement that the book is "effective on both a personal and societal level." What does she mean? Surely the book is interesting and rewarding for individual readers; it has a good "story." But what does "societal level" mean? Does she mean the book presents useful social commentary, ideas that we would do well to know because they may help us solve the problem? Ultimately, readers must guess. Readers who are guessing what something means are distracted readers. All Trina needs to do, however, is to use more precise or accessible language ("societal" is misused, and the source of the confusion) and to add a sentence to clarify what she means.

Despite this loose string, however, she does provide sufficient context to help readers understand her thesis statement. Her claim that awareness will be the instrument for escaping and resolving the problem gets her back on track. Finally, her thesis is directly stated—Pecola is the human sacrifice that brings Claudia to awareness and allows her a metamorphosis, a transformation and an escape from her suffering. The thesis statement is sufficiently complex while remaining clear. At the introduction's end, readers are interested and waiting to see her argument.

Does Trina establish a voice and make an effective connection with her reader? She earns positive evaluations here. Her voice is a no-nonsense voice. Her stance is analytic. She understands how the book works and seems capable of explaining it to readers. Her verbs, "probes," "suggests," and "shows," are forceful and suggestive. She uses language effectively, indicating that she is a competent thinker and writer, someone to be trusted and believed. In the body of her essay, Trina indeed demonstrates her competence by explicating her thesis effectively, showing her understanding of the novel.

Be mindful of these criteria whenever you write or read an introduction. Though developed for the highly structured argumentative essay form, they will serve you well when evaluating any introduction.

ASSIGNMENT: WRITE AN INTRODUCTION

It is now time to return to the revised body of the argumentative essay you completed a while ago. Compose an introduction for your essay. Remember the functions and types of introductions. Complete an evaluation of your introduction and then test it on your peers to see how well it fits with the rest of your essay. Revise in light of their evaluations.

CONCLUSIONS

Like introductions, conclusions require special consideration. As the name suggests, the purpose of the conclusion is to end the essay, to bring it to some sort of satisfying close. The introduction has established the context and the thesis, and the body has developed and proved the argument. Now the conclusion must tie all the parts together into a neat package. But this "neat package" must be more than an empty summary of all that came before it. Rather, the conclusion allows writers the opportunity to say: "This is the significance or application of the argument. This is what it really means."

Structuring Essays with Conclusions

Review Figure 6-1 of the basic argumentative essay form (page 146) to gain a sense of the dynamics of the whole essay. Look closely at the diagram and you will see why a conclusion should not be a simple summary restatement of the argument. Given the brevity of the essay—thesis statement, defense, and conclusion in four paragraphs—a summary is either an admission that the argument was not well enough presented to be understood the first time through or an insult to the reader. Neither alternative results in a satisfactory conclusion to an essay.

Often a summary conclusion originates in the natural but not always appropriate human impulse to bring episodes to a close. But not every essay or piece of writing needs a formal conclusion. If your task is to make a point quickly and thoroughly, to provide your reader with information for immediate use, then you do not need a separate conclusion. The final sentence of the body of your essay will suffice.

Summaries are not categorically bad. In longer essays they often serve as transitions signaling the end of one segment of an argument and preparing the reader for the next. When appropriate, they are important tools. They are not, however, sufficient for concluding an argumentative essay.

They are not sufficient, but they are part of a conclusion. A summary can be used like a transition in the body of an argument. A concluding paragraph might begin with a *recapitulation*. Review the diagram. The recapitulation need not be a direct restatement of the thesis statement; it can be a paraphrase. However, it must restate what you have proved and provide direction for the rest of the paragraph. As the first sentence of a paragraph, it has the same responsibility any topic sentence has.

Types of Conclusions

What are the functions and types of conclusions? Basically, the conclusion must complete the argument, and it can do this in a number of ways. In each case, the conclusion must *recontextualize* the thesis statement by reestablishing the reason the essay was written or restating the problem the essay tried to solve. This done, the conclusion can then take the argument in the body and develop a *personal application* or discuss its *personal significance*. For example, the analysis of the problem of racism in *The Bluest Eye* lends itself effectively to a personal application conclusion. The theme of awareness as an instrument of transcendence, crucial in Claudia's growth as a character, can be applied to some personal situation in which the writer was a victim of oppression.

There may, in fact, be noteworthy comparisons between the plight of blacks in a racist society and the position of students in school. These comparisons could make for an interesting conclusion to an essay. Some view students as inhabiting a basically oppressive environment. Students are expected to accept and obey rules although they are rarely permitted to participate in formulating these rules. The awareness that develops in Claudia and enables her to deal with her situation might also allow students to be better able to deal with their plight. For example, "Witnessing Claudia's ability to deal with oppression through awareness may help students understand and cope with their powerlessness" could serve as the topic sentence for an effective personal application conclusion.

Personal significance conclusions are slightly different. Rather than talking about how to put what has been learned in the argument to work solving a personal problem, a writer would consider what the argument means, how it has caused growth or change. For example, *The Bluest Eye* may tell the story of Claudia's coming to awareness, but it also educates readers, leading them toward awareness, which can help them avoid participating in such oppression. For example, a topic sentence for a personal significance conclusion could be, "Witnessing the destructive power of hate and racism in *The Bluest Eye* makes me determined not to perpetuate such oppression by supporting racist institutions." Such a conclusion would focus on how the writer understands the effects of racism and will no longer participate. Such a discussion would be an apt conclusion for an argumentative essay on *The Bluest Eye*.

Another kind of conclusion works by putting the specific argument developed in the thesis into a *larger context*, applying it to a significant, on-going problem. In this case the writer will be showing how *The Bluest Eye* is a specific example of a much larger system for solving similar problems.

For example, throughout history humans have used awareness as a weapon against tyranny. And through awareness, humans have discovered that sympathy and understanding can help find solutions to seemingly unsolvable problems. Awareness leads to mobilization which in turn can result in liberation. This is the pattern in *The Bluest Eye* as in many other books and throughout history. Awareness and acceptance are the instruments Hester Prynne uses in *The Scarlet Letter* to turn her guilt into her means of salvation. Not only a tool of personal liberation, awareness and mobilization were the primary weapons of the civil rights movement in the 1960s. They are means humans have long used to correct injustice. *The Bluest Eye* is another example of this pattern at work. A sample topic sentence for such a larger-context conclusion would be: "Morrison's *The Bluest Eye* illustrates the power of personal awareness to liberate humans from unjust bondage, standing as another example among many of the tradition of human liberation."

Yet another kind of conclusion presents an *evaluation* of the topic at hand. After arguing a thesis and showing mastery of *The Bluest Eye*, a writer might use the conclusion paragraph to evaluate the credibility of the book. There is a problem in *The Bluest Eye* that deserves attention. Namely, the narrator, Claudia, does not seem to be sufficiently contrasted to everyone else to merit the transformation she experiences.

Some have called this a weakness in the book. Some view Claudia as an unbelievable heroine who neither earns nor deserves her transcendence. This weakens the book and compromises its point about awareness and liberation. Thus, a writer might ask, "Why should I believe this book? Why should I take it seriously?" Such criticism put in relation to the argument of the essay could provide the basis of a solid concluding paragraph. A sample topic sentence would be: "Indeed, Morrison's *The Bluest Eye* illustrates the destructive power of hate and the constructive power of love, but is Claudia sufficiently developed as a character to serve as a credible example?" Such a conclusion, of course, would have to be related to the rest of the paper; it could not introduce completely new material, nor could it open a discussion that would take more than a paragraph to develop adequately. Despite these limitations, evaluation is a frequently used conclusion strategy.

Evaluating Conclusions

Although there are other examples of concluding paragraph strategies, the four mentioned here should provide you with plenty of ideas for developing effective conclusions to your own essays. To put this information to work, let's take a look at Alex Tanner's conclusion to "Burden of Hate." Read the conclusion, and answer the questions for analysis which follow.

Conclusion

In The Bluest Eye, Morrison shows one way--through love--that man can find meaning in his life. Indeed, that theme is very popular in existential literature. In this new, godless age, however, meaning in life can take many forms. Since man's suffering is--to a large extent-- unique, a man must find meaning and purpose within himself alone. The way he carries his burden is different from the way any other man will bear his; whereas Camus's Sisyphus overcomes his oppressive fate through scorn, Morrison's Claudia overcomes hers through love.

EVALUATION QUESTIONS: CONCLUSIONS

1. Of the four kinds of conclusions, which is used?
2. Does the topic sentence of the conclusion provide an adequate recapitulation of the argument? Does it provide sufficient direction for the reader to anticipate the rest of the paragraph?
3. Is the body of the paragraph sufficiently developed? Does it require special information not available to readers to make sense? Does it recontextualize the thesis?
4. Does the conclusion demonstrate the writer's competence? How?
5. Does the conclusion provide closure?

Alex's is a modest but effective conclusion to his essay. He places *The Bluest Eye* into the *larger context* of existential literature. Doing this he returns to the existentialism theme he introduced in the introductory paragraph. He is closing the circle, completing the argument. Some may quibble with Alex's topic sentence, claiming it is incomplete because it does not include a recapitulation as well as the new topic. A revision might combine the two sentences, like this: "By illustrating the power of love to help man find meaning in his life, Morrison places *The Bluest Eye* in the tradition of existential literature."

Given the length of the conclusion, some may wonder about its level of development. It does recontextualize the argument. However, Alex needs to be sure that his audience will be familiar with his reference to Camus's Sisyphus. If he is not, then he should add some basic background information. He could do this fairly easily in a revision. It is not a major problem. However, he needs to avoid introducing significant new information, for such is not the purpose of a conclusion.

Despite this potential problem with background information, Alex shows sufficient control over his material to demonstrate his competence, especially in light of his effective use of evidence in the body of the paper. Revision would take care of any weaknesses. Yes, the conclusion provides closure by combining restatement and recontextualization. Alex demonstrates that he understands the book, and he has helped readers understand it more effectively through his essay and its conclusion.

ASSIGNMENT: WRITE A CONCLUSION

Write a one-paragraph conclusion for the argumentative essay that you have already drafted. Follow the preceding suggestions in terms of types and purposes. Submit the conclusion for peer response using the same questions used to evaluate Alex's conclusion. Keep all this in mind—determining whether a conclusion is needed, constructing and completing the paragraph, and meeting the goals of closure, recontextualization, and demonstration of competence—when you revise.

Now, put all the various parts together, edit and proofread carefully, and prepare a final copy to submit for evaluation.

ASSIGNMENT: ONCE MORE FOR MASTERY

You have received plenty of new information, new procedures, and writing practice in this chapter. In order to make assimilation more manageable, you have written the argumentative essay in three stages. First, you composed the thesis statement and defenses, evaluated them, got peer responses, and revised. Second, you added an introduction, evaluated it, and again revised based on peer responses. Finally, you wrote a conclusion, evaluated it, and revised after getting responses from peers. In the end, you produced a complete argumentative essay.

The argumentative essay uses a simple and flexible structure. Built around the thesis statement that suggests the meaning of the paper and the structure and method of defense, it is a form for which you will find many uses. It is not unlike a jeep. It may not be very pretty to look at, but it holds up well in hard terrain and gets you where you want to go.

Because of the general usefulness of the form and because putting the essay together in stages as you did may not have given you sufficient practice, you should write another argumentative essay. Keep it simple, using the form we have developed and following the procedures we have learned. Decide on a common topic or a small and manageable list of topics familiar to all in your class or writing group so that they can participate in the argument. Then, formulate your thesis and develop your paragraphs of defense. Evaluate. Revise. Draft your introduction and evaluate it. Draft your conclusion and evaluate it.

During the discovery process, use invention techniques and research and consultation procedures in order to make sure you know enough to write intelligently, that you know how you feel about the topic to conceive an effective thesis statement and argument. Use close reading techniques to anticipate difficulties and solve them while drafting.

When revising, use the various evaluation criteria developed in this chapter to examine your thesis statement, your paragraphs of defense, your introduction, and your conclusion. Have your peers consider each of these parts when you get peer responses. Use the draft self-evaluation to bring yourself back into your essay after analyzing the peer responses. Then, revise. Finally, edit and proofread aggressively to create the best final essay that you can.

Master this essay form now. It will be one of the most helpful for you through the rest of your writing career.

CHAPTER 7

Writing a Persuasive Essay

INTRODUCTION: FROM INFORMING TO PERSUADING

Thus far, writing essays has given you practice in the various phases of the composing process, especially with discovery and revising, and with basic structures like the argumentative essay form, which you will be able to adapt for use in many writing situations. You have also practiced informative writing, one of the most common types of WRITING FOR THE OUTSIDE. The primary purpose of informative writing is getting useful information to particular audiences.

Within the broad spectrum of informative writing, however, there are some subtle differences of purpose. In narratives and descriptions, the audience observes and the writer is responsible for making information clear, understandable, and usable. In personal significance and argumentative essays, however, interpretation and argument assume great importance. The writer must not only communicate certain information but also a particular attitude toward that information. The success of these more complex kinds of informative writing, in fact, depends upon the writer's establishing a relationship with the reader that fosters trust, acceptance, and credibility. Information, no matter how significant, will not be put to work if its source is unreliable or mistrusted.

The relationship between writer and readers becomes central when we move from informative writing to persuasive writing. We saw that the success of argumentative essays depends upon the writer's ability to make readers understand, evaluate, and accept an argument. In persuasion, the relation between writer and readers becomes even more intense. In persuasion, the writer must move readers to action. In fact, persuasion is not successful unless it makes readers act. The result may be to lead readers to confirm or change their attitudes toward an issue, to purchase a product, to pass legislation, or to elect a candidate. Regardless, there must be action.

In this chapter, you will write a persuasive essay. You will select a controversial issue, develop a position, and write an argument that convinces readers of the validity of your position and the soundness of your plan of action. Your job will not be complete until you have motivated your audience to act.

ABOUT PERSUASION: LOGICAL, ETHICAL, AND PATHETIC APPEALS

Persuasion is at work around us almost constantly. Advertising, perhaps the most common example of persuasion, tries to sell us something at almost every turn. In its work, commercial advertising uses a variety of tactics. One common tactic is the logical appeal, an appeal to reason. "Logical" comes from the Greek *logos* meaning "the word." It works by engaging the audience in a more or less explicit debate concerning the credibility or correctness of some claim. Generally advertisers use statistics and expert testimony to argue the claim. Classic examples include statements like "Four out of five doctors surveyed recommend aspirin X."

Two elements combine to make this appeal successful. The first is research. In this case, the research uses statistical analysis. Not just one or a small number of those surveyed, but four out of five make the recommendation. That is a high average, an impressive research finding. But the statistic would be of questionable value if not for the second element, expert testimony. Doctors who are professionals and experts at recommending drugs were surveyed. When a majority of experts makes a recommendation, their recommendation carries weight. The authority, the strength of the appeal to reason, resides in its use of research and expert testimony.

Another important appeal used in advertising is the "ethical" appeal. *Ethos*, derived from the Greek concept of character or personality, is the set of assumptions that inform the beliefs and customs of a person or culture. They are the unconscious or unexpressed reasons why people act as they do. Ultimately, these assumptions are codified and embodied in familiar ideas like the "American work ethic." *Ethos* is related to the idea of ethics and ethical behavior—how righteous people are expected to act. In persuasion, the ethical appeal causes us to buy or believe something because someone like us has bought or believed it.

Good examples of the ethical appeal at work include advertisements for laundry detergents. In terms of cost and quality, there is very little difference between most detergents. In fact, these similarities preclude the use of the logical appeal because there is no reasonable argument about which product is better than the other. Thus, advertisers must depend on something else to sell the product. They choose an audience, analyze its characteristics, and tailor their advertisements directly to the audience. The commercial reflects the advertiser's sense of the audience's self-concept.

Most laundry detergent advertisements focus on a central character. Often there is an attractive but not overly glamorous woman with a child or children doing something completely normal such as sitting on the front porch. Most often the children are very cute, the kind of children anyone wanting children would want. The central character, Mom, is someone advertisers believe the audience will want to emulate. Everything is arranged to project happiness, stability, and competence, so buyers, desiring a similar situation, will get on the bandwagon, and buy the product. Think of all the advertisements that sell products not by reason or argument, but by identification with an exemplary person. All are instances of the ethical appeal.

The final persuasive appeal is the "pathetic" appeal. It is based in the Greek *pathos*, the quality that evokes pity or compassion in us. The pathetic appeal, sometimes called the emotional appeal, convinces us of the value of a product by suggesting that harm will come to us or others if we do not buy the product. It does not argue from authority or project an attractive central character, it raises fear.

Frequently this appeal takes the form of a scare tactic. In a commercial for a local power company, a woman's car breaks down at night on a dark road. Just a short way up the road, however, bright street lights turn the night into day. A little girl is out walking her dog in the safety of the street lights. A voice comes over the scene as the woman begins to jog toward the safety of the street lights announcing that "75 per cent of all personal attacks happen in the dark." The commercial continues, supplying more information about crime and the dark.

That commercial is not selling light; it is selling fear. The appeal is to the emotions, the pathetic appeal. We pity the victims of the dark; we fear becoming victims. Convinced of the potential danger, we light the night with electricity, adding profits to the coffers of the power company. Other kinds of products like smoke detectors, burglar alarms, even fire insurance employ the pathetic appeal in their advertisements to get us to buy them.

The Appeals at Work in Essays

No doubt you have seen these appeals at work in advertising. How about in writing? Our writing so far has not considered persuasion *per se*; nevertheless, it is at work in the sample student essays. To some degree, persuasion is an element in all public writing. Writers persuade us to keep reading by convincing us that what they are saying is worthwhile. Variations of the persuasive appeals do the convincing.

Look back at some of the essays we analyzed and see if the appeals are not at work. Remember Marie Turner's objective description of the injured, comatose motorcyclist (pages 115–17)? What kept us interested in reading was the nature of the information involved. It was available only to an expert. Her descriptions of certain apparatus such as the respirator, her organization using the hierarchy of life-threatening injuries, and her reference to sounds inside the body that are known only to doctors and nurses characterize her expert stance. The expert stance involves a logical appeal, the appeal to reason. The same appeal is at work in Alex Turner's essay on *The Bluest Eye* (pages 150–52). But Alex's authority does not come from his expert stance as much as from his effective use of research. He discovers evidence and constructs a logical argument by closely researching the book.

The ethical appeal is what makes Albert Johnson's personal narrative of the second-grade autobiography (pages 88–91) an effective piece of writing. We are like Albert; we have had similar experiences. We believe him because he is like us. His character, reflected in the voice he uses in the essay, is recognizable and convincing. The same is at work in Lynn Hardin's personal significance essay (pages 135–37).

Something close to the pathetic appeal is at work in Karen Evan's impressionistic description of the funeral (pages 122–24). What brings us into the story is both our sadness at the death of her friend and our horror at the suicide. Karen uses the fact that there is something wrong with the world to shock us into thinking about often-ignored subjects like death, suicide, and salvation. We become involved because we know we will sometime confront the same problem.

LOG EXERCISE: Analyzing Appeals

To make sure you understand how the appeals work, complete the following analysis in your Learning Log. First, spend some time watching TV. Rather than as a passive observer or consumer, however, watch as a rhetorical critic. Analyze at least four commercials, summarizing their content and determining what persuasive appeals or combinations of appeals are being used to sell the products. You may want to videotape the commercials so you will have them available for review and research.

Next, examine the editorial page of your local newspaper or the letters to the editor section of a national magazine. Clip four editorials or letters, place them in your Log, and analyze the appeals used in them. Which are effective? Which are not? Why?

Finally, analyze the appeals used in two of the essays you have completed for this course. Make specific reference to particular uses of the persuasive appeals. Be prepared to share the results of your analysis with your class.

Evaluating Subjects for Persuasion: Four Questions

Knowing what persuasion is and how it works, we must now decide on a subject, establish our position, master the subject, analyze our audience, anticipate and neutralize opposition, and, finally, produce the essay.

The need to write persuasively confronts us frequently. In school, teachers make assignments, and we must write to persuade them that we are knowledgeable and competent and should be rewarded with a good grade. At work, supervisors put us to work on a project, and we must convince them and potential clients not only that we can complete the project, but also that ours is the best way to do it. In our political lives, we are struck by some incident of injustice or incompetence, and we feel compelled to write the editor of the local newspaper to express our opinion and suggest an alternative plan of action. Each of these instances involves persuasion.

For this essay, however, we will use a particular procedure, so we can practice evaluating a subject's potential for persuasion. The subject must be controversial, and you must feel strongly about it. The class must limit itself to one or two subjects. Your writing group will form around a specific subject. Do not form a group around a specific position on an issue because that would limit your ability to discover all the possible arguments for and against your position. Working with people who are arguing opposing sides allows you and them to anticipate counter arguments and work to neutralize them.

Here is the procedure for selecting one or two subjects all can use for the essay. First, as a class, brainstorm a list of potential subjects for a persuasive essay. The brainstorm should produce many alternatives because controversy surrounds us always. A typical list might include abortion, capital punishment, smokers' rights, nuclear weapons policy, local school board policies, surrogate parenting, "quiet hour" regulations in college dormitories, school prayer, lowering the drinking age, and more. After brainstorming a substantial list, start evaluating; try to determine which ones would be most interesting and productive.

The class has the right to challenge and reject subjects on the brainstorm list. Often arguments erupt. They are interesting because they help identify inadequate subjects for persuasion. For example, classes often eliminate abortion for two reasons. First, it is too emotionally charged and will probably result in a shouting match rather than in a productive dialog. Second, attitudes toward the morality of abortion depend on scientific, socioeconomic, and philosophical arguments about which the class probably does not have sufficient information nor room in a short essay to address adequately. Abortion, in this particular instance, is an overly complex topic.

Other classes eliminate smokers' rights because arguments for smokers' rights are untenable. So much evidence points to the harmful effects of smoking that writers are uncomfortable arguing for such a harmful habit. Arguing smokers' rights is the equivalent of championing disease and bad health. Some will challenge school board policies because many class members are not from the locality and feel the subject is irrelevant. Preparing themselves to write knowledgeably about local issues would require extensive research on a subject in which they have little interest.

Some will challenge and eliminate quiet hours in the dormitories as a subject because they believe they can have no real impact. In such an embattled situation, reasonableness will never win; good time and energy will be wasted writing essays that preach to the already converted. Frustration and futility are not the aims of persuasion. Sometimes instructors will eliminate certain subjects based on their long experience reading persuasive essays. Lowering the drinking age is such a case; it invites dumb arguments. Instructors will eliminate the subject and will save students from the trap.

But agreeing on a common subject is worth the effort. It is possible to avoid traps like those mentioned above and select powerful and manageable subjects. Let the following questions help you evaluate your interest in and readiness to write about a subject for persuasion:

1. Am I sufficiently interested in the topic? Am I moved, and do I have a position I believe in which is workable enough for me to advertise as a plan of action?

    2. Is my position arguable?
       This question entails three subordinate questions:
       A. Are there at least two reasonable sides to the argument?
       B. Is there objective evidence available to support my position?
       C. Is my solution or plan of action workable?
    3. Do I know enough about my subject to write persuasively?
    4. Who are my readers? How do they feel about this subject? And how can I
       influence them?

    Mindful of the range of questions we must ask ourselves about subjects for persuasion, we can now consider each in some detail.

    The first group of questions deals with your relation to the subject. Successful persuasion depends on your ability to communicate conviction and commitment to your audience. Nothing can lead to ineffective persuasion more quickly than writing about an issue that you neither care about nor consider important. Affirmative responses to these questions assure that you have the prerequisite motivation to do the work needed to produce effective persuasion.

    The second question considers the nature of the subject and the stand you will take. Not all positions are arguable. Smokers' rights provides a good example. One of the obvious arguments against smokers' rights is saving the lives of smokers and their co-workers or families. Writing against saving lives doesn't make much sense. It's an untenable position. While the Constitution may preserve your right to do as you please, does individual liberty permit you to make choices about someone else's life, about the lives of your co-workers or family members who are poisoned by the smoke you introduce into their environment? To argue for smokers' rights, you would have to anticipate and neutralize the argument about saving lives.

    This question of arguability is a key one. It involves three related issues. First, the subject must have two arguable sides. For example, establishing a position that claims the United States should work to avoid war is hardly a position with two arguable sides. What sane and reasonable person would argue that as a country the United States should work to start a war? The position fails as a result of the subject that does not have two sides. Thus, it is not arguable. The same problem exists with abortion as a subject. At base, the issue involves personal belief with scientific, socioeconomic, and philosophical evidence available to support a variety of positions. As a writer trying to salvage the subject, you would need to shift the focus to something arguable like the issue of legislating regulations about such a personal issue. Can the government establish rules dictating behavior in such circumstances? That would be a multifaceted and arguable subject.

    Second, your argument will require the careful use of evidence. It will succeed if you can use illustration and analysis to demonstrate the reasonableness of your claims. Do not choose a subject for a persuasive essay that will require you to depend on an emotional appeal. There must be factual evidence you already know or you can uncover through research. The subject must not in itself limit your persuasive strategies by being without evidence, without logical ground.

    Third, your solution must be workable. For example, an argument against abortion might have as its solution three parts: (1) the community must provide effective sex education and assure adequate availability of birth control measures to prevent unwanted or unplanned pregnancies; (2) the community must guarantee adequate medical and economic support for all women who, despite education and birth control, conceive unplanned babies; (3) the community must support these unplanned children after they are born. This three-part solution seems workable, even obvious. So obvious, in fact, that it is self-evident. Why has it not been tried before? It probably has been, and it has not worked. Thus, this and most other self-evident solutions are essentially unworkable and not appropriate for persuasion. Unless you can suggest a new and workable solution, you should avoid subjects that offer self-evident solutions.

Here's an important point about persuasion. To be effective, you must not only establish a position, you must also suggest a solution. This two-part requirement differentiates it from the typical argumentative essay that includes a position and elaboration, but no solution. In persuasion, the solution you offer will most often be explicit. You will be arguing some concrete plan of action. Education to encourage effective birth control to avoid the need for abortion is an explicit solution. However, at other times you will be arguing against some recommendation or plan, a constitutional amendment for the balanced budget, for example. When you argue against a proposition, your recommendation is to make no change, to *maintain the status quo*. You are recommending that matters continue as they have. This is an implicit rather than explicit plan of action.

If a subject has passed these first evaluations—interest and motivation, and arguability—then it is time to consider the third question. Do you know enough about the subject? For many writers, this is a particularly helpful question. Often they have great feelings, intense passions, about subjects, but when they sit to write, they find that they do not know where the feelings or the position comes from. They cannot produce evidence and argue logically for their position.

But question 3 is not designed to identify what you ought not write about. It can help you develop a plan to tap your motivation and direct you to find more information. The question helps you determine how much and what kind of research you need to do to prepare to write. For example, suppose you are assigned or choose to write for smokers' rights. First, you must neutralize your opposition's winning argument that smoking harms both smokers and their associates. You know that such an argument is based on medical research. You also know that medical research is a very complex source of evidence.

The nature of the evidence opens a door for you. Can you develop an argumentative edge by challenging the validity of the evidence? Were the experiments conducted in laboratory or normal living conditions, on humans or on lab animals? Can you find some anomaly in the research that you can use to challenge the conclusions? Did lab rats get cancer from passive smoke administered in doses likely only to be encountered in the middle of a forest fire? Are the results found in lab rats necessarily expected in humans also? If you can raise such challenges, you can argue that smokers should maintain their rights until more reliable or conclusive evidence is available. At least you can give it a try.

Finding an argumentative angle raises another question implicit in the third question: Are you *competent* to write about the subject? Do you know how the research was completed and where it is reported? Do you know how to use the library's journal collections and government documents section to find relevant information? Do you have basic competence in science and mathematics or are you willing to train yourself or consult an expert? Do you know how to develop and complete your argument after you have limited and defined the problem? Answering these questions takes you beyond motivation to determining what research you must do and whether you are capable of completing that research effectively.

The first three questions consider writers and their relationships to subjects. They also consider the subjects themselves and how complex and accessible they are to writers. But the final question may be the most crucial to effective persuasion. Understanding the special needs of audiences is the art of persuasion. Mastery can come only after long work and practice. What we can do here and now is develop ways to analyze audiences so our efforts are more productive.

AUDIENCES

Most writers can never be sure exactly who their audience is. They know that an audience is a group of people and that no two people are the same. At best they *estimate* who their audience will be. From this estimate they imagine an audience and write with it in mind.

The problem with audience is not a new one for you. It is involved in all writing, not only in persuasion. Your work in the PDJ demonstrated that you are a multifaceted individual; in fact, you are many audiences for yourself. Writing essays reinforced this, teaching you that you have a private and public self. Writing the personal narrative and the personal significance essay forced you to take important, personally meaningful material and shape it for a general audience. In order to do this you had to make yourself that general audience first. You were translating private meaning to public terms.

Writing descriptive essays involved a slightly more complex meaning-making process. In the objective description, you were trying to remove yourself from the scene. Since this is really impossible, you had to choose a particular aspect of your self, a persona, and make that persona the eyes and mouth of the scene. Remember how Marie Turner used the persona of the expert and the details it provided her in the description of the comatose young man? Remember also how she had to temper that expert persona through revision because her draft was not reaching her audience? First, she wrote to herself, to her approximate audience, then she developed a more precise sense of audience based on the actual responses of her peers. You have had similar practice and experience. You have already created audiences for yourself, written to them, and then tested the accuracy of your approximation against the response of your peers. And you put their responses to work for you during revision.

In persuasion, however, your sense of audience is so crucial to the success of an essay that you need to develop systematic guidelines to help you create for yourself an audience that most resembles the one you are trying to convince. The first problem is to determine whether you are addressing a specialized or general audience.

Specialized Audiences

Specialized audiences do not normally present a great problem. A specialized audience is a known group with common experience, information, vocabulary, and expectations. When you write for such an audience, you will have expert information developed from your training, experience, and research that will be structured by the conventions of your discipline and expressed in its vocabulary. In fact, much of your undergraduate training will be an introduction to the conventions and vocabulary of your discipline.

General Audiences

But how do you write to a general audience sharing neither common experience, information, vocabulary, nor expectations? What you need are some guidelines for developing a comprehensive image of the projected general audience.

First, you must assume that your audience will include reasonable people and that you can use the rules of normal behavior to predict their actions and reactions to your argument. You trust that they are not excessively biased concerning your issue. You assume that they can understand your logic and language, and that they can be persuaded if you make the argument complete and accessible to them.

Given these assumptions about a general audience, you should be asking yourself continuously as you write:

Are my position, argument, and solution all reasonable?
Do I believe them and should others believe them?
Are they complete and accessible?

Analyzing Audiences

Having thoroughly questioned yourself in these regards, you can fine-tune the image you have of your audience by considering the following questions. Remember, you are working on approximations and should, when possible, test your assumptions on trial audiences like that available through your writing group before you revise.

1. How old are the members of my audience? Will age affect their attitudes and responses to my topic and argument?
2. Will my audience consist mainly of one sex? Will sex affect their attitudes and responses and reactions to my topic and argument?
3. Will my audience have particular religious, political, or social beliefs that I

must take into consideration to avoid alienating them from me, my subject, and my argument?

4. How much education is my audience likely to have? What socioeconomic class do they represent? How might this affect their attitudes toward my subject and argument?

5. How much direct experience does my audience have with my subject? Do I need to provide considerable general background? Do they have special knowledge or experience that I can put to work for me?

As you choose and develop the subject for your persuasive essay, use these questions to assess your audience and its influence on your argument. Remember, persuasion is effective only inasmuch as it moves readers to believe or act. This should convince you of the importance of analyzing your audience.

Of course, this analysis is valuable in other writing situations, not just in persuasion. Considering these questions, in addition to trying out drafts on real audiences, will make sure you are moving from WRITING FOR THE INSIDE to WRITING FOR THE OUTSIDE in which your purpose is to have a particular effect on a particular audience.

ESSAY #6: WRITING A PERSUASIVE ESSAY

ASSIGNMENT: SELECT A SUBJECT

All the questions and procedures we've discussed can help you evaluate potential subjects for persuasive essays. Consider your motivation and background, the arguability of your position, your knowledge of and research resources for the topic, and your audience. Eliminate troublesome subjects and avoid common traps that lead to ineffective persuasion. A little bit of work and thinking at the beginning can save a lot of work and frustration later.

Work hard with your classmates to decide upon a limited number of subjects that all can use productively. You will probably want to choose timely issues that tap current national or international controversies that have received considerable attention in newspapers and national newsmagazines. Thus, you will not have a difficult time finding information and discovering the sides of the issue.

But timely subjects often merge with broader, timeless ones. Groups working to return prayer to the public schools are raising long-standing constitutional issues involving the relation between church and state. Surrogate parenting involves the right of humans to buy and sell other humans. On one level, this can be viewed as the equivalent of slavery, a problem the United States tried to solve through its Civil War. The timelessness of a subject encourages a depth of research and a long-term payoff for the writer. The problem will not disappear tomorrow; the principle upon which you base your solution will probably apply to a broad range of incidents. Regardless of the issues you and your classmates agree upon, make sure they lend themselves to effective persuasion.

RESEARCHING AND DISCOVERING THE SIDES OF AN ISSUE

Having chosen a subject following the guidelines developed above, now you can begin to work through the discovery phase of the writing process. To write effective persuasion, writers need a comprehensive understanding of their subject. The following procedure should help you gain greater control of your subject by forcing you to research and discover the sides of an issue and the reasons supporting them.

The following group exercise employs several of the strategies for discovery suggested in our discussion of the composing process, especially problem formulation, journal writing, research, and talk with colleagues. The exercise will help you explore your subject and find reasons to support your position.

Step One

First, organize groups of four or five around the subjects the class has chosen. Thus, if nuclear disarmament policy, the balanced budget amendment, and surrogate parenting were selected as common subjects for all the class to work on, then smaller groups should form around each of these. Those interested in nuclear disarmament policy will work as one group, those interested in the balanced budget amendment will form another, and so forth.

Prepare for your next group meeting by completing a personal assessment of your position on the subject. You participated in the selection of the subject and placed yourself in a particular group, so you obviously have an opinion and know some reasons why you feel as you do. Supplement your understanding by working through several of the invention procedures presented in the Appendix. Your job is to state your position clearly and to articulate the reasons supporting your position. You do this in preparation for learning the other sides of the issue.

Step Two

Articulating your own position is not enough. In addition, you must discover reasons supporting the opposite side. If, for example, your group has decided to work on the constitutional amendment permitting school prayer, then each member is required to write and bring to class two lists: one list must include three reasons for the amendment with brief explanations defending school prayer; the other list must include three reasons against the amendment with brief explanations condemning prayer in the public schools. Prepare the lists so that when you present them to the group they cannot determine what side you favor. Complete enough research so that you are well informed on each side of the issue. Your goal is to find and develop reasons on both sides of the issue.

Step Three

At your next group meeting, share the lists. Because all the members of the group are working on the same subject, you will generate a comprehensive set of reasons supporting all the sides of the issue. After hearing all the lists, then the group should begin considering which of the sides has the strongest support.

When writers complete this exercise, they frequently make an interesting observation. Many of them change their position—or feel less confident in their original position—as a result of making the lists and hearing all the reasons on both sides. At the same time, they see that a persuasive argument must be well researched and well written. To write effective persuasion, you must move beyond the intensity and passion of private writing like that done in the PDJ. You must elaborate and articulate personal beliefs clearly, to yourself and others. One of the great benefits of writing and working through the writing process is that you must examine your beliefs and confirm them or change them as a result of what you discover.

Step Four

The final part of the procedure involves sharing information by swapping sources for reasons on both sides of the issue. It is not enough for you to have a comprehensive list of reasons; you also need sources to consult to find more information in order to understand and ultimately be able to refute counter arguments. Your peers, especially those who are arguing the side opposite yours, can help you get started by providing a starting point for your search for more information. They can direct you to library sources or individuals who can help you develop and clarify your argument.

By the end of this exercise, you will know more about your own position and the arguments against your position than you knew before. You have come to know yourself, your subject, your position, and its opposition. All this is solid preparation for writing a persuasive essay.

STRUCTURING PERSUASIVE ARGUMENTS: STRAWMAN, STRAWMAN WITH DEFENSE, AND CONCESSION

Having accumulated all this material, now you must organize it and structure a convincing argument. Writers construct persuasive arguments using three basic formats. The first is the argumentative essay form, which you already understand and have practiced. The writer makes a statement and then proceeds to develop and defend it. The problem with the argumentative essay form when used for persuasion, however, is that it does not consider the opposition. One of the prerequisites of effective persuasion is anticipating and dealing with the opposition.

The other approaches, strawman and concession, allow you (1) to put the opposition to work for your side or (2) to concede important opposing views but to argue another more compelling point to bring readers to your side. For the purpose of simplicity, we will consider these as three-paragraph formats with each paragraph performing a particular function within the whole essay.

Strawman

Strawman arguments entail proving your position by refuting its opposition. They succeed because you discount the other side. A strawman is an argument with a flaw; it stands only precariously and does not have much substance. Like a man made of straw, it has no bones. You set it up, so you can come along and knock it down. When you knock the strawman down, your position wins by default. But the other side must be seriously enough flawed so that you can knock it down and destroy it.

In a strawman essay, as illustrated in Figure 7-1, the introduction functions like any other introduction. It establishes the context, catches the reader's attention, reveals the writer's stance, and advertises the thesis. Rather than introducing parts that dictate the structure of the rest of the essay, however, the strawman's thesis statement asserts your position on the issue. The second paragraph contradicts the thesis and presents an opposing view. The third paragraph refutes this opposing view. Your argument stands as a result of having refuted the opposition.

A brief example may help you better understand the structure. After an introduction, you assert the following thesis statement, which is your position on the

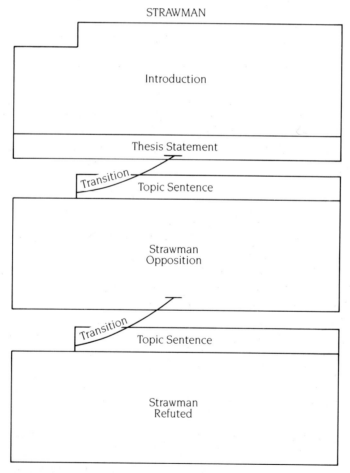

Figure 7-1
The Strawman Format

importance of learning to write well in college: "Writing is perhaps the most important skill any student can learn in college." Note that the thesis statement does not specifically anticipate the arguments that will follow.

The body of the paper includes the strawman opposition and that opposition refuted. The paragraph following the introduction presents the opposing view, that learning to write in college is not crucial to later success because bosses and higher-level employees will make their subordinates do the writing. It is the old saw that secretaries do all the writing.

The third paragraph refutes this opposition, which is easily done by arguing that if supervisors do not know how to write well, they will not be able to evaluate and correct their subordinates' work. Moreover, supervisors are responsible for work done under them. When problems develop, supervisors may be fired or demoted as a result of the poor quality work done by their subordinates. An old sports adage claims, "It's easier to replace a coach than to hire a whole new team." There really is no need to prove the assertion of the thesis statement because the opposition has been so thoroughly refuted. Understanding the argument that not knowing how to write effectively seriously jeopardizes chances for subsequent success should persuade reasonable people that they need to learn to write well in college.

But using the strawman strategy alone raises problems. Because the argument works primarily by refutation and negation, it often lacks force. If readers suspect that you have purposefully weakened the opposition in your second paragraph in order to refute it later, they will doubt your credibility and reject your argument. In addition, if your readers can produce opposing arguments of equal merit to the one you dismiss, then your assertion lacks adequate justification.

Strawman with Defense

One of the ways of dealing with the potential weakness of the simple strawman strategy is to add a strong argument in support of your thesis. As a diagram, the strawman with defense is shown in Figure 7-2, on page 186. Note how this format collapses the two strawman paragraphs of the previous diagram into one and adds a paragraph introducing and developing a strong positive defense of the assertion made in the thesis statement.

Obviously, the third paragraph must include a transition taking the reader back to the assertion of the thesis and introducing the positive argument. In terms of the learning-to-write-well-in-college example, the transition and topic sentence might read, "In addition to enabling supervisors to evaluate the work of subordinates, learning to write enhances communication and problem-solving skills that are prerequisites for advancement in business." The major supporting argument becomes the relation between effective writing and business leadership potential, a relationship which can be easily documented.

The strawman-with-defense format convinces readers that you cannot only anticipate and refute opposition to an argument, but that you can also provide substantive additional support for your position. Generally, it is more convincing than the simple strawman. There is no need for a conclusion to this type of paper. You have already proved your point, which is the assertion of your thesis statement.

STRAWMAN WITH DEFENSE

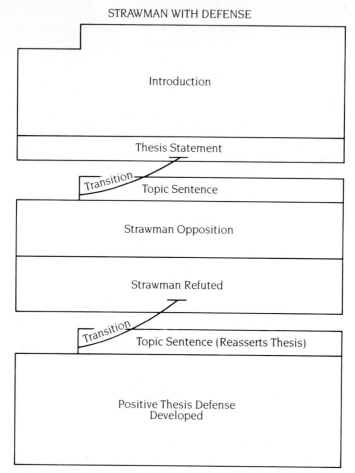

Figure 7-2
The Strawman with Defense Format

Concession

There are some issues in which the opposition to your position is so strong that it cannot be ignored or refuted. In such instances, as an effective persuader, you cannot let an audience believe you are not aware of this opposition. To ignore significant opposition would seriously impair your power to convince. Such situations have led to the development of another format for persuasion, concession.

The concession format resembles the strawman in terms of its introduction and thesis statement as shown in Figure 7-3. The thesis statement asserts your position. The second paragraph, however, is devoted entirely to developing the significant opposition to your argument. The final paragraph begins with the *concession* that admits the validity of the opposing argument but then introduces another consideration, a consideration so important that it overrides the opposition.

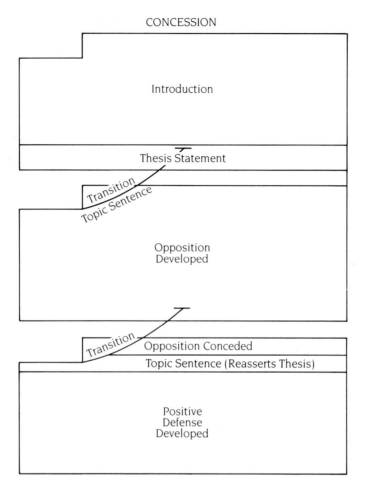

Figure 7-3
The Concession Format

An example might work this way: You have introduced the issue of the school prayer amendment and have taken as your stance the position that the amendment permitting school prayer is unnecessary because individuals already have the right to begin their day in prayer—at home. The primary opposition to this assertion is that the amendment would guarantee the right to public, collective prayer in school, which is currently denied by Supreme Court ruling. Developing this argument, the opposition to your position, would entail proving certain points, especially the value of collective prayer and the right of public assembly. You might reason that prayer is analogous to patriotism, which is permitted and encouraged by the public recitation of the Pledge of Allegiance. In addition, you could claim that schools should develop healthy public values, which is why cheating or dishonesty in school is generally punishable by expulsion, and that school prayer teaches proper values. Finally, you would assert that faith and trust in God are concepts at least as important as the ones "officially" taught in the school curriculum. These are all potential arguments for the amendment that you must anticipate and concede or neutralize. You can develop these opposing points of view with confidence, however, because your final paragraph will argue your position forcefully and persuade your audience to believe and act as you desire.

The arguments for school prayer carry weight, and an effective persuader would have to concede them. The concession would appear as a transition in the topic sentence of the third paragraph. The rest of the topic sentence, however, would assert the greater, more important consideration to be developed in the rest of the paragraph. The paragraph might begin like this: "Indeed, public school prayer teaches important values, but it nevertheless contradicts a fundamental belief for which our revolutionary forebears died—the separation of church and state." The transition concedes the potential benefit. But the balance of the sentence introduces the greater consideration that will win the argument, the constitutional principle of separation of church and state. The rest of the paragraph would deal with this issue and its importance to the American way. Given the brevity and organization of the essay, there is no need for a conclusion.

You will see several examples of this reasoning and the various tactics that can be used in its support in the sample essay to be presented shortly.

Flexible Structures

Here is an important point. For this assignment and others through the course, our model formats are convenient aids for learning argumentative strategies. They provide valuable practice. However, in many instances you will need to adjust and develop them in response to particular writing assignments. An essay may not have three paragraphs but three units of argument. A position may have more than one primary opposition that you must refute or concede. It might have two or three. In such a case, the whole essay would be structured as a sequence of strawmen, refutations, concessions, and other arguments supporting your thesis. The diagrams and simplified structures are introduced for the sake of convenience, to help you see and master the concepts. Do not be limited by them; adapt and expand them to your own needs and purposes.

ASSIGNMENT: DRAFT A PERSUASIVE ESSAY

You have already selected a subject and completed the group exercise designed to make you aware of the various sides of your issue. You have completed any additional research this exercise indicated you needed to complete to strengthen your position. Now you must draft a version of your persuasive essay. Use the best structure for your argument. Once you have a strong first draft of your essay, read the student sample and the section on essay mapping. They will teach you another procedure for evaluating the structure of your essay.

A Student Sample with Analysis

The sample you are about to read demonstrates how adaptable the strawman and concession techniques are when put to work defending a position. The writer, Alex Tanner, whose "Burden of Hate" on *The Bluest Eye* served as a sample of the argumentative essay form, has prepared this persuasive essay using the procedures we have discussed. He has completed the subject evaluation procedure and the in-class exercise designed to generate an extensive list of pros and cons on the issue. He has completed the audience analysis. His essay is an argument against the proposed constitutional amendment to permit prayer in school. Read it closely to analyze the persuasive strategies Alex uses throughout the essay.

Alex Tanner
Essay #6
Persuasive Essay
                Sorry Mr. Reagan, This Is America

  For most of American history, educational institutions placed a strong emphasis on religion. Prayer in school was as natural as prayer in church. With the growth of public school education, however, came the question of whether religion and government-backed education should mix. After a bitter debate, the Supreme Court, in 1962, ruled that in order to preserve the separation of church and state, prayer would not be allowed in public school. The debate has far from ceased, though. Recently, President Reagan proposed an amendment to the Constitution stating, in effect, that prayer in school shall not be prohibited. Reagan feels strongly that, although no student should be forced to participate, voluntary prayer should become embedded in the public school system. Such government interference is intolerable because it not only endangers freedom to practice religion, but also contradicts the American spirit of freely embracing all religions and traditions.
  Supporters of Reagan's amendment and voluntary school prayer try to sell their view by emphasizing again and again that no student will be forced to participate in prayer exercises. They argue that a child who does not wish to comply, or whose beliefs are different and do not allow him to join, can ignore the prayer or, better yet, leave the room. The advocates are certainly kind to grant such a liberty.

What Reagan and his followers fail to grasp, or perhaps choose to ignore, is that ''voluntary prayer,'' especially in younger age groups, is far from being entirely voluntary. Social interaction in a child's school years is extremely important and has serious permanent effects on a person's behavior and personality. It is unfair and harsh for a teacher to ask an eight–year–old child to leave the classroom because the rest of the class is going to have a prayer session. The student is ostracized from his peers and exposed to ridicule simply because he exercises his right to freedom of religion as preserved in the First Amendment of the Constitution. Reagan's amendment basically tramples the rights of the minority in favor of majority wishes. Indeed, the conflict is not entirely between––as Reagan sees it––believers and non–believers, but between believers and other believers. Perhaps Reagan and his supporters encourage prayer in public schools because they assume that ''their'' prayer will be the one used.

The purpose of this paper is by no means to belittle the importance of prayer or the importance of religion in our society. Indeed, teaching children religion and religious traditions at an early age ecourages worthy morals and good citizenship. That view is the main reason behind parental support of prayer in public school. Is, however, public school the appropriate place and situation for such important spiritual teaching?

If the amendment passes, children, who are required by law to attend school, will be at the mercy of school officials who not only would direct prayer activity, but also would determine its content. Certainly the officials would try to make the prayer general and impersonal to offend as few as possible, thus eliminating all individuality and feeling. More important, however, is that such worship can have nowhere near the moral impact as worship in church or the influence of the family at

home.   It is ridiculous and irresponsible to put the
government in charge of religious teaching and personal
communication with God; it is not the purpose of
government, nor should the government purport to assume
such responsibility.

Indeed, people come from all regions of the earth to
America in order to worship their God as they see fit,
without interference from government.   The mixture of all
religions and traditions is the substance and the spirit
of America.   Public school is a place where diverse people
come together to pursue a common goal.   Conversely,
churches, synagogues, and shrines are places where similar
people come together to worship God.   Our present school
system is one of the best opportunities for different
cultures, traditions, and religions to mix and interact
freely.   That free atmosphere, which represents the true
spirit of America as the ''melting pot'' of the world,
must remain clear of the boundaries and walls that
Reagan's proposed amendment would surely raise.

Though not perfect, Alex's is a convincing essay. To summarize, Alex opposes
the amendment for two reasons: government intervention in matters of prayer and
religion endanger the freedom to practice religion, and government intervention in
the school prayer issue contradicts the spirit of America as the melting pot. Because Alex is arguing against the amendment, an argument to keep things as they
are, to maintain the *status quo*, he need not propose a plan of action. His action is
resisting change and stopping the proposed amendment. He will be successful if
he convinces us of the inadvisability of the amendment.

Evaluating Drafts: Essay Mapping

With persuasion, it is not enough for us to say an essay works or it does not.
We need to examine its structure and argument and analyze it. We need a procedure that will allow us to evaluate closely, to determine what is working and what
is not, and to make concrete suggestions to aid revision. Essay *mapping* is an analytic technique designed to foster close reading. It complements peer critiquing
and draft self-evaluation with which you are already familiar, but it is very specifically tailored to work with persuasion.

Use the essay mapping technique when reworking a draft before submitting it
to peer reviewers. It is a self-editing technique that requires you to check what you
planned to say and do in the essay against what you really said and did in the

draft. Many writers claim that essay mapping is the most helpful self-editing procedure they know.

Most simply stated, the essay map requires a writer to reduce each paragraph
in the essay into one or two sentences that explain *what* the paragraph is saying,
how it is saying it, and *why*. The map tries to answer the question: how does this
paragraph contribute to the essay as a whole? The best way to organize an essay
map is to break it into paragraph-by-paragraph *abstracts* that pay attention to the
what, how, and why of the particular paragraphs.

Consider the following essay map of Alex's essay, "Sorry Mr. Reagan, This Is
America":

Essay Map:
Alex Tanner's ''Sorry Mr. Reagan, This Is America''

Paragraph 1:
Introduces the problem of the proposed Reagan school
prayer amendment through a discussion of the history of
public education and the Supreme Court rulings on school
prayer. Thesis states opposition on two grounds: (1) it
violates individual right to free practice of religion and
(2) it contradicts American principle of religious and
cultural tolerance.

Paragraph 2:
Establishes opposition by arguing that the amendment
will not mandate participation in prayer, that students
can choose not to participate.

Paragraph 3:
Questions and refutes opposition by arguing that normal
social pressures, especially peer pressure which compels
common behavior in groups of children, will make it
unlikely that students will not participate. Criticizes
proposed amendment because it tramples minority rights.

Paragraph 4:
Raises another opposition by providing positive
argument in defense of religion and prayer. Concedes
their value. However, questions whether schools should be
trusted with responsibility for instilling religious
values.

Paragraph 5:

   Develops question of government's capability to
interfere in religious matters by attacking a government-
designed prayer as generic and essentially
meaningless. Contrasts this kind of prayer with private
and family prayer and finally <u>refutes opposition</u> by
stating that government cannot supervise an individual's
private relation with God.

Paragraph 6:

   Elaborates theme of America as melting pot which was
introduced in the thesis and describes the role of schools
in the integration of cultures and religions. Warns that
school prayer amendment could alter and impair this
function thereby providing a <u>final refutation</u> of
amendment.

   Study the paragraph abstracts to make sure you see how each addresses the
what, how, and why of each paragraph. Look at paragraph 6. The "what" is that
America is a melting pot, that schools are integrators, and that the nature of school
prayer could impair this function. The "how" is a description of integration through
the open atmosphere of religion-free schools. Why does Alex need the paragraph?
What function does it serve? It refutes an opposition to his position.

   Having completed the essay map of Alex's essay, what suggestions might we
give him to make the essay more effective? One suggestion would direct him not
to change his position, but to revise the essay by rephrasing more simply and
directly in order to develop certain ideas more clearly.

   One area Alex needs to work on is the phrasing of his thesis: "Such government interference is intolerable because it not only endangers freedom to practice
religion, but also contradicts the American spirit of freely embracing all religions
and traditions." After completing the abstract of paragraph 6, readers have a clear
idea of the role of schools in the melting pot phenomenon that is America. However, Alex does not forecast that argument in his thesis statement. If he were to
expand it, perhaps by adding a phrase like "a phenomenon encouraged through
nonreligious public education," to include the idea that the school prayer amendment would substantially change the function of public schools in America, readers
would be better prepared and more quickly agree with the concepts of paragraph
6 and his thesis statement.

   Another suggestion would ask Alex to consider making the thesis statement a
straightforward assertion of his opposition to the amendment by dropping from it
the reasons for his opposition. In complicated persuasion, the thesis statement
should establish the position, not the reasons. The body of the essay will present

and argue the reasons. In Alex's case, the thesis statement is packed, perhaps overloaded, with information. Reducing it to a statement of his position would solve the problem of information overload. The revised thesis statement might read, "Such government interference in schools is unacceptable; the amendment should be rejected." On the whole, however, the essay map indicates the strength of his argument.

ASSIGNMENT: ESSAY MAPPING

Complete an essay map of the draft of the persuasive essay you have already prepared. Then use what you learn about the structure of your argument and the strategies of your paragraphs to revise your draft before submitting it for peer review.

While the value of the essay map is obvious in persuasive essays, it is also a helpful drafting procedure with all essay assignments.

ASSIGNMENT: REVISE YOUR PERSUASIVE ESSAY

We have covered a broad range of topics in the process of writing the persuasive essay. We have considered the nature of persuasion and developed an awareness of the three primary appeals. We have established criteria for evaluating subjects for persuasion, assessed our readiness to write, and learned how to analyze an audience. We have learned how to select a good subject for persuasion.

After selecting a subject, we researched our subject, gathered information, and became aware of both sides of the issue. Next we considered some common persuasive essay formats and by examining the sample essay saw how to adapt them for a particular writing assignment. Finally, we learned essay mapping, a powerful self-evaluation procedure especially useful during drafting.

Having come this far, now it is time to revise the essay and put it into its final shape. Here's what to do:

1. Test your draft against a real audience using the argumentative essay peer critique questions (page 148).
2. Use peer responses and self-evaluation to complete the revision.
3. Edit and proofread to create the best essay possible.

POSTSCRIPT: A FINAL TEST

You have completed quite an elaborate procedure to write this persuasive essay. You have made sure that the subject is appropriate and that you have mastered it sufficiently to persuade effectively. Following all these steps has allowed you to write an effective persuasive essay for submission to your instructor for evaluation. There is another step you can take, an opportunity you should not overlook. Send your essay off to test its effectiveness on an audience beyond your peers and instructor.

For example, if you have written on an issue in contemporary politics, you can send it to your local, state, or federal governmental representatives. Revising the essay to fit into a letter format should not be difficult. Check a handbook for the appropriate letter format, and follow it. You will need to consider your audience when you revise, but that should not affect the body of your argument and your plan of action. Lists of governmental representatives and their addresses are often published in newspapers. The telephone directory and local political organizations are also sources for addresses.

Not only legislators, but also newspapers and magazines are potential targets for your letter. If you have written on a social or political issue, you might send your argument, again revised for the new audience and occasion, to the opinion page of your newspaper or to the local chapter of the interest group concerned with the issue. The opinion page exists to publish readers' viewpoints. You are a reader, and you surely have a viewpoint. The president of the local Nuclear Freeze organization would be a good audience for persuasive letters dealing with the issues of national defense and armament. Reading your local newspaper or checking the local phone book are ways to find who and where to send your essay.

Why do this? The purpose should be obvious. You want to send your essay into the the world to see if it will do the work you have designed it to do. Your goal has been to change minds and inspire action. Test yourself. See if you get a response. Perhaps you can begin a dialog that will have a long-term effect on you and your correspondents. This assignment is not really complete until you have tried your work on a public audience and determined whether you have had an impact.

PART THREE

WRITING THE INSIDE OUT

CHAPTER 8

Writing the Ethical Essay

INTRODUCTION

You have learned quite a bit about the process of writing, about developing ideas and structuring essays, and about informing and persuading audiences. In fact, you have learned enough already to write successfully for school. Many courses would end now, but we will attempt one more ambitious project.

Near the beginning of this book, we tried to answer the question, "What makes writing good?" In the process, we discovered all the elements that make up writing: subject, language, purpose, structure, and audience. But we determined that one element suffuses all the others—the writer. Implicitly or explicitly, the writer is at the center of all writing. Further, we concluded that one of writing's most important functions is its ability to help writers discover themselves and use their discoveries to make connections with readers. One of our definitions of good writing emphasized this above all else: "Good writing expresses the writer's self honestly and evokes a personal response in the reader."

To that end, we have worked with the writer always at the center, WRITING FROM THE INSIDE OUT. We worked in stages. We began by WRITING FOR THE INSIDE exclusively and mastered the major functions it serves: self-development, learning, and problem solving through keeping academic and personal journals. With this firm grounding, we began WRITING FOR THE OUTSIDE, paying close attention to the process of writing for a public audience with a specific purpose in mind. We learned how to structure paragraphs and essays, to organize evidence, and to use language precisely. We discovered that we make promises as we write and that it is our reponsibility to keep those promises by meeting our readers' expectations. Whether we accomplished our original purpose, informing or persuading our readers, determined if we were successful or not.

Now it is time to complete the process and bring the inside and outside together in a special way. You are an aware person and a practiced writer. You will now write a longer essay articulating personal beliefs and explaining or defending your conduct in a specific instance to a specific audience. In the process you will establish a sense of identity with a community and become a member.

We will call this the "ethical" essay. We use ethical here in the same sense we used it when discussing the ethical appeal when writing persuasive essays. Derived from the Greek concept of character or personality, an individual's or culture's ethics embody the set of assumptions informing all belief and custom. Ethics, expressed or unexpressed, are why people act as they do. Based on this concept, a dictionary would define "ethical," as in an ethical decision, as conforming to moral standards or conforming to standards of conduct of a given profession. Your "ethical" essay will be similarly concerned with standards of conduct.

Underlying the concept of ethics is an ancient Indo-European idea, even more ancient than the Greek, based in the root word, *swedh*. In this sense, ethics means the essential quality of one's own character. To be ethical means to be you, to express your "you-ness." Ethics gets to your nature as a person, why you think or believe a certain way, why you act as you do.

The ethical essay requires you to sort through all you have discovered about yourself, put the pieces together into a coherent whole, and explain yourself to an audience. Your audience is a particular community to which you belong or would like to belong. Thus, if you are discussing personal dilemmas, such as abortion or surrogate parenting, your audience would be that community most involved in the controversy, say the Roman Catholic church or the American Medical Association's ethics committee.

The point of the ethical essay is that you must investigate something personally relevant and important to you, discover the basis for your feelings and actions, and explain and justify them to a specific public audience. You must make the personal public; you must write your inside out. This WRITING THE INSIDE OUT integrates all you have learned in this course as no other essay can.

This essay will be longer than the others you have written. It will probably run to a length of five pages or more. In it, you will write about a subject that interests you deeply and has relevance beyond school. You will assess your knowledge of the subject and research it in order to establish personal authority. Once you have developed this authority, you have earned the right to make statements that others should consider significant. Your purpose will be to articulate your beliefs about the subject to an informed community. Doing this you exercise your right and responsibility as a moral individual and citizen.

THE ETHICAL ESSAY: AN INITIATION

In one sense, writing the ethical essay resembles a knight's quest and subsequent initiation into his king's court. The knight has learned the fundamental rules and practices of the court, the code by which he must act. He experiences the trials of the quest and risks his life in order to prove his understanding and acceptance of the code. He slays the dragon or defeats a sworn enemy of the court. Having proven both his personal worth and battle prowess, the king recognizes him in a ritual by administering an oath and receiving him as a fully privileged member of the court.

Coming as the final assignment in this course, the ethical essay serves as both your quest and initiation. You have had your period of practice. You have learned the basic rules and purposes of writing, and it is time for you to test yourself and assume complete responsibility. In this case, however, the court is a community. You are seeking membership in the community of educated and morally responsible citizens.

Writing and Community

Comparing the writing of an ethical essay to an initiation into a particular community may strike you as odd. But it is not. Look around. From the editorial page of local newspapers to the newsletters published by churches, social organizations, or businesses, we are constantly bombarded with appeals to our ethics; we are constantly asked to join communities or reconfirm our membership in them. Our society is a collection of many separate and sometimes conflicting communities. We are members of several communities and probably of several subcommunities within them. We may even be members of two communities at odds with one another. Problems arise when we are not aware of our membership or not aware of the consequences of membership. Sometimes we become overly committed members of a community and lose our sense of self and personal identity.

Writing is constantly used to proclaim community ideologies and membership. Examine any serious publication whose purpose goes beyond providing simple information. From *The Atlantic Monthly* to *Playboy*, from *Soldier of Fortune* to *Cosmopolitan*, one of the central purposes of the many articles these magazines publish is articulating the ethics of the community represented by their readership and the code of conduct those members should practice. Each writer who is published contributes to the expression of the ethics of that community. By nature of publication, the writer becomes part of the community's leadership. The time has come for you to contribute and to lead.

The following exercises introduce you to some of the many forms an ethical essay can take. Analysis will show the variety of stances writers can assume in relation to their audience and community. Pay close attention. Use what you learn now when you write your ethical essay.

Belief and Community

Let's look at *The New Yorker* magazine. Though mostly famous for its humorous cartoons and witty essays, it has its serious side. Read several consecutive weeks of "Notes and Comments," the introductory column of "The Talk of the Town." In it, the editors focus on some significant current event and view it from a particular perspective. They evaluate the behavior of those involved. In doing so, they fit the event into an overall scheme, their ethic, their view of the world. In the process, they help their readers to find a way of thinking about the event. Thus, readers are made to feel a part of a larger community. That the readers largely agree with the point of view consistently announced in the magazine is why they buy it in the first place.

LOG EXERCISE

Read the following "Notes and Comments" from the April 26, 1986, issue of *The New Yorker*. The writer establishes a perspective which views the space shuttle *Challenger* disaster as one of a series of similar disasters such as the Bhopal chemical and Three Mile Island nuclear accidents. All these disasters have their origin in technology. In addition, they illustrate the human tendency to solve technological problems by creating even greater problems, which sometimes result in death and large-scale human suffering. This pattern calls into question our ability to survive our own technological sophistication.

Read the article and respond to the following questions in your Log:

1. Audience: How does the writer relate to the audience? Is this relationship formal or informal? What assumptions is the writer making about the readers' knowledge of current events? Is the writer assuming a certain attitude of the readers concerning the value of technology and the perfectibility of humankind?

2. Structure: How does the writer organize information and structure the argument? Is the main idea stated at the beginning of the article in a thesis statement or is it withheld and asserted near the end? What significance do you attribute to this kind of organization?

3. Language: How does the writer use language to further the argument and maintain a relationship with the audience? Consider the level of the vocabulary and any analogies or metaphors the writer uses and the effect these have on the audience.

NOTES AND COMMENT

[1]In the nuclear age, human survival has, for the first time in history, been made a feat of human competence — has become as secure only as the fail-safe machines that hold our nuclear arsenals in check. [2]It was hard not to give a thought to this new circumstance when we saw the space shuttle Challenger vanish in a ball of smoke — hard, watching this rocket with its seven passengers, not to think of those thousands of other rockets, in their silos, on which the fate of nearly five billion people rides. [3]Even the fact that by cruel coincidence the explosion was beamed directly into classrooms all over the country suggested that there might be lessons we were all supposed to learn from the event. [4]The investigation of the causes of the accident goes on, but it has now taken a twist familiar to the public from investigations of other recent technical disasters, such as the one at Three Mile

Source: *The New Yorker*, April 21, 1986.

Island, or the one at Bhopal. [5]The search begins for the technical flaw—the faulty chip, the missing wire in the computer, the stuck valve—that will explain the accident. [6]And the flaw eventually turns up. [7]But the investigation continues, and it turns out that this very flaw had been pointed out by someone, that there had been memos, telephone calls, arguments. [8]In fact, as we find out how much the engineers foresaw, our faith in strictly technical expertise may rise. [9]But gradually the search moves from such arcane matters as computer glitches and eroded O-rings to such mundane ones as scheduling, loan payments, profit margins, bureaucratic inertia, political pressures. [10]Now it is not the flaws of machines that the investigators are looking into but those of human beings. [11]Yet they are an old story—as old as mankind. [12]The truth about the matter at hand can sometimes be found, and amends made, but not even the most brilliant Presidential commission can find the loose wire in the human brain or the faulty connection in the human heart which led to the error. [13]Nor can the expenditure of any hundreds of millions of dollars renovate these particular components of the procedure for the next launch. [14]All of which should say something to us about the wisdom of staking our survival as human beings on human perfectibility.

Analysis

An ethical essay expresses the moral beliefs and approved code of conduct within a specific community. Consider the following analysis of "Notes and Comments" based on the questions noted earlier; it will provide you with some help in making important choices about audience, organization, and language when you write your essay.

1. Audience

How does the writer relate to the audience? The relationship between the writer and audience in this essay is quite familiar. The writer addresses them as if they were acquaintances. But the writer is not so familiar as to violate the principles of public writing.

The writer has made certain assumptions about the audience based on knowledge of the readership of the magazine. They are familiar with the events noted in the article, interested in them, and capable of connecting them into a pattern from which lessons can be drawn. The writer addresses a community of educated, relatively well-informed and morally concerned readers.

Introducing the survival theme shows another assumption. The writer believes the audience is, if not fearful, at least concerned with the future of the species. The audience is skeptical; they have not been fooled by all the progress technology has caused in the last century and a half. They see that all this progress has caused huge, perhaps unsolvable problems, and some may long for "the good old days" when things were simpler. But those days are gone forever.

At the same time, the writer assumes the audience to be morally concerned. Readers probably view the world and all its people as connected, as part of the human web. They believe that individuals and nations share a responsibility to one another over time and space.

We know all this by the wide range of events the writer mentions, the level at which they are considered, and the way they are connected into a theme. The writer depends on a sense of like-mindedness within the community which will allow agreement upon the "lessons" these disasters offer.

2. Structure

How does the writer organize the article, and what is the significance of this organization? Looking closely at the article, we can see that it has a typical three-part structure including an introduction with a thesis, a body with a strawman and a defense, and a conclusion.

The introduction includes sentences 1 to 3. It begins with a generalization about human survival in the nuclear age, places this in the context of the *Challenger* accident, and ends with a thesis-like claim that there are "lessons" to be learned. The thesis states the purpose; the writer is going to consider the problem and raise our awareness.

The first part of the body of the article, sentences 4 to 7, makes a strawman of the ability of technology to discover solutions to problems. Notice how the length of sentence 6 stands in contrast to the majority of sentences in the essay. Its abruptness calls attention to the strawman, the ever present "flaws" that eventually turn up. The problems had previously been detected and solutions proposed, but for some reason they were ignored. Our "faith in strictly technological expertise may rise."

The second part of the body presents a defense. Sentences 8 to 10, shift the concern from technological problems to human problems, "mundane" ones like bureaucratic inefficiency and human greed. The writer places contemporary events within the larger perspective of human history. Doing so reinforces the sense of like-mindedness, the philosophical and moral familiarity of writer and the community of readers.

The conclusion, from sentence 11 to the end, develops the greater context. A short sentence signals the shift. The disasters are part of "an old story—as old as mankind." Neither brilliance nor money can solve the fundamental problem of human imperfection. The end is ominous; the writer leaves the audience with a problem but does not offer a solution.

This is significant. Some ethical essays are written solely to bring a long-term human problem before an audience. The writer of "Notes and Comments" intends only for readers to connect the incidents and become aware of the problem. They are challenged to solve the problem for themselves. However, because writer and readers share community values and a code of conduct, any solutions devised would be acceptable. In fact, sharing potential solutions would establish a dialog leading to greater understanding, perhaps even a resolution of the problem.

3. Language

What about the writer's use of language? How does it reflect both the purpose of the essay and relationship between the writer and readers? The writer uses language, especially pronouns and metaphor, to establish a relationship and offer readers a way of thinking about the problem.

Language establishes a sense of honest familiarity and directness, reinforcing the bond of community. The writer does not use specialized vocabulary. In fact, it is pleasantly direct. Faulty chips or stuck valves cause the accidents. There is no technical obfuscation like that which characterizes official inquiries where bureaucrats babble along, trying to avoid admitting anything, never assuming responsibility for failure. "Partial malfunction of the fuel oxidation release mechanism," a bureaucrat's obfuscation, becomes a "faulty valve."

At the same time there is a certain degree of technological language, indicating that the writer knows the subject and expects the same of the audience. "Eroded O-rings" is such an example. In addition, the writer depends on certain key words and concepts throughout, such as "fate," "lessons," "faith," "flaws," and "human perfectibility." Through these terms, readers connect with the overall problem examined in the article. Here the writer trusts the intelligence, education, and sensitivity of the audience. He depends on their ability to read closely and understand the point.

This trust in the audience is further illustrated by the use of first-person plural pronouns "we" and "us" throughout. The writer is not working with any problem, but with "our" problem. This brings the reader into the article, reinforcing community and familiarity. This is not so much an article as it is a conversation among friends.

Also remarkable is the writer's use of metaphor. Near the end of the article, the writer discusses human problems in technological terms: no one will find "the loose wire in the human brain or the faulty connection in the human heart which led to the error." Literally, there are no wires in the brain or connections in the heart. But the influence of technology has been so great in our world that we have begun to see things, even human things, in the terms technology offers. This is part of the problem.

The conflict between the subject and the language in which it is described reinforces the message of the article. Human problems cannot get a quick technological fix because there is no wire to be replaced, no connection to be fixed. Our nature is imperfect and imperfectible. Technology cannot save us from ourselves. In the metaphor, the writer uses technology as an implicit argument against itself. The language appeals to the skepticism of the audience and reflects, if not an anti-technological bias, at least a vein of distrust in the audience. Again, community and the values and code of conduct held in that community are helping the writer make the point.

Analyzing "Notes and Comments" in terms of the writer's relationship to audience, organization, and language should sensitize you to the kinds of problems you will confront when writing your essay. Your purpose is first to discover for yourself how you feel and why you feel that way, and then to express your view clearly enough to give your readers a perspective from which to consider the problem or to understand your point of view. Success is measured by your ability to connect with a community of readers.

The Authoritative "I"

Another example, Paul Fussell's "My War," illustrates an alternative approach to the ethical essay. More than simply raising awareness of a problem, Fussell solves it by explaining and analyzing his actions. Rather than relating to the audience as a member of a community with shared experiences, he establishes himself as largely isolated and alienated—opposed to the community. Rather than using a simple three-part structure, he uses a variety of structures and strategies designed to emphasize the significance of the experience and its consequences. Rather than familiar language with an occasional, clever metaphor, he combines erudite literary reference with concrete, sometimes shocking imagery.

LOG EXERCISE

Read "My War," by Paul Fussell, a teacher, literary critic, contemporary social commentator, and veteran of the European theatre of World War II. "My War" appears as the final essay in Fussell's collection *The Boy Scout Handbook and Other Observations* (New York: Oxford University Press, 1982). In the first paragraph, "foregoing pages" refers to the final section of the book that includes nine essays addressing contradictions between the real images and experiences of World War II and histories and stories that celebrate and glorify the war. The photographs of the dead soldier on the gun mount and the hanged partisans appear in "The War in Black and White." After reading, respond to the following questions in your Log.

1. Meaning: Summarize the essay in no more than two paragraphs. What does Fussell say? What is his purpose?

2. Audience: Does Fussell use a formal or informal stance? Does he address readers as insiders or outsiders; that is, does he expect his audience to have had similar experiences? Does he depend on this shared experience to make his point? Provide specific references.

3. Structure: How does Fussell structure his essay? Does one idea follow another logically from beginning to end, as it does in argumentative or persuasive essays, or does he alternate argument with various narrative structures such as dramatic incidents and anecdotes? How does structure reinforce his point?

4. Language: How does Fussell's language contribute to his essay? Is it a shared, common language that all find easy to understand? Or does Fussell use language to create a distinctive, personal voice? Does this contribute to the credibility of his essay? How? Does he use any striking metaphors? How do these contribute to his overall purpose?

MY WAR

Paul Fussell

1   I recognize that in the foregoing pages I have given the Second World War a bad press, rejecting all attempts to depict it as a sensible proceeding or to mitigate its cruelty and swinishness. I have rubbed the reader's nose in some very noisome materials—corpses, maddened dogs, deserters and looters, pain, Auschwitz, weeping, scandal, cowardice, mistakes and defeats, sadism, hangings, horrible

Source: Paul Fussell, *The Boy Scout Handbook and Other Observations.* New York: Oxford Univ. Press, 1982.

wounds, fear and panic. Whenever I deliver this unhappy view of the war, especially when I try to pass it through a protective screen of irony, I hear from out-
raged readers. Speaking of my observations on the photograph of the ruined sailor
on his ruined gunmount, for example, a woman from Brooklyn finds me "callous,"
and focusing on my remarks about the photograph of the German soldiers engaged
in hanging the partisan boy and girl, she says,

> As the daughter of survivors of the Holocaust, it is beyond my com-
> prehension how Mr. Fussell can ramble on about the "respectabil-
> ity" and "normality" of the Germans . . . while a young girl hangs
> from a rope and a young boy, his hands bound behind his back,
> waits to be hanged. While this photograph should elicit pathos and
> anger at seeing young lives being so cruelly blotted out, Mr. Fussell
> is concerned about the "almost frivolous touch" of the "two colored
> decorative rope, suggestive of a bathrobe cord or gift tie."

In short, my approach has been "insensitive": I have demonstrated an "overwhelming deficiency in human compassion." Another reader, who I suspect has
had as little empirical contact with the actualities of war face-to-face as the cor-
respondent from Brooklyn, found the same essay "black and monstrous" and concluded that the magazine publishing it "disgraced itself." It seems like the old
story of punishing the messenger for bringing bad news. But one has always known
that irony has a hard time of it in this country, especially irony reflecting some
skepticism about the human instincts for reason and virtue.

How did I pick up this dark, ironical, flip view of the war? Why do I enjoy
exhibiting it? The answer is that I contracted it in the infantry, and I suspect I
embraced it with special vigor once I found how it annoyed people who had not
fought at close quarters in terrible weather and shot people to death and been hit
by a shell from a German gun. My view of the war is a form of revenge. Indeed,
the careful reader will have discerned in all the essays in this book a speaker who
is really a pissed-off infantryman, disguised as a literary and cultural commentator.
He is embittered that the Air Corps had beds to sleep in, that Patton's Third Army
got all the credit, that non-combatants of the Medical Administrative and Quarter-
master Corps wore the same battle-stars as he, that soon after the war the "enemy"
he had labored to destroy had been re-armed by his own government and positioned to oppose one of his old Allies. "We broke our ass for nothin'," says Sergeant Croft in *The Naked and the Dead*. These are this speaker's residual complaints while he is affecting to be annoyed primarily by someone's bad writing or
slipshod logic or lazy editing or pretentious ideas. As Louis Simpson says, "The
war made me a foot-soldier for the rest of my life," and after any war foot-soldiers
are touchy.

2   My war is virtually synonymous with my life. I entered the war when I was
nineteen, and I have been in it ever since. Melville's Ishmael says that a whale-
ship was his Yale College and his Harvard. An infantry division was mine, the
103rd, whose dispirited personnel wore a colorful green and yellow cactus on their
left shoulders. These hillbillies and Okies, drop-outs and used-car salesmen and
petty criminals were my teachers and friends.

How did an upper-middle-class young gentleman find himself in so unseemly a place? Why wasn't he in the Navy, at least, or in the OSS or Air Corps administration or editing the *Stars and Stripes* or being a general's aide? The answer is comic: at the age of twenty I found myself leading forty riflemen over the Vosges Mountains and watching them torn apart by German artillery and machine-guns because when I was sixteen, in junior college, I was fat and flabby, with feminine tits and a big behind. For years the thing I'd hated most about school was gym, for there I was obliged to strip and shower communally. Thus I chose to join the R.O.T.C. (infantry, as it happened) because that was a way to get out of gym, which meant you never had to take off your clothes and invite—indeed, compel—ridicule. You rationalized by noting that this was 1939 and that a little "military training" might not, in the long run, be wasted. Besides, if you worked up to be a cadet officer, you got to wear a Sam Browne belt, from which depended a nifty saber.

When I went on to college, it was natural to continue my technique for not exposing my naked person, and luckily my college had an infantry R.O.T.C. unit, where I was welcomed as something of an experienced hand. This was in 1941. When the war began for the United States, college students were solicited by various "programs" of the navy and marine corps and coast guard with plans for transforming them into officers. But people enrolled in the R.O.T.C. unit were felt to have committed themselves already. They had opted for the infantry, most of them all unaware, and that's where they were going to stay. Thus while shrewder friends were enrolling in Navy V-1 or signing up for the pacific exercises of the Naval Japanese Language Program or the Air Corps Meteorological Program, I signed up for the Infantry Enlisted Reserve Corps, an act guaranteeing me one extra semester in college before I was called. After basic training, advancement to officer training was promised, and that seemed a desirable thing, even if the crossed rifles on the collar did seem to betoken some hard physical exertion and discomfort—marching, sleeping outdoors, that sort of thing. But it would help "build you up," and besides officers, even in the Infantry, got to wear those wonderful pink trousers and receive constant salutes.

It was such imagery of future grandeur that in spring, 1943, sustained me through eighteen weeks of basic training in 100-degree heat at dreary Camp Roberts, California, where to toughen us, it was said, water was forbidden from 8:00 a.m. to 5:00 p.m. ("water discipline," this was called). Within a few weeks I'd lost all my flab and with it the whole ironic "reason" I found myself there at all. It was abundantly clear already that "infantry" had been a big mistake: it was not just stupid and boring and bloody, it was athletic, and thus not at all for me. But supported by vanity and pride I somehow managed to march thirty-five miles and tumble through the obstacle course, and a few months later I found myself at the Infantry School, Fort Benning, Georgia, where, training to become an officer, I went through virtually the same thing over again. As a Second Lieutenant of Infantry I "graduated" in the spring of 1944 and was assigned to the 103rd Division at Camp Howze, Texas, the local equivalent of Camp Roberts, only worse: Roberts had white-painted two-storey clapboard barracks, Howze one-storey tar-paper shacks. But the heat was the same, and the boredom, and the local whore-culture, and the hillbilly songs:

> Who's that gal with the red dress on?
> Some folks call her Dinah.
> She stole my heart away,
> Down in Carolina.

The 103rd Division had never been overseas, and all the time I was putting my rifle platoon through its futile exercises we were being prepared for the invasion of southern France, which followed the landings in Normandy. Of course we didn't know this, and assumed from the training ("water discipline" again) that we were destined for the South Pacific. There were some exercises involving towed gliders that seemed to portend nothing at all but self-immolation, we were so inept with these devices. In October, 1944, we were all conveyed by troop transports to Marseilles.

3.   It was my first experience of abroad, and my life-long affair with France dates from the moment I first experienced such unAmerican phenomena as: formal manners and a respect for the language; a well-founded skepticism; the pollarded plane trees on the Av. R. Schuman; the red wine and real bread; the *pissoirs* in the streets; the international traffic signs and the visual public language hinting a special French understanding of things: *Hôtel de Ville, Defense d'afficher;* the smell of Turkish tobacco when one has been brought up on Virginia and Burley. An intimation of what we might be opposing was supplied by the aluminum Vichy coinage. On one side, a fasces and *Etat Français.* No more Republic. On the other, *Liberté, Egalité, Fraternité* replaced by *Travail* (as in *Arbeit Macht Frei*), *Famille,* and *Patrie* (as in *Vaterland*). But before we had time to contemplate all this, we were moving rapidly northeast. After a truck ride up the Rhone Valley, still pleasant with girls and flowers and wine, our civilized period came to an abrupt end. On the night of November 11 (nice irony there) we were introduced into the line at St. Dié, in Alsace.

We were in "combat." I find the word embarrassing, carrying as it does false chivalric overtones (as in "single combat"). But synonyms are worse: *fighting* is not accurate, because much of the time you are being shelled, which is not fighting but suffering; *battle* is too high and remote; *in action* is a euphemism suited more to dire telegrams than description. "Combat" will have to do, and my first hours of it I recall daily, even now. They fueled, and they still fuel, my view of things.

Everyone knows that a night relief is among the most difficult of infantry maneuvers. But we didn't know it, and in our innocence we expected it to go according to plan. We and the company we were replacing were cleverly and severely shelled: it was as if the Germans a few hundred feet away could see us in the dark and through the thick pine growth. When the shelling finally stopped, at about midnight, we realized that, although near the place we were supposed to be, until daylight we would remain hopelessly lost. The order came down to stop where we were, lie down among the trees, and get some sleep. We would finish the relief at first light. Scattered over several hundred yards, the two hundred and fifty of us in F Company lay down in a darkness so thick we could see nothing at all. Despite the terror of our first shelling (and several people had been hit), we slept as soundly as babes. At dawn I awoke, and what I saw all around were numerous objects I'd miraculously not tripped over in the dark. These objects were dozens of dead German boys in greenish-gray uniforms, killed a day or two before by the company we were relieving. If darkness had hidden them from us, dawn disclosed them with open eyes and greenish-white faces like marble, still clutching their rifles and machine-pistols in their seventeen-year-old hands, fixed where they had fallen. (For the first time I understood the German phrase for the war-dead: *die Gefallenen*.) Michelangelo could have made something beautiful out of these forms, in the *Dying Gaul* tradition, and I was startled to find that in a way I couldn't understand, at first they struck me as beautiful. But after a moment, no feeling but shock and horror. My adolescent illusions, largely intact to that moment, fell away all at once, and I suddenly knew I was not and never would be in a world that was reasonable or just. The scene was less apocalyptic than shabbily ironic: it sorted so ill with modern popular assumptions about the idea of progress and attendant improvements in public health, social welfare, and social justice. To transform guiltless boys into cold marble after passing them through unbearable fear and humiliation and pain and contempt seemed to do them an interesting injustice. I decided to ponder these things. In 1917, shocked by the Battle of the Somme and recovering from neurasthenia, Wilfred Owen was reading a life of Tennyson. He wrote his mother: "Tennyson, it seems, was always a great child. So should I have been but for Beaumont Hamel." So should I have been but for St. Dié.

After that, one day was much like another: attack at dawn, run and fall and crawl and sweat and worry and shoot and be shot at and cower from mortar shells, always keeping up a jaunty carriage in front of one's platoon; and at night, "consolidate" the objective, usually another hill, sometimes a small town, and plan the attack for the next morning. Before we knew it we'd lost half the company, and we all realized then that for us there would be no way out until the war ended but sickness, wounds, or oblivion. And the war would end only as we pressed our painful daily advance. Getting it over was our sole motive. Yes, we knew about the Jews. But our skins seemed to us more valuable at the time.

4   The word for the German defense all along was clever, a word that never could have been applied to our procedures. It was my first experience, to be repeated many times in later years, of the cunning ways of Europe versus the blunter ways of the New World. Although manned largely by tired thirty-year-old veterans (but sharp enough to have got out of Normandy alive), old men, and crazy youths, the German infantry was officered superbly, and their defense, which we experienced for many months, was disciplined and orderly. My people would have run, or at least "snaked off." But the Germans didn't, until the very end. Their uniforms were a scandal—rags and beat-up boots and unauthorized articles—but somehow they held together. Nazis or not, they did themselves credit. Lacking our lavish means, they compensated by patience and shrewdness. Not until well after the war did I discover that many times when they unaccountably located us hidden in deep woods and shelled us accurately, they had done so by inferring electronically the precise positions of the radios over which we innocently conversed.

As the war went on, the destruction of people became its sole means. I felt sorry for the Germans I saw killed in quantity everywhere—along the roads, in cellars, on roof-tops—for many reasons. They were losing, for one thing, and their deaths meant nothing, though they had been persuaded that resistance might "win the war." And they were so pitifully dressed and accoutered: that was touching. Boys with raggedy ad hoc uniforms and *Panzerfausts* and too few comrades. What were they doing? They were killing themselves; and for me, who couldn't imagine being killed, for people my age voluntarily to get themselves killed caused my mouth to drop open.

Irony describes the emotion, whatever it is, occasioned by perceiving some great gulf, half-comic, half-tragic, between what one expects and what one finds. It's not quite "disillusion," but it's adjacent to it. My experience in the war was ironic because my innocence before had prepared me to encounter in it something like the same reasonableness that governed prewar life. This, after all, was the tone dominating the American relation to the war: talk of "the future," allotments and bond purchases carefully sent home, hopeful fantasies of "the postwar world." I assumed, in short, that everyone would behave according to the clear advantages offered by reason. I had assumed that in war, like chess, when you were beaten you "resigned"; that when outnumbered and outgunned you retreated; that when you were surrounded you surrendered. I found out differently, and with a vengeance. What I found was people obeying fatuous and murderous "orders" for no reason I could understand, killing themselves because someone "told them to," prolonging the war when it was hopelessly lost because—because it was unreasonable to do so. It was my introduction to the shakiness of civilization. It was my first experience of the profoundly irrational element, and it made ridiculous all talk of plans and preparations for the future and goodwill and intelligent arrangements. Why did the red-haired young German machine-gunner firing at us in the woods not go on living—marrying, going to university, going to the beach, laughing, smiling—but keep firing long after he had made his point, and require us to kill him with a grenade?

5   Before we knew it it was winter, and the winter in 1944−1945 was the coldest in Europe for twenty-five years. For the ground troops conditions were unspeakable, and even the official history admits the disaster, imputing the failure to provide adequate winter clothing—analogous to the similar German oversight when the Russian winter of 1941−1942 surprised the planners—to optimism, innocence, and "confidence":

> Confidence born of the rapid sweep across Europe in the summer
> of 1944 and the conviction on the part of many that the successes
> of Allied arms would be rewarded by victory before the onset of
> winter contributed to the unpreparedness for winter combat.

The result of thus ignoring the injunction "Be Prepared" was 64,008 casualties from "cold injury"—not wounds but pneumonia and trench-foot. The official history sums up: "This constitutes more than four 15,000-man divisions. Approximately 90 percent of cold casualties involved riflemen and there were about 4,000 riflemen per infantry division. Thus closer to 13 divisions were critically disabled for combat." We can appreciate those figures by recalling that the invasion of Normandy was initially accomplished by only six divisions (nine if we add the airborne). Thus crucial were little things like decent mittens and gloves, fur-lined parkas, thermal underwear—all of which any normal peacetime hiker or skier would demand as protection against prolonged exposure. But "the winter campaign in Europe was fought by most combat personnel in a uniform that did not give proper protection": we wore silly long overcoats, right out of the nineteenth century; thin field jackets, designed to convey an image of manliness at Fort Bragg; and dress wool trousers. We wore the same shirts and huddled under the same blankets as Pershing's troops in the expedition against Pancho Villa in 1916. Of the 64,008 who suffered "cold injury" I was one. During February, 1945, I was back in various hospitals for a month with pneumonia. I told my parents it was flu.

That month away from the line helped me survive for four weeks more but it broke the rhythm and, never badly scared before, when I returned to the line early in March I found for the first time that I was terrified, unwilling to take the chances which before had seemed rather sporting. My month of safety had renewed my interest in survival, and I was psychologically and morally ill-prepared to lead my platoon in the great Seventh Army attack of March 15, 1945. But lead it I did, or rather push it, staying as far in the rear as was barely decent. And before the day was over I had been severely rebuked by a sharp-eyed lieutenant-colonel who threatened court martial if I didn't pull myself together. Before that day was over I was sprayed with the contents of a soldier's torso when I was lying behind him and he knelt to fire at a machine-gun holding us up: he was struck in the heart, and out of the holes in the back of his field jacket flew little clouds of tissue, blood, and powdered cloth. Near him another man raised himself to fire, but the machine-gun caught him in the mouth, and as he fell he looked back at me with surprise, blood and teeth dribbling out onto the leaves. He was one to whom early on I had given the Silver Star for heroism, and he didn't want to let me down.

As if in retribution for my cowardice, in the late afternoon, near Engwiller, Alsace, clearing a woods full of Germans cleverly dug in, my platoon was raked by shells from an 88, and I was hit in the back and leg by shell fragments. They felt like red-hot knives going in, but I was as interested in the few quiet moans, like those of a hurt child drifting off to sleep, of my thirty-seven-year-old platoon sergeant—we'd been together since Camp Howze—killed instantly by the same shell. We were lying together, and his immediate neighbor on the other side, a lieutenant in charge of a section of heavy machine-guns, was killed instantly too. And my platoon was virtually wiped away. I was in disgrace, I was hurt, I was clearly expendable—while I lay there the supply sergeant removed my issue wristwatch to pass on to my replacement—and I was twenty years old.

6   I bore up all right while being removed from "the field" and passed back through the first-aid stations where I was known. I was deeply on morphine, and managed brave smiles as called for. But when I got to the evacuation hospital thirty miles behind the lines and was coming out from the anesthetic of my first operation, all my affectations of control collapsed, and I did what I'd wanted to do for months. I cried, noisily and publicly, and for hours. I was the scandal of the ward. There were lots of tears back there: in the operating room I saw a nurse dissolve in shoulder-shaking sobs when a boy died with great stertorous gasps on the operating table she was attending. That was the first time I'd seen anyone cry

in the whole European Theater of Operations, and I must have cried because I felt that there, out of "combat," tears were licensed. I was crying because I was ashamed and because I'd let my men be killed and because my sergeant had been killed and because I recognized as never before that he might have been me and that statistically if in no other way he was me, and that I had been killed too. But ironically I had saved my life by almost losing it, for my leg wound providentially became infected, and by the time it was healed and I was ready for duty again, the European war was over, and I journeyed back up through a silent Germany to re-join my reconstituted platoon "occupying" a lovely Tyrolean valley near Innsbruck. For the infantry there was still the Japanese war to sweat out, and I was destined for it, despite the dramatic gash in my leg. But thank God the Bomb was dropped while I was on my way there, with the result that I can write this.

That day in mid-March that ended me was the worst of all for F Company. We knew it was going to be bad when it began at dawn, just like an episode from the First World War, with an hour-long artillery preparation and a smoke-screen for us to attack through. What got us going and carried us through was the conviction that, suffer as we might, we were at least "making history." But we didn't even do that. Liddell Hart's 766-page *History of the Second World War* never heard of us. It mentions neither March 15th nor the 103rd Infantry Division. The only satisfaction history has offered is the evidence that we caused Josef Goebbels some extra anxiety. The day after our attack he entered in his log under "Military Situation":

> In the West the enemy has now gone over to the attack in the sector between Saarbrücken and Hagenau in addition to the previous flashpoints. . . . His objective is undoubtedly to drive in our front on the Saar and capture the entire region south of the Moselle and west of the Rhine.

And he goes on satisfyingly: "Mail received testifies to a deep-seated lethargy throughout the German people degenerating almost into hopelessness. There is very sharp criticism of the . . . entire national leadership." One reason: "The Moselle front is giving way." But a person my age I met thirty years later couldn't believe that there was still any infantry fighting in France in the spring of 1945, and puzzled by my dedicating a book of mine to my dead platoon sergeant with the date March 15, 1945, confessed that he couldn't figure out what had happened to him.

7   To become disillusioned you must earlier have been illusioned. Evidence of the illusions suffered by the youth I was is sadly available in the letters he sent, in unbelievable profusion, to his parents. They radiate a terrible naïveté, together with a pathetic disposition to be pleased in the face of boredom and, finally, horror. The young man had heard a lot about the importance of "morale" and ceaselessly labored to sustain his own by sustaining his addressees'. Thus: "We spent all of Saturday on motor maintenance," he writes from Fort Benning; "a very interesting subject." At Benning he believes all he's told and fails to perceive that he's being prepared for one thing only, and that a nasty, hazardous job, whose performers on the line have a life expectancy of six weeks. He assures his parents: "I can get all sorts of assignments from here: . . . Battalion staff officer, mess

officer, rifle platoon leader, weapons platoon leader, company executive officer, communications officer, motor officer, etc." (Was it an instinct for protecting himself from a truth half-sensed that made him bury *rifle platoon leader* in the middle of this list?) Like a bright schoolboy, he is pleased when grown-ups tell him he's done well. "I got a compliment on my clean rifle tonight. The lieutenant said, 'Very good.' I said, 'Thank you, sir.' " His satisfaction in making Expert Rifleman is touching; it is "the highest possible rating," he announces. And although he is constantly jokey, always on the lookout for what he terms "laffs," he seems to have no sense of humor:

> We're having a very interesting week . . . , taking up the carbine, automatic rifle, rifle grenade, and the famous "bazooka." We had the bazooka today, and it was very enjoyable, although we could not fire it because of lack of ammunition.

He has the most impossible standards of military excellence, and he enlists his critical impulse in the service of optimistic self-deception. Appalled by the ineptitude of the 103rd Division in training, he writes home: "As I told you last time, this is a very messed up division. It will never go overseas as a unit, and is now serving mainly as a replacement training center, disguised as a combat division."

Because the image of himself actually leading troops through bullets and shellfire is secretly unthinkable, fatuous hope easily comes to his assistance. In August, 1944, with his division preparing to ship abroad, he asserts that the Germans seem to be "on their last legs." Indeed, he reports, "bets are being made . . . that the European war will be over in six weeks." But October finds him on the transport heading for the incredible, and now he "expects," he says, that "this war will end some time in November or December," adding, "I feel very confident and safe." After the epiphanies of the line in November and December, he still entertains hopes for an early end, for the Germans are rational people, and what rational people would persist in immolating themselves once it's clear that they've lost the war? "This *can't* last much longer," he finds.

The letters written during combat are full of requests for food packages from home, and interpretation of this obsession is not quite as simple as it seems. The C and K rations were tedious, to be sure, and as readers of *All Quiet on the Western Front* and *The Middle Parts of Fortune* know, soldiers of all times and places are fixated on food. But how explain this young man's requests for "fantastic items" like gherkins, olives, candy-coated peanuts (the kind "we used to get out of slot-machines at the beach"), cans of chili and tamales, cashew nuts, devilled ham, and fig pudding? The lust for a little swank is the explanation, I think, the need for some exotic counterweight to the uniformity, the dullness, the lack of point and distinction he sensed everywhere. These items also asserted an unbroken contact with home, and a home defined as the sort of place fertile not in corned-beef hash and meat-and-vegetable stew but gum drops and canned chicken. In short, an upper-middle-class venue.

Upper-middle-class too, I suspect, is the unimaginative cruelty of some of these letters, clear evidence of arrested emotional development. "Period" anti-Semitic remarks are not infrequent, and they remain unrebuked by any of his addressees. His understanding of the American South (he's writing from Georgia) can be gauged from his remark, "Everybody down here is illiterate." In combat some of his bravado is a device necessary to his emotional survival, but some bespeaks a genuine insensitivity:

Feb. 1, 1945

Dear Mother and Dad:

Today is the division's 84th consecutive day on line. The average is 90−100 days, although one division went 136 without being relieved. . . .

This house we're staying in used to be the headquarters of a local German Motor Corps unit, and it's full of printed matter, uniforms, propaganda, and pictures of Der Führer. I am not collecting any souveniers [*sic*], although I have had ample opportunity to pick up helmets, flags, weapons, etc. The only thing I have kept is a Belgian pistol, which one German was carrying who was unfortunate enough to walk right into my platoon. That is the first one I had the job of shooting. I have kept the pistol as a souvenier of my first Kraut.

It is odd how hard one becomes after a little bit of this stuff, but it gets to be more like killing mad dogs than people. . . .

Love to all,
Paul.

8   The only comfort I can take today in contemplating these letters is the ease with which their author can be rationalized as a stranger. Even the handwriting is not now my own. There are constant shows of dutifulness to parents, and even grandparents, and mentions of churchgoing, surely anomalous in a leader of assault troops. Parental approval is indispensable: "This week I was 'Class A Agent Officer' for Co. F, paying a $6000 payroll without losing a cent! I felt very proud of myself!" And the complacency! The twittiness! From hospital, where for a time he's been in an enlisted men's ward: "Sometimes I enjoy being with the men just as much as associating with the officers." (*Associating* is good.) The letter-writer is more pretentious than literate ("Alright," "thank's," "curiousity"), and his taste is terrible. He is thrilled to read Bruce Barton's *The Man Nobody Knows* ("It presents Christ in a very human light"), Maugham's *The Summing Up,* and the short stories of Erskine Caldwell. Even his often-sketched fantasies of the postwar heaven are grimly conventional: he will get married (to whom?); he will buy a thirty-five-foot sloop and live on it; he will take a year of non-serious literary graduate study at Columbia; he will edit a magazine for yachtsmen. He seems unable to perceive what is happening, constantly telling his addressee what will please rather than what he feels. He was never more mistaken than when he assured his parents while recovering from his wounds, "Please try not to worry, as no permanent damage has been done."

But the shock of these wounds and the long period recovering from them seem to have matured him a tiny bit, and some of his last letters from the hospital suggest that one or two scales are beginning to fall from his eyes:

> One of the most amazing things about this war is the way the bizarre and unnatural become the normal after a short time. Take this hospital and its atmosphere: after a long talk with him, an eighteen-year-old boy without legs seems like the *normal* eighteen-year-old. You might even be surprised if a boy of the same age should walk in on both his legs. He would seem the freak and the object of pity. It is easy to imagine, after seeing some of these men, that *all* young men are arriving on this planet with stumps instead of limbs.
>
> The same holds true with life at the front. The same horrible unrealness that is so hard to describe. . . . I think I'll have to write a book about all this some time.

But even here, he can't conclude without reverting to cliché and twirpy optimism:

> Enough for this morning. I'm feeling well and I'm very comfortable, and the food is improving. We had chicken and ice cream yesterday!

He has not read Swift yet, but in the vision of the young men with their stumps there's perhaps a hint that he's going to. And indeed, when he enrolled in graduate school later, the first course he was attracted to was "Swift and Pope." And ever since he's been trying to understand satire, and even to experiment with it himself.

It was in the army that I discovered my calling. I hadn't known that I was a teacher, but I found I could explain things: the operation of flamethrowers, map-reading, small-arms firing, "field sanitation." I found I could "lecture" and organize and make things clear. I could start at the beginning of a topic and lead an audience to the end. When the war was over, being trained for nothing useful, I naturally fell into the course which would require largely a mere continuation of this act. In becoming a college teacher of literature I was aware of lots of company: thousands of veterans swarmed to graduate schools to study literature, persuaded that poetry and prose could save the world, or at least help wash away some of the intellectual shame of the years we'd been through. From this generation came John Berryman and Randall Jarrell and Delmore Schwartz and Saul Bellow and Louis Simpson and Richard Wilbur and John Ciardi and William Meredith and all the others who, afire with the precepts of the New Criticism, embraced literature, and the teaching of it, as a quasi-religious obligation.

9   To this day I tend to think of all hierarchies, especially the academic one, as military. The undergraduate students, at the "bottom," are the recruits and draftees, privates all. Teaching assistants and graduate students are the non-coms, with grades (only officers have "ranks") varying according to seniority: a G-4 is more important than a G-1, etc. Instructors, where they still exist, are the Second and First Lieutenants, and together with the Assistant Professors (Captains) comprise the company-grade officers. When we move up to the tenured ranks, Associate Professors answer to field-grade officers, Majors and Colonels. Professors are Generals, beginning with Brigadier—that's a newly promoted one. Most are Major Generals, and upon retirement they will be advanced to Lieutenant-General ("Pro-

fessor Emeritus"). The main academic administration is less like a higher authority in the same structure than an adjacent echelon, like a group of powerful congressmen, for example, or people from the Judge Advocate's or Inspector General's departments. The Board of Trustees, empowered to make professorial appointments and thus confer academic ranks and privileges, is the equivalent of the President of the United States, who signs commissions very like Letters of Academic Appointment: "Reposing special trust and confidence in the . . . abilities of ——, I do appoint him," etc. It is not hard to see also that the military principle crudely registered in the axiom Rank Has Its Privileges operates in academic life, where there are plums to be plucked like frequent leaves of absence, single-occupant offices, light teaching loads, and convenient, all-weather parking spaces.

I think this generally unconscious way of conceiving of the academic hierarchy is common among people who went to graduate school immediately after the war, and who went on the G.I. Bill. Perhaps many were attracted to university teaching as a post-war profession because in part they felt they understood its mechanisms already. Thus their ambitiousness, their sense that if to be a First Lieutenant is fine, to work up to Lieutenant-General is wonderful. And I suspect that their conception of instruction is still, like mine, tinged with Army. I think all of us of that vintage feel uneasy with forms of teaching which don't recognize a clear hierarchy—team-teaching, for example, or even the seminar, which assumes the fiction that leader and participants possess roughly equal knowledge and authority. For students (that is, enlisted men) to prosecute a rebellion, as in the 1960's and early 70's, is tantamount to mutiny, an offense, as the Articles of War indicate, "to be punished by death, or such other punishment as a court-martial shall direct." I have never been an enthusiast for The Movement.

In addition to remaining rank-conscious, I persist in the army habit of exact personnel classification. For me, everyone still has an invisible "spec number" indicating what his job is or what he's supposed to be doing. Thus a certain impatience with people of ambiguous identity, or worse, people who don't seem to do anything, like self-proclaimed novelists and poets who generate no apprehensible product. These seem to me the T-5's of the postwar world, mere Technicians Fifth Grade, parasites, drones, noncombatants.

Twenty years after the First World War Siegfried Sassoon reports that he was still having dreams about it, dreams less of terror than of obligation. He dreams that

> the War is still going on and I have got to return to the Front. I complain bitterly to myself because it hasn't stopped yet. I am worried because I can't find my active-service kit. I am worried because I have forgotten how to be an officer. I feel that I can't face it again, and sometimes I burst into tears and say, "It's no good, I can't do it." But I know that I can't escape going back, and search frantically for my lost equipment.

That's uniquely the dream of a junior officer. I had such dreams too, and mine persisted until about 1960, when I was thirty-six, past re-call age.

10   Those who actually fought on the line in the war, especially if they were wounded, constitute an in-group forever separate from those who did not. Praise or blame does not attach: rather, there is the accidental possession of a special empirical knowledge, a feeling of a mysterious shared ironic awareness manifesting itself in an instinctive skepticism about pretension, publicly enunciated truths, the vanities of learning, and the pomp of authority. Those who fought know a secret about themselves, and it's not very nice. As Frederic Manning said in 1929, remembering 1914–1918: "War is waged by men; not by beasts, or by gods. It is a peculiarly human activity. To call it a crime against mankind is to miss at least half its significance; it is also the punishment of a crime."

And now that those who fought have grown much older, we must wonder at the frantic avidity with which we struggled then to avoid death, digging our foxholes like madmen, running from danger with burning lungs and pounding hearts. What, really, were we so frightened of? Sometimes now the feeling comes over us that Housman's lines which in our boyhood we thought attractively cynical are really just:

> Life, to be sure, is nothing much to lose;
> But young men think it is, and we were young.

Analysis

Fussell's essay makes readers confront the life-long impact that war experience can have on individuals and society. We will focus for the moment, however, on the questions presented earlier. We will see that "My War" has such an impact on us because it is an ethical essay.

1. Meaning

What does Fussell say? Why does he write? To summarize, Fussell reflects on his experiences as a young combat officer in Europe during World War II and demonstrates how these experiences have shaped the way he looks at life. He presents a chronology of his earliest experiences, focusing especially on ironies like enlisting in a junior college ROTC program in order to avoid athletics and close male contacts. His enlistment ultimately puts him in battle as a field officer at the age of 20. The chronology continues, presenting his initial European combat experiences paying particular attention to his first encounter with the war dead, and ultimately focusing on his admission of cowardice in battle, his injury, and the death of his friend, the platoon sergeant. After the chronology, Fussell analyzes his wartime behavior, criticizing himself harshly. Then he illustrates how the lessons learned in the army influence his life today. He ends by asserting the final effect of the war on him and others like him: "a mysterious shared ironic awareness manifesting itself in an instinctive skepticism about pretension, publicly enunciated truths, the vanities of learning, and the pomp of authority." He also learns that for humans, war is both crime and punishment: we violate each other through war and suffer the punishment by having to live our lives knowing what we did.

Why did Fussell write the essay? He writes for two reasons. First, he writes to defend his "dark, ironical, flip view of the war" against certain criticism he has received. The "protective screen of irony" he uses is the best and perhaps the only way to capture the essence of war. He knows; he is an insider, both a victim and a victimizer. Second, in order to defend himself, he must better understand and communicate the life-shaping power the war experience had on him. His vague outrage at both his critics and at his ill-luck in having suffered the war experience must become a coherent and credible statement of belief. He demonstrates the loss of innocence, the general suffering, and the ultimate human folly and failure that is war. He generalizes from his personal experience to connect it with that of other thoughtful persons who have endured war, and he shapes it through the essay so even those who do not have the experience can understand.

2. Audience

How does Fussell relate to his audience? How does this relationship contribute to the essay? Fussell deals with the problem of audience from the very beginning. In the first paragraph he mentions that one of his motives for writing is to deal with criticism he has received from certain audiences. He establishes a series of experienced/inexperienced, insider/outsider, informed/uninformed relationships. Simply stated, those who have the experience understand how his irony works to capture the essence of war while protecting him from its horror; those who have not experienced war will not understand and will falsely accuse him of "deficiency in human compassion." Setting these oppositions, he proceeds to discuss his experience, establish the legitimacy of his view, and disprove his critics. He has compassion aplenty; it is private and pervasive. It is his life.

Beyond this level of insider/outsider, an opposition designed initially to exclude the uninformed and inexperienced, Fussell further isolates himself by striking quite a formal relationship with his audience. He stays close within his personal experience, which is limited and specific. He does not spend much time explaining for a general audience. When he does use an analogy, his sources are not normal experience, but uncommon experience, especially art. He describes the fallen soldiers as "like marble": "Michelangelo could have made something beautiful out of these forms." Note also his frequent references to literature. Such references largely exclude a general readership. At first it would seem that Fussell's stance isolates him from readers, but its ultimate effect is creating a strong sense of solidarity with the limited readership familiar with his experiences and a strong authoritative personal voice for those familiar with his materials.

Rather than working to establish a broad-based sense of community, Fussell depends on a stance of isolated authority. Unlike the writer of "Notes and Comments," Fussell stands as an individual whom readers must accept or reject on his own terms. And those terms are explicit, not implicit and unstated. His immediate community includes a very small in-group of combat veterans along with those inexperienced readers who can appreciate and respond to his authoritative voice. In the end, however, his community is all humanity, a perverse humanity that inflicts war upon itself.

3. Structure

How does Fussell structure his essay? How does structure contribute to his meaning? Fussell uses a variety of structures in his essay. Section I establishes the context of the essay: he is writing to defend his point of view toward war and to explain that this view is the view of all experienced foot-soldiers. This is the main idea the essay will demonstrate.

Sections 2 through 6 present a chronology of his war-related experiences, from junior-college ROTC through basic training, from first combat to hospital and back to battle, cowardice, and its consequences. Each section focuses on an important incident emphasizing the irony and unreasonableness of war. This is especially the case when Fussell comments on the German Army's desperate but futile defense of a lost cause. "What were they doing? They were killing themselves; and for me, who couldn't imagine being killed, for people my age voluntarily to get themselves killed caused my mouth to drop open."

Fussell organizes the body of the essay using chronology, with climactic order governing each section. Thus, Fussell leads readers deeper and deeper into the war's futility and horror. In terms of reason and logic, however, Fussell uses quick shifts of scene and the accumulation of detail rather than argument and explanation to make his points. He uses this strategy consciously. He notes at the beginning of section 3 that the pace of the war is mind-boggling. The soldiers move too quickly to understand their plight: "But before we had time to contemplate all this, we were moving rapidly northeast." He creates the same situation for his readers; he moves us quickly from one scene to another, not allowing us to understand, trusting that all the separate instances will combine to make sense upon contemplation.

Section 7 begins a sequence of reflection and analysis. He begins with a very brutal analysis of his wartime behavior. He analyzes himself with a cold eye, using the pronoun "he" as if the essay were a psychological case study. He includes "empirical" data. For example, he analyzes his letters home, criticizing their foolishness. In a sense, this harsh analysis exemplifies the negative effect of the war experience. He has been hardened and isolated—even from himself. And he has lived his postwar life that way.

Section 9 ends the analytic segment with some cockeyed humor. He cannot see the world except through the hierarchies he learned in the army. He views colleagues and students as if they had "spec numbers." The students who participated in the "Movement" against the Vietnam war of the 60s and 70s become mutineers. Irony seems his purpose here because these same protesters helped to end that war and saved many from the same nightmares Fussell suffers until he passes re-call age.

Section 10 is a conclusion that takes us back to the purpose of the essay. He asserts his membership in the limited and private community of combat veterans and generalizes its immediate effect: "instinctive skepticism" about almost everything, especially about readers who have "little empirical contact with the actualities of war" but who nevertheless call him " 'black and monstrous.' "

In sum, Fussell combines argumentative and narrative structures in his essay. The main idea implied in section 1 is developed by the accumulation of details through the chronologically organized narrative, and then analyzed through criticism of his behavior and the effect the war has had on his life. The conclusion articulates the consequence, the generalization concerning the skepticism rooted in the war. Fussell uses the writer's tools to discover and communicate his feelings about the effect war has on combat veterans. He writes the ethical essay to turn his vague outrage into a credible defense of his beliefs.

4. Language

How does Fussell's language contribute to the essay's effectiveness? Fussell uses language to create a tension between him and his audience. He uses indirection and negative phrasing early to criticize those who attack him though they have no experience on which to base their attack. He does not accuse his critics of never having been in combat; he "suspects" they have had "little empirical contact" with the "actualities of war." Such strategies make readers slow down in order to understand the meaning. He wants us to slow down, not take what he is saying lightly. We cannot breeze through; we must deal with him.

In addition, Fussell uses literary techniques such as irony throughout the essay to avoid having to explain everything. He asserts a strong, personal voice, an experienced and authoritative voice. He is not someone we have a conversation with. The essay is not a dialog; rather, it is a monolog, something like a formal lecture. Fussell ultimately proves his point through self-deprecation, which can only work if we believe his authoritative voice. This man who seems so smart and so experienced admits to being a coward? We wonder how we would have responded.

Further, Fussell depends on striking images of horror, such as the battle dead "with open eyes and greenish-white faces," to bring readers to certain conclusions. He combines harsh imagery and irony to show just how honorably brave and fatally foolish war can make us: "but the machine gun caught him in the mouth, and as he fell he looked back at me with surprise, blood and teeth dribbling out onto the leaves. He was one to whom early on I had given the Silver Star for heroism, and he didn't want to let me down." The literal and figurative clash. We are attracted and repelled. This is how he makes his point.

Summary

Fussell's essay exemplifies the opposite end of the spectrum of ethical essays from "Notes and Comments." Rather than creating an immediate community, it asserts individual identity, explains the sources of that identity, and legitimizes it. Rather than creating someone like us who is concerned with human perfectibility and survival in a technological age, he asserts his separateness from us as if he does not care what we think. Thus he illustrates the reality of human imperfectibility that we must live with. He creates an authoritative voice that causes us to confront a real human problem—war. War, both crime and punishment, is a human phenomenon that exceeds time and community. It is a problem all responsible moral individuals must consider, and Fussell's essay gives us some powerful insights to help our thinking.

The Challenge of the Ethical Essay: The Authoritative Self

One of the finest examples of an extended ethical essay is Henry David Thoreau's *Walden*. It demonstrates the ethical essay's power to reveal the essence of belief. Moreover, in the expression of those beliefs Thoreau provides a model for living that has influenced generations of readers and had a huge impact on the politics of several nations. Combining both ends of the spectrum of the ethical essay, Walden employs both the authoritative "I" of "My War" and the implicit sense of community used in "Notes and Comments." A slow and careful reading of Walden reveals a depth of thinking, common sense and wisdom, and a joy in living that is refreshing in our days of artificial stimulation and conspicuous consumerism. You may want to read or reread it.

Walden is also a book about WRITING THE INSIDE OUT. Thoreau plumbs the depths of self to discover what is permanent and important, so he can shape and report his findings for others. Thoreau addresses this process near the beginning of Walden:

> For a long time I was a reporter to a journal, of no wide circulation, whose editor has never yet seen fit to print the bulk of my contributions, and, as is too common with writers, I got only my labor for my pains. However, in this case my pains were their own reward.

The "journal" Thoreau alludes to here is his own personal journal, the repository of his insights and reflections on his everyday life. His journal is not unlike the one you learned to keep earlier. The personal journal, for you and for Thoreau, is its own reward.

However, Walden is the fruit of that labor, the recomposed journal of his days by the pond. As editor he has finally discovered material worth publishing. Walden is the capstone, the ultimate product of the education, experience, and reflection of Henry David Thoreau. As such it is a very large but very effective example of an ethical essay. Write your essay in that same spirit and with that same ambition. Now, like Thoreau, you are to be your life's own boss, your journal's own editor.

Within Walden, Thoreau addresses the problem of education. His criticism, in fact, provides a strong defense for writing ethical essays. He denounces the tradition that sees education as leisure, as a retreat from the world, as approximating experience rather than providing experience itself. Thoreau objected to education that requires repeating facts rather than discovering knowledge. In the system he rejects, the way to success seems to be to follow the rules, to do what we are told. Our own educational system frequently sends these messages. We are encouraged to be "good little girls and boys," to complete the exercises, write the assigned number of words, and repeat what our teachers have said without necessarily thinking about facts or issues and understanding how we feel about them or how we should act. Too often our educations are like lab experiments in basic chemistry: follow the procedures exactly, measure the chemicals carefully, and weigh the salt that precipitates from the solution. No surprises; the same amount always precipitates. Ho hum. Nothing new.

Thoreau argues for a different system. Listen as he debates an imaginary proponent of the old system:

> "But," says one, "you do not mean that students should do work with their hands instead of their heads?" I do not mean that exactly. . . . . I mean that they should not *play* life, or *study* it merely,

> while the community supports them at this expensive game, but
> earnestly *live* it from beginning to end. How could youths better
> learn to live than by at once trying the experiment of living.

Thoreau here emphasizes the need for real experience as the basis for education. And writing is largely how Thoreau integrates his experience, draws its lessons, and announces them to the world at large. Writing is instrumental in his education. So too have we learned that the process of writing, while a way to learn anew, is a powerful instrument for reflecting, reconsidering experience, evaluating it, and synthesizing its lessons. Writing the ethical essay requires us to go beyond playing and studying, beyond reporting what others have thought and said. We must live the experiment of our lives, reflect and evaluate, and put ourselves down on paper.

The Dynamic of the Ethical Essay

The ethical essay demands a special kind of writing. It requires that we integrate what we have learned about writing for ourselves and for others. We begin by WRITING FOR THE INSIDE, with ourselves as the primary audience and with the purpose of discovering personal meaning in the process. Then we make our discoveries available to a larger and more distant audience. As we discover meaning and shape it, our audience should simultaneously be understanding our meaning and discovering insights about themselves.

The thoughtful interaction of writer and readers is the goal of this essay. Its success depends on sympathy, on "like-feeling," whose source is the interaction between writer and reader. Sympathy helps readers appreciate the writer's struggle to discover meaning and helps writers appreciate the reader's willingness to participate in the struggle toward meaning. In the process, we grow as writers and readers—as humans. Through the process, we recognize the beliefs and values that guide our behavior and the behavior of others. We recognize the sources of our values and can evaluate them. Thus, we assert an identity and proclaim membership in a community.

In *Walden*, Thoreau writes so that interaction between writer and readers can occur. He objects to superficial or impersonal writing, which belongs to no one and is directed to no one. He abhors writing in which there is no "I" working to create a "we." He wonders who would want to read soulless, disembodied writing that does not require the reader to participate. He knows that he does not.

In reality, disembodied writing occurs for a number of reasons. Sometimes necessity prevails. An informative purpose may require writers to withdraw, causing the information to stand entirely on its own. Thoreau would praise these writers. Sometimes pragmatism prevails. Some choose to write impersonally in order to accomplish a limited purpose, to pass a course or complete a mundane job, with the least expense of time and energy. Thoreau would criticize these writers. But too often ignorance or inexperience prevails. Many write impersonally because they have no alternative; they know only examples of dead and impersonal writing. Thoreau would educate these writers.

Beyond Egotism

For Thoreau, to be impersonal is to be dishonest. In *Walden*, he plans a radical departure from the norm. In the process, he questions the legitimacy of overly formal, impersonal writing:

> In most books, the I or first person, is omitted; in this it will be retained; that, in respect to egotism, is the main difference. We commonly do not remember that it is, after all, always the first person that is speaking.

Here Thoreau is not bragging about his egotism. Rather, he claims all writing is egotistic; writing is fundamentally an assertion of self, the product of ego. This egotism can sometimes be obscured or hidden behind an objective third person. Thoreau, on the other hand, constantly assumes responsibility for his writing and ideas. He will not mask his insights behind an objective third person. He advertises his personal responsibility up front. Challenging his readers, he says, "If you don't like what I'm saying or if you don't agree, argue with me. Here I am."

This dynamic resembles the way "Notes and Comments" requires the reader to fill in the answer to the problem and provide a plan of action, and the way Fussell challenges readers to refute his point of view by denying the validity of his experience. Taking chances, accepting risks, putting self on the line, accepting responsibility—these are the goals and potential rewards of the ethical essay for both writers and readers.

Thoreau uses the word egotism and raises an important issue concerning ethical essays. Generally, egotism carries a negative connotation: an excessive concern or obsession with self. Many assume egotism is unhealthy, but this assumption, especially in the context of the ethical essay, deserves scrutiny. Is keeping the self and its discovery of meaning a central concern necessarily egotistical or unhealthy?

No. The essay's success depends upon the sympathy developed between writer and readers and the simultaneous discovery of meaning this sympathy permits. If the writing remains egotistical, it is unsuccessful or incomplete. If it does not move beyond WRITING FOR THE INSIDE, if it remains the same writing that would appear in an unrevised journal entry, then it has not moved beyond the egotistical to establish the sympathy of an effective ethical essay. Sympathy between writer and readers does not mean readers must agree and assume the writer's position on issues. Rather, readers must understand the writer's position *and* understand their own positions better, whether they agree or not. In this sense, the ethical essay is the opposite of egotistic.

An ethical essay must be honest and authentic. Unlike persuasion in which a writer sometimes assumes a stance in order to get a reader to do or believe something, an ethical essay requires the writer to articulate the self as it is, or is becoming, then and there.

Again, Thoreau provides some insight here. After questioning the objectivity of formal "I-less" writing, he admits the source of his confidence, the reason he writes with the "I"; he knows and believes in himself: "I should not talk so much about myself if there were anybody else whom I knew as well." He goes further and makes personal honesty a prerequisite of good writing: "Moreover, I, on my side, require of every writer, first or last, a simple and sincere account of his own life, and not merely what he has heard of other men's lives." Rather than a deficiency, the personal-ness of the essay becomes its strength.

So far we have discovered that the ethical essay must go beyond the egotism of WRITING FOR THE INSIDE; it must engage a reader directly and create sympathy, the dynamic through which understanding and growth become possible. In the same way that the exercises in the PDJ forced you to establish a dialog among different aspects of your self and through that dialog created opportunities for growth and learning, so does the ethical essay require you to strike a sympathetic relationship between you and your readers in order to stimulate understanding and growth.

Essay #7: The Ethical Essay

The true test of your understanding of the ethical essay is writing one. Having read and analyzed some sample essays, and having understood their purpose, now it is your turn to create a true representation of yourself and your feelings about an issue of importance and, through this, to invite your readers to a clearer understanding of themselves and their attitudes toward the issue. Your job is articulating your beliefs, explaining your behavior in some key situation, and justifying your code of conduct. Aim for a length of five typed pages or more. As usual, you will work through the essay in segments.

DISCOVERY

Choosing a Subject

Select a subject which is large enough to fit the purpose of the essay yet is still manageable. The subject must force you to the edge of your abilities as a thinker and writer and beyond the neat structures we have practiced so far. The subject must cause you and your reader to learn about yourselves and the world. Take a chance and accept the challenge. Writers find that the best ethical essays are grand failures. These are essays they can never quite finish but can never forget.

You are free to explore any subject that is of interest to you. But it must be significant. An ethical essay is not merely an opinion about something; it is a reasoned and structured argument or response to a significant issue directed to a public audience. Relations between parents and children or between mates, the role of education, the consequences of contemporary materialism, the challenge of technology, the need for developing mature religious beliefs—these are just a few potential ethical essay subjects. Of course, these are subjects that frequently came up in your PDJ. It is an excellent place to look for prospective subjects.

The procedure is basically the same as for other essays. First you must choose a subject, discover what it is and how you feel about it, discover through research what others have felt and written about it, and use all this information to formulate your position. Then your task is to articulate this position so readers can under-stand and sympathize—in the sense we have been using "sympathy"—and come to know themselves better as a result. In the ethical essay, you work like a pro-spector: you survey the area, stake a claim, assay the quality of the ore you dis-cover, mine its rich veins of meaning, and mill it so it becomes useful for others.

Staking a Claim: Making a Survey

How do you go about staking a claim on a subject? Your first job is surveying the land in order to determine a potentially rewarding area to mine. Where should you look? If you are like most writers who have completed the PDJ, you encoun-tered two or three themes that consistently came to the surface as primary con-cerns.

Lynn Hardin's experience with her PDJ is a good example. Throughout her PDJ she wrote about her boyfriend and their plans to marry and live a mainstream American middle-class life together. These plans and her discontent with waiting for them to be realized almost became obsessions. In addition, she wrote about how constrained she felt, about how she seemed to be spinning wheels and getting nowhere.

These same issues come to the fore in her personal significance essay where she considered her PDJ concerns in a different light. She discovered that she was not really happy, that their plans were not really her plans, that they had been imposed on her and she resented them. These themes—portentous plans and a personal sense of powerlessness—served as an interesting outcropping of rocks in the field that Lynn surveyed while preparing to write her ethical essay.

In fact, the conflicts and transitions she was experiencing eventually became her subject. The issue in particular was maintaining relationships through periods of growth and change. Read this excerpt from an early draft of her essay where she is getting right to the heart of the issue:

Lynn Hardin
Ethical Essay (Draft)

''Mr. Right''

I've always felt that to have a full, well-rounded
life, I needed to be absolutely surrounded by people. I
wanted not only to associate with people, but to be
completely involved in their lives. I wanted to be an
intrinsic part of their lives, just as I wanted them to be
an intrinsic part of my life. This sort of intimacy was
easy enough to acquire through ''best'' friendships with

other girls. But intimacy did not come so easily in relationships with the opposite sex.

I spent seventeen years of my life in active pursuit of ''Mr. Right.'' When I found him, or thought I did, I fell hard. After all, it was my senior year in high school, and it seemed to be the most appropriate time to find someone to share the rest of my life with. And I was just beginning a new life for myself. So I did share a part of my life with him, at least one year of it. I spent an entire year wrapped up with him, planning my whole future in him. After a while, though, my search for intimacy and togetherness was stymied by an almost overwhelming longing for independence.

The principle reason the relationship failed is that I was starting a new life. The transition from high school to college is an enormous one. In one sense it is helpful to have someone with you to help you through, but in another sense that same person can be like a millstone around the neck.

Beginning a college education is probably the greatest undertaking anybody ever faces. A relationship can often be strained because the two participants are not the same persons they once were. But there is often enough understanding to withstand the strain without buckling under. However, understanding is not enough. Space and time are essential. People have to be willing to accept the fact that they are going through major changes. Former promises cannot always be kept. Old dreams no longer fit into the new life.

The excerpt exemplifies ethical essay writing. As we read, we sense a person speaking truly of herself, coming to understand her behavior, and in the process helping readers understand themselves. In addition, we also see Lynn surveying a field and staking her claim. In an interview about her choice of this subject, she claimed that she did not choose the subject as much as it chose her. The theme of transition and conflict had crashed over her in waves, first in her PDJ, and later in her personal significance paper; she could not ignore it.

You too must survey your PDJ and other writing and reading throughout the course and discover an interesting outcropping around which you will stake your claim.

Extracting and Assaying the Ore

Having completed the survey and staked a claim, the concern you will examine, you need now to extract some ore and complete an assay to discover what valuable minerals it contains. You need to find exactly what you are working with. The process involves gathering and evaluating information to see how it best fits together. The quality of your ore can be tested through any one or a combination of the discovery techniques used so far. Consider using informal techniques like journal writing and talking with colleagues and experts as well as reading and formal library research. The nature of your subject will determine which combination of these techniques will help you most.

If your subject is a personal dilemma like Lynn's, talking with friends, especially those who have already confronted the problem, may be helpful. Remember that research can take many forms. Do not discount the value of information you can gather by talking with colleagues. But remember Thoreau's warning to go beyond the reporting of other people's lives. In this essay, you are the researcher and your subject and its relation to your life is your central concern. Collecting what others have written is not enough; you must use what you discover to come to your own conclusions and make your own statement.

Another powerful way to begin thinking in productive ways is through reading literature. No matter how unique your experience and the subject you derive from it may seem, you are not the first or only one to deal with the problem. The history of literature is largely an investigation of human potential and problems. Reflecting on all you have read, you may discover that when Shakespeare's Hamlet determines "to be or not to be, that is the question," he is asking the same question you are asking right now. And you may also find that his behavior offers you approaches to the problem your subject contains. You should read, explore, and remember the wisdom literature offers as you complete the discovery process for this essay.

Formal library research is another productive way to gather information, especially if your subject involves public controversy. When solving a problem, several heads are better than one. Your job is to make yourself a collaborator with the best and the brightest who have considered the problem and whose findings have been collected in the library. Searching out what experts have discovered about a controversy and evaluating their findings and solutions gives you more material to use. The standard methods of library research—which involve gathering sources through the card catalog and subject indexes, reading and note taking, synthesizing the various information into a structured account of other researchers' findings, using quotations and citations, and compiling a reference list to properly credit your collaborators—might help you prepare your essay. Consult the Appendix discussion of using a college writing handbook (pages 271–73) for more information.

But formal research in the library is not the only nor necessarily the best way to gather information about your subject. Interview an authority, confer with your instructor, write more in your journal—whatever. Gather as much information as you can. Later, as you are drafting and revising your essay, you will find it better to have extra information, even if you do not use half of it, than to be without enough.

Once you have gathered the information, the ore for your essay, then you need to assay it to find its rich minerals. The assay, or the evaluation, requires you to separate, categorize, and reformulate the information you have collected. Techniques you learned while writing previous essays will help you put the information into a coherent logical framework to inform the argument in your essay.

Effective ethical essays depend upon logic and reason to establish the source and context and to justify the position advanced. You saw this at work in Fussell's essay, which used argumentative essay strategies embedded within the narrative frame of the war experience. Reason and logic help establish sympathy between you and your readers. You do not want your experience and the lesson culled from it to be so personal that they are relevant only to yourself. You must use reason and logic to make the experience and the lesson understandable to your readers.

Thus, when Lynn chose transition and conflict as her issues, she focused on maintaining personal relationships as her theme because she could safely assume that most of her readers either had had the same experience or knew someone who did. She discovered the potential for sympathy through brainstorming. When she listed her memories and began to organize them according to hierarchies, she discovered that she was not alone in her predicament. Her list included several friends who were experiencing the same shock of transition and the break-up of close relationships. The brainstorming helped her determine that her experience was general and had more potential for development.

To organize and develop her essay Lynn used chronology to focus on a particular episode during her senior year in high school: falling in love with "Mr. Right." Then through analysis of the actors and their actions, she moved deeper and deeper into the episode to discover her motives and their significance. Finally, she was able to move beyond the immediate situation and make a generalization: transition and conflict are indicators of change; major changes can threaten and destroy previously healthy personal relationships. But the process is a normal one which she will survive: "Old dreams no longer fit into the new life." She may not have realized her dreams, but she has gained a new life.

Lynn's use of brainstorming and other analytic techniques allowed her to assay her subject and determine that it was significant and valuable for a general audience. What needs to be noted most is how her discovery procedures meet the specific needs of her subject and purpose. You may need to try several different procedures to find the best one for your subject.

ASSIGNMENT: SELECT AND MASTER A SUBJECT

Use the information and techniques suggested previously in this section to determine the subject for your essay, assess your readiness to write, and complete research and other analytic activities to prepare yourself to draft your essay.

DRAFTING

Digging the Mine

Just as the prospector who has discovered a rich vein of gold below the earth's surface has to construct a strong and dependable mine shaft that will not fall in as miners extract the valuable ore, so do you have to design and build a structure for your ethical essay that will make your discovery easily available to your readers. As you have seen with both "Notes and Comments" and "My War," ethical essays exceed the constraints of the argumentative and simple persuasion essay formats. Since this essay addresses issues more complex than previous essays have, you will need to write more.

To accommodate this increased complexity, you will need to design your own structure. You will probably combine several of the structures you have already practiced. Note that even the brief excerpt from Lynn's essay uses elements of personal narrative in the initial paragraph, argumentative essay strategy in the second paragraph, and persuasive structures including a concession in the middle of the third paragraph: "However, understanding is not enough." Similarly, Fussell's essay combines elements of narrative, argumentative, and persuasive essay formats. You will have to experiment as you shape the conclusions you derive from all the information collected during the discovery process for your public audience.

ASSIGNMENT: DRAFT AND MAP YOUR PERSONAL ESSAY

Though you may be designing a new structure as you write your essay, you should use procedures learned previously to evaluate that structure. Pay close attention to the shape your paper is taking as you draft. After you have completed a draft, map your essay following the procedures presented earlier (pages 191–94). The essay map requires you to consider what each paragraph in your essay is saying, how it is saying it, and why. As you map your essay draft, you are asking how each paragraph contributes to the essay as a whole. The essay map will help you get your essay in the best shape possible before you try it out on your peers.

REVISING

Milling the Ore

Having written the draft, now you must purify what you have extracted from the mine and put it on display for others to inspect and use. This process of milling the ore is best accomplished by getting responses from your peers. Reading and responding to your draft, your peers will be inspecting the rough ore your mine produced through the discovery and drafting processes. Use their responses and the confidence and expertise you have gained already to create a significant personal statement about an important issue.

We discovered earlier that tailoring peer responses to the purpose of an essay helps readers provide specific information for use during revision. In this case, we can tailor the peer responses by recasting the characteristics of ethical essays discussed earlier as questions our peers can respond to. Basically, successful ethical essays exhibit three characteristics:

1. The writer makes a personal statement that exceeds egotism by being relevant to readers.
2. The writer demonstrates a control of the issue based on experience and research.
3. The writer establishes a relationship of identity and sympathy with the readers.

Rephrased, these characteristics constitute the peer critique questions:

PEER CRITIQUE QUESTIONS

Answer the following questions when providing peer responses to the ethical essay:

1. Is the essay personal but not egotistic? Specifically, how does the writer solve the problem of making sense to and for self only? Summarize the essay in a few sentences. Establish how the position expressed is relevant to you.
2. Does the essay contain an authentic and authoritative voice? Does the writer seem honest and believable? Does the writer of the essay seem adequately informed and legitimately able to defend the position assumed? Does the writer move beyond immediate personal experience and establish a general context for the issue and position? Should the writer have considered any important opposing points of view? Suggest specific areas the writer should research or points of view the writer should consider before revising the paper.
3. Does the writer establish a dynamic of sympathy with you as reader? What "angle" does the writer use to draw you into the essay? Briefly explain what you have learned about yourself as a result of reading this essay.

EVALUATING ETHICAL ESSAYS

A Student Sample with Analysis: Sympathy and Common Experience

The ethical essay is a challenge, but it is a challenge this course has prepared you to accept. The following student samples illustrate how writing this essay can help writers realize their potential as mature, contributing community members.

The first sample, Trina Chamber's "Liberated Woman or Normal College Student?" deals with a question many of us have asked ourselves: "What am I doing at college?" The essay presents Trina's solution. She is cultivating a love for learning and an intense interest in a particular subject. In the second essay, "Florence Nightingale Wasn't Just a Camp Follower," Marie Turner articulates her belief in an individual's responsibility for her own actions, a belief developed through her eighteen years of professional experience as a nurse. Though different in both structure and substance, both are strong examples of the opportunity this essay provides writers to discover and articulate beliefs and claim membership in a community.

Trina Chamber's "Liberated Woman or Normal College Student?" considers a number of important concerns including the nature of college, the meaning of learning, relationships with parents and friends, and more. Through the essay, Trina explains her discovery of the meaning of education, asserts her belief in the value of learning, and claims membership in the university community.

Trina makes reference to *Zen and the Art of Motorcycle Maintenance* by Robert Pirsig. As she was reading and researching her essay, she uncovered similarities between her quandary and that of its hero. The book traces the narrator through his discovery and integration of self. He was fragmented by the competing responsibilities of each of his roles. These included student, teacher, father, motorcycle mechanic, and technical writer. In order to survive, he developed a neat set of categories by which he could manage these responsibilites without overlap. Despite the categories, he was not managing his life very well. In fact, certain incidents had previously landed him in an insane asylum. The book begins when he discovers that his problem now threatens the mental health of his young son, Chris.

Throughout the book, Pirsig is greatly concerned with the problem of underlying form: the reason for being, the fundamental identity and purpose of things. Underlying form is the unifying concept that finally allows the narrator to accept his various roles, develop an integrated self, and help his son. This is the same theme Trina develops in her essay, though in the context of her own discovery of self and purpose—her own underlying form.

Read Trina's essay several times and respond to it using the peer critique questions presented earlier. You will be reading the finished draft that Trina submitted to peers for response.

Trina Chambers
Essay #7: Ethical Essay

            Liberated Woman or Normal College Student?

    Through the course of the semester, I have learned many
things about myself and the university environment.
Confused and aimless before, I have just pulled many of
these discoveries together. My problem was that I didn't

really know how to channel all that incoming stuff; I
didn't see anything in it for me. After reflecting on my
PDJ, and reading and analyzing Pirsig's Zen and the Art of
Motorcycle Maintenance (NY: Bantam Books, 1976), I now
realize that I have been experiencing the anxiety and the
exhilaration of personal growth and change which is
central to the learning process. Now that I understand, I
am energetic and hungry for all it has to offer me.

     When I first arrived here, tormenting questions--''What
is college?'', ''Why am I here?'', and ''What is my place
in relation to this institution?''--nagged at me constantly,
occupying my thoughts 24 hours a day. I was truly
obsessed, as is evident in almost every entry in my
PDJ. I was yet to discover what the underlying form
(thanks, Mr. Pirsig) of the school was, and what it had to
offer its students, me included. I would look at the
overall barren appearance of the institution--the cement
walkways, too-neatly manicured lawns, motel-like dorm
rooms--and think that this place seems intended for a stay
not too long, and that certainly no fruit would be borne
here for me. Even though I'd been told not to judge a
book by its cover, and had made similar mistakes in the
past when prejudgement and prejudice had plagued me, I'd
been led astray by the school's physical appearance. I
had not penetrated its surface.

     I also was disgusted by the way I thought that, as
Pirsig notes:

          Schools teach you to imitate. If you don't
          imitate what the teacher wants you get a
          bad grade. Here, in college, it was more
          sophisticated, of course; you were supposed
          to imitate the teacher in such a way as to
          convince the teacher you were not
          imitating, but taking the essence of the
          instruction and going ahead with it on your
          own. That got you A's. Originality on the

        other hand could get you anything--from A
to F (p. 172).

I loathed conformity, strove for originality, and
determined that the university environment seemed to
contradict these fundamentals that I held so highly.
    What I had been unable to see was what had actually
been surrounding me the whole time. I had just been
looking at it from the wrong perspective, not taking
notice of the university's underlying form and internal
meaning and purpose--learning. Actually, that statement
probably is not wholly correct, for I feel underlying form
is what each individual <u>needs</u> it to be, what is good
personally and provides a center of focus. I realized
that what I had been searching and crying out for was
something that I'd already tasted, and craved more of--
learning.
    Perhaps it was, in Pirsig's terms, an ego problem. I
was like Pirsig's son struggling up the mountain, wanting
only for the climb to be over, unable to enjoy myself
along the way. Pirsig writes:

> He's here but he's not here. He rejects
> the here, is unhappy with it, wants to be
> farther up the trail but when he gets there
> will be just as unhappy because then <u>it</u>
> will be ''here.'' What he's looking for,
> wants, is all around him, but he doesn't
> want that because it <u>is</u> all around
> him. Every step's an effort, both
> physically and spiritually, because he
> imagines his goal to be external and
> distant (p. 190).

    I don't know. I was feeling parched and void. The
things that had been my whole life before, my family, my
friends, my high school, my music, had all seemed to slip

away. I was left with huge gaps and a yearning for
something to fill them.

My realization, my understanding and acceptance of my
place in the university, did not come about overnight, by
any means. One of the greatest factors in my enlightenment,
what allowed me to find a ''home base,'' was finding a
subject that really ''turned me on.'' This is what
happened when I discovered theater. Each day I look
forward to class. Everything is so new and exciting and
challenging that I have no trouble finding the energy I
need to devote to rehearsals, reading and attending plays,
and watching TV to study individual actors and learn their
techniques. I am limited only by the amount of time in a
day! It's great! Not only has it filled the large
creative gap that had formed in me, but it has also given
me a much-improved outlook on other aspects of school.
Theater has helped me to find a center, a focus.

A recent conversation with my boyfriend also helped me
to see the light that actually had been blinding me all
along. He is in much the same predicament as I was, with
similar feelings of directionlessness. We differ because
he hasn't been turned on yet, and he is choosing to divert
his attention from college because he doesn't think
there's anything here for him. Of course, I've argued
that he hasn't looked closely enough; but I've argued from
my angle, with my newly inspired ambition and love of
learning. I have not changed his mind. The ends just
don't meet.

It might be awful to say, but, if anything, this
discrepancy between us has reinforced my attitude towards
the university and learning. He has made me see that now,
at 18 years old, basically completely taken care of, open-
minded, ambitious, and, yes, full of gaps, I am at the
prime time for learning and for other good things to take
place. The way those gaps are filled, and what fills
them, will constitute my underlying form, which is what
will be the future me. Seeing the problem reflected in

the mirror of my boyfriend has helped me see myself in a better perspective. Unfortunately, he has been hurt.

Understanding that the underlying form of the future me is in process now helps me resolve certain conflicts I am having with my parents, conflicts I frequently wrote about in my PDJ. They want me to be practical, economically oriented, and guaranteed a good job when I finish college. But I'm <u>not</u> practical--at least not yet; money is not my number one priority now, and who knows what I'll be doing when I'm finished with school. But, they're the fund-providers, and I love them very much, and would like very much to please them. But these conflicts are resolved, or at least tempered, by the intensity I now have for school and for finding something that I will enjoy doing for the rest of my life. I am going to strive to stay turned on like this always. I must be choosy and somewhat selfish in my decisions, and must not be negatively persuaded by outside influences. After all, the quality I find, take part in, and contribute to <u>is</u> my responsibility. Isn't that right, Mr. Pirsig?

My discoveries have given me much peace of mind. I know there are rough times ahead, but at least now I have a center of focus and a direction in which to head. I have found something that I really like, and, though I may change my mind in the future, it has helped me to resolve many of the incongruities that plagued me. I realize how important the decisions and choices that I will be making in the next four years or so are for the evolving me. And I realize that these decisions must be made by me and only me.

———————

Trina's essay is an effective ethical essay by most of the criteria mentioned earlier. In its present form, it is not a perfect essay; there are some technical problems she will have to attend to in revision. In fact, it is a "grand failure" in the best sense of the term. It cannot be finished, yet it cannot be forgotten.

There is plenty to like about this essay. Reminiscent of the hymn "Amazing Grace" with its line, "I once was lost, but now am found/ Was blind but now I see," the overall attitude of the essay is most attractive. Trina describes an insight that enlightens her, helps her understand why she is in school and what she should be doing there. In this large sense, this positive, upbeat (Trina calls it "turned-on") sense, the essay calls out a positive response in readers. It connects and creates the dynamic of sympathy by its honesty and enthusiasm, and its resolve to confront the future healthfully.

In terms of the peer critique questions, the essay succeeds on several levels. In terms of the first evaluation question, Trina explains her insight that purposefulness—having a sense of what she is doing and why—motivates her, inspires her, to actively engage in school and affirms her sense of self. Her interest in learning about theater is the source of her sense of purpose and the source of a feeling of membership in a community. She discusses the implications of this insight in terms of her relationships with her boyfriend and her parents, stating that her sense of purpose strengthens her against their questions and doubts. In fact, she knows she belongs by recognizing that her boyfriend does not.

It is an ambitious essay. Because the problems she addresses are interesting and are applicable to almost anyone who has left home to go to college, the essay assumes a relevance for readers beyond Trina herself. While the essay may be specifically about her involvement with theater, it is also about any person's discovery of an intense interest in some subject or project and how that makes life enjoyable. Thus, the essay is personal but not egotistic.

On another level, the essay is about enthusiasm and the need to have a positive attitude toward life and living. In an interesting little prose poem, Charles Baudelaire discusses the phenomenon of enthusiasm and its role in shaping a positive attitude toward life. He uses the metaphor of inebriation—drunkeness—to describe total involvement in an activity: Be it wine, or love, or poetry—get drunk!

GET DRUNK!

Charles Baudelaire

One should always be drunk. That's all that matters; that's our one imperative need. So as not to feel Time's horrible burden that breaks your shoulders and bows you down, you must get drunk without ceasing.

But what with? With wine, with poetry, or with virtue, as you choose. But get drunk.

And if, at some time, on the steps of a palace, in the green grass of a ditch, in the bleak solitude of your room, you are waking up when drunkenness has already abated, ask the wind, the wave, a star, the clock, all that which flees, all that which groans, all that which rolls, all that which sings, all that which speaks, ask them what time it is; and the wind, the wave, the star, the bird, the clock will reply: "It is time to get drunk! So that you may not be the martyred slaves of Time, get drunk; get drunk, and never pause for rest! With wine, with poetry, or with virtue, as you choose!"

Source: Charles Baudelaire, *Twenty Prose Poems*, Michael Hamburger, trans. London: Jonathan Cape, 1968.

For Trina her drink is theater and her desire to learn about acting. For another it may be writing and trying to help others learn to write and enjoy writing. What is it for you? The essay is about enthusiasm, about Trina's and about the enthusiasm with which we should all confront life. Focusing on this common theme, she avoids the trap of egotism and makes an important statement about a generally relevant concern.

The second evaluation question concerns the writer's voice, whether it seems honest and informed. Trina's paper succeeds in this respect. Trina takes a chance at the beginning of the essay with her confession that through most of the semester she felt "confused and aimless." She claims she was obsessed by the nagging question: "What am I doing here?" At the same time, she mentions that she has just connected many discoveries and found some answers. This stance—I have a problem and I think I've solved it—is very effective in establishing a sense of "presence," a connection between a writer and her readers. While the writer is clearly Trina Chambers and so the product of her singular experience, it could also be anyone who has had this problem and has solved it. Because she writes with an authentic voice, the essay is the real thing, not just a school exercise she is completing as an obligation. She is working out a real problem. She seems honest; readers believe her.

How does Trina take care of the problem of projecting herself as "informed?" Remember Thoreau and his assertion that he knows himself best. Obviously this paper is about Trina, and she knows herself. But that is not enough. What makes the essay most credible is Trina's use of evidence. Note how she makes reference to both her PDJ and *Zen and the Art of Motorcycle Maintenance*. She has gone back to her PDJ and analyzed it. She has abstracted recurring themes and connected them with her present problem. She has found the problem, done her research, and become an authority as a result.

Note also that she uses Pirsig's concept of "underlying form" as the central and unifying concept of the essay. Rather than remain inside her own experience and language, she uses Pirsig's terminology and in so doing makes herself a part of a tradition which, as Pirsig establishes in his book, goes all the way back to the Greeks. She steps out of her immediate context and joins a long established tradition. Not just Trina Chambers but also Pirsig and Plato are part of the struggle toward identity, self-confidence, and group membership. By joining the larger tradition, Trina adds "authority" to her voice.

Does this strategy work? Some critical readers might say she has made a noble effort to expand her argument into the larger tradition, but that she has failed. This may be a valid criticism. The problem is that she borrows the concept of "underlying form" whole from Pirsig—("Thanks, Mr. Pirsig"). She does not establish a context nor does she elaborate the concept. She uses it as Pirsig does. She does not, however, prove that she sufficiently understands the concept to "own" it herself.

She could solve this problem by taking a paragraph or two to define "underlying form" as Pirsig uses it, at the same time explaining its relation to the long tradition of inquiry going back to Plato. She needs to state explicitly how she is using the term. This minor and manageable revision would solve the problem of authority in Trina's voice. Did you, as a peer respondent, suggest a similar revision?

Such revisions are an opportunity to make a good essay even better. Remember your responsibility to provide accurate and usable responses that will help writers during revision.

The third evaluation question asks whether Trina establishes a relation of sympathy between her and her readers. Trina's peers responded with enthusiasm suggesting that they were drawn into the paper, that the spark of sympathy existed for them. But how does she do it? What "angle" does she use to bring us into her essay? What does she teach us about ourselves?

This is a difficult question to answer because Trina's paper succeeds through the interaction of tone and message. Basically the paper is a demonstration of its own thesis: that purposefulness and enthusiasm are means of extracting the most from life. And its tone is one of enthusiasm and open-mindedness. In essence, the essay demonstrates the value of its argument by its argument. Thus, as readers we become witnesses and participants; we experience the "sympathy" that makes an ethical essay work.

The essay begins by asserting the value of Trina's discovery of interest in theater and demonstrates how this inspires her, giving her a sense of purpose and resolve more than adequate to counter the immediate personal problems she encounters with school, her boyfriend, and her parents. The essay further argues that purposefulness is a prerequisite for satisfaction and personal fulfillment. As a consequence, the essay exists on two levels: Trina's problem with its solution *and* the general statement about humans and their need for purposefulness. This expansiveness, individual experience becoming human experience, an individual voice merging with the human voice, is another means Trina uses to create sympathy. Her honesty, her directness, her joy in finding purpose, her enlightenment—all these characteristics combine to make the essay effective. All of them together create the sympathy.

Hearing Trina's voice connecting with the human voice allows us as readers to make another important connection, the connection in which we learn about ourselves. When we discover that the essay is really about enthusiasm, and that the claim originates in Trina's personal experience, then Trina has sensitized us and helped us bring our own memory and experience to the essay. As a result, we see ourselves in her. We remember our own important discoveries about positive attitudes, about enthusiasm and our personal responsibility to make the best of any situation. Or we are encouraged to look for similar means of getting "turned on" in our own lives. Through Trina's essay, we are brought to our own experience and are reinvigorated, reconvinced of the value of our insights. It works for Trina; it works for us as readers. We are together; we share sympathy.

It is not so important that readers agree with the message of an ethical essay as it is that the essay bring us back to ourselves *through* the writer. We saw it happen in Trina's essay which is based on a common experience. We are members of the human community dealing with common problems. She has proved herself to be an authoritative voice on one problem and its solution. We accept her contribution. She has informed us and has caused us to revitalize our connection with the human community. More important than teaching us any particular lesson, any specific information, more important than convincing us that she is right or persuading us that we should study theater, she has forged a bond between us. By discovering who she is, she has reminded us of who we are. This is the purpose of the essay.

A Student Sample with Analysis: Sympathy and Uncommon Experience

The second sample essay serves as model of a different approach to the assignment. Marie Turner's "Florence Nightingale Was Not Just a Camp Follower" does not describe a single insight and its consequences for informing a life. Rather, it addresses a professional dilemma Marie and other nurses confront every day: nurses act and their actions have a direct life-and-death impact on their patients' lives; they must act responsibly.

Like "Notes and Comments" and "My War," these two student essays stand on different ends of a continuum. Trina uses an insight to begin to break through a problem. Enthusiasm and hope that the insight will indeed solve the problem make the essay succeed. Marie, on the other hand, uses her extensive nursing experience to illustrate and justify a solution to a serious professional problem. The essay is credible; it succeeds because the problem has been solved. Her continuing to work testifies to her solution. While Trina experiences an insight and generalizes her conclusions, Marie reflects on experience to prove that she has successfully handled a problem. Trina is joining a community; Marie is reporting the consequence of long experience as a member of a community. Trina's belief is rooted in some experience and hope. Marie's comes from expert experience. Trina teaches us by letting us believe we as readers are like her. Marie uses her special knowledge, her professional authority, to *teach* others, especially nurses, how to live. The differences are striking, yet both are successful essays.

Marie Turner
Essay #7: Ethical Essay

Florence Nightingale Wasn't Just a Camp Follower

Today's newspaper carried the story of a nurse in Tennessee who killed a patient with an overdose of insulin, an accidental overdose, but an accident which can't be retracted or helped by a sincere, ''I'm sorry.'' The accident occurred when the nurse misread an order for 5 units of regular insulin I-V every hour for four hours. She read and gave 50 units of regular insulin I-V every hour for four hours. This is all that is reported in the paper, not whether the nurse is prone to

mistakes, not whether she was under more stress than usual
at the time of the error, not even whether she was
experienced, respected by her peers, or a nice lady. We
can surmise that there will be a lawsuit, else, why a
newspaper story? And we know that nice lady or not,
experienced or not, stressed or not, her mistake caused
the death of a human being, and it cannot go unnoticed.

As a fellow nurse, I am not about the business of
condemning my colleague, nor of exonerating her, for her
actions and the resulting tragedy. I am trying only to
make plain my feelings about personal responsibility and
accountability. The importance of individual accountability
for my actions is equal in my personal and professional
life, but I will deal here only with my professional
accountability.

The story in today's paper offers evidence of a fact
known to most health care professionals. Nurses can kill
people. When I went to nursing school I wasn't taught
immediately that I was going to be able to kill a person,
because this knowledge would have been much more than I
wanted to know early in my education. First I had to be
hooked on the idea that I could actually make a positive
difference in a person's life, and the better nurse I
could be, the more difference I could make. Here was my
first reason for learning as much as I could learn.

Then gradually I began to learn that not everyone can
be helped with drugs and surgery, some can only be comforted
and cared for while they await death. Now I needed to
learn something of this difference, and to begin to
recognize that sitting and listening can sometimes work
more miracles and relieve more pain than morphine. This
was a new concept, but one I began to appreciate as I
slowly lost my fear of holding the hand of a dying man or
woman.

Finally, I learned that, as a nurse, I could cause the
death of another. This concept far outweighed holding
death's hand on the fear scale. I discovered that I could
cause death without even giving it a thought. As a matter

of fact, carelessness is much more frequently a cause of death than is malice. My God! It's so simple to do. All it takes is inattentiveness, laziness, or ignorance. So there it was, another reason to learn all I could. Perhaps, this reason seems less noble than the others, but I could never underestimate its importance, or the competence it could produce.

The nurse in Tennessee was giving insulin not for the specific purpose of reducing the patient's blood sugar, its most common use; she was giving it because it has the property of driving potassium into the cell, thereby reducing serum potassium levels. Her patient had dangerously high serum potassium levels, and reduced renal function, or other methods would no doubt have been employed. She needed to know that her patient was seriously compromised by the risks of renal failure, by cardiac arrhythmias due to the elevated serum potassium, and now by the use of insulin. Maybe she knew these things. Maybe she was not familiar with the use of insulin for the reduction of potassium, maybe she thought 50 units of I-V insulin every hour was a reasonable dose in this setting. More likely though, she was busy, stressed, and unfamiliar with a number of things. She probably thought she was carrying out the doctor's orders, just doing as she was told, and didn't give it another thought. Repeating the mistake three times suggests she couldn't have been thinking very clearly about her actions. As it turns out, the doctor had written a perfectly reasonable order, the nurse read the order inaccurately, made an error and caused harm to the patient. Given the limited information in the newspaper account, there can be no doubt where the responsibility lies.

Would the picture change if the doctor had written the order for 50 units instead of for 5 units?

About five years ago, in another place, I was working one night on a medical unit, and I was given a message by another nurse, along with a new order for one of my

patients. The doctor had spoken to this nurse, giving an
order for a drug in a dosage that was nearly guaranteed to
kill the patient. I questioned the nurse. She said she
was certain of the order. In fact, she had repeated it
back to the doctor for confirmation before she hung up the
phone. What a way to start a shift!

After consulting with my supervisor and the pharmacist,
who both agreed that the dose was inappropriate, I called
the doctor, confirmed that the order was understood, and
questioned the appropriateness of the medication. After
some discussion, I told him that I could not give the
drug. He was not pleased to have his order thwarted, and
actually came to the unit later in the shift to discuss
his displeasure with me. He seemed impatient as I tried
to explain about being accountable for my actions. Then
he sought to relieve my anxiety on that account.

In his view, I had discharged my responsibility in the
matter by questioning the order. Once he confirmed that
the order was, indeed, what he intended, I was then to
give the drug with a clear conscience, knowing the
responsibility to be his. He maintained this to be the
case even if he told me to give strychnine. Bizarre!

I showed him where he could find the drug, telling him
that he should feel free to give it, but I maintained that
I would not give it. In his turn, he too, chose not to
give the drug.

In spite of his threats to ''have my job,'' I remained
employed. The patient wasn't killed by either of us that
day. Neither of us suffered more than the discomfort of
the situation.

The question of error was removed from this situation.
There was no doubt regarding the drug, the dosage, or the
intent of the doctor. Giving the medication would, quite
possibly, have not caused anyone to bat an eye, even if
the patient had died as a result. In fact, his death and
the drug might not have been connected except by me; the
patient was, after all, an old man. Giving the drug would

have certainly been a way to avoid the unpleasant confrontation that refusal provoked. But giving the drug would have been a violation of all that I have come to believe about my responsibility to others and myself to behave in a responsible manner.

Those of us occupying positions in which we wield power over others must recognize the responsibility joined inseparably to that power. The ability to preserve or not preserve, to make a positive difference in a person's life, is not just a job, it is, quite realistically, a trust which cannot be abused.

The fact that life and death decisions are made daily by doctors and by nurses is a burden that they must bear. The burden can be lightened, but not removed, by an educated conscience and by the habit of prudent behavior. It isn't enough for me to say that I shouldn't cause harm to come to another. This will only keep me from kicking an old man in the street. Unless I add the imperative to learn the consequences of certain actions and to follow through on that knowledge, I haven't satisfied the requirements of responsible behavior.

On occasion it will be uncomfortable to follow through with responsible behavior; more often though, the results are worth the momentary discomfort. There have been many occasions when I questioned a doctor's orders, presented the physician with questions and showed great reluctance to follow the order. The first time such an occasion occurred, I called the doctor with my problem. He listened and then asked me to identify myself again. When I did identify myself, he laughed a little and said, ''Well, Marie, you're young.'' Then he gave me a quick but thorough class on the theory behind giving comparatively large doses, ''loading doses,'' when first starting a patient on digitalis. He followed this with this advice, ''Keep on asking questions when you've got them.'' I gave the drug, have given many similar doses since then, and have always remembered to ask the questions. Most times the questioned order leads to some discussion, sometimes to changed orders, and sometimes to short courses on the whys and wherefores of certain actions. Only three times in eighteen years have I been made to feel acutely uncomfortable because of my questioning. In all three instances I maintained my position because it was the only right thing to do, and in all three instances I believe I kept a patient from dying by my hand.

The Report From the Board of Nursing: (15, No. 1 [Spring 1985], Albuquerque, NM) states, ''Licensure is the responsibility of the individual. Individuals cannot work under another individual's license.'' Neither can I work on another's conscience. I am responsible for my actions and will be held accountable for my actions legally and morally. Thus, in light of the power I have because of my profession, I must also accept the responsibility to know all I can reasonably know in my area of practice and must behave prudently based on that knowledge. This responsibility of mine encompasses not just the need to develop my abilities to do, but the need to recognize limits and, when necessary, refuse to do.

Marie's paper can stand on its own. In your analysis, consider why it succeeds. Complete the evaluation questions and discuss them with a peer or as a class activity.

ASSIGNMENT: REVISE YOUR ESSAY

Use the ethical essay peer critique questions to get several reactions to the finished draft of your essay. In the same way the questions helped us evaluate the student samples, you can use it to check whether your draft is on track.

Responses to Question 1 will help you determine whether you need to re-cycle into the discovery phase in order to work more on moving your personal meanings outward for the public audience. In addition, the summaries will let you know whether the structure you designed placed significant information in prominent positions and contributed to your readers' understanding. Responses to Question 2 will help you check whether you communicated your position clearly, whether you established an honest and authoritative voice. Peer responses may also make you aware of other considerations that could strengthen your essay. Responses to

Question 3 will check the relationship you have struck with your readers and help you determine whether you established sufficient sympathy for them to learn from your essay.

Consider the peer responses and complete a self-assessment to bring you back to your work. Then begin reshaping and rephrasing, editing and proofreading. Use the information and experience provided by evaluating both Trina's and Marie's essays and all that you have learned about yourself and writing in the course while revising your essay. Assert the authority of your experience and claim membership in a community as Trina and Marie did. Take this final opportunity to put all you have learned about WRITING FOR THE INSIDE and WRITING FOR THE OUTSIDE to work WRITING THE INSIDE OUT.

The Writer's Resources

INTRODUCTION

You have abundant personal resources that, once developed, will help you become a good writer. Personal experience, natural language competence, and previous training, combined with awareness of the writing process and plenty of practice will guide you through the many choices confronting you as a writer.

To make good choices, however, you must be aware of alternatives. To discover alternatives, you must be familiar with the writer's basic resources. These include *invention*, which is the process of investigating a subject so you can discover what you know and want to write about it, and *basic language skills*, which include your ability to select appropriate words and to use grammar, mechanics, and style for writing correct and effective sentences. This appendix will discuss these subjects and provide you with procedures and exercises designed to help you gain control of them. As a writer, you are responsible for learning about these resources and developing the skills that will allow you to use them effectively.

ON INVENTION

INVENTION: DISCOVERING AND EVALUATING IDEAS FOR WRITING

Invention may seem a strange term to use in reference to writing, but it is part of a tradition that goes as far back as the ancient Greeks. Simply stated, invention is the process of discovering and developing ideas for use in writing. It provides procedures that help us manage and organize ideas in the discovery phase. It guides us as we explore our experience and knowledge and warns us when we lack knowledge or information so we can consult other sources of information. Obviously, invention activities are most useful during the earliest stages of writing, when we are trying to master our subject, to understand it so we can determine what we want to say about it to our audience.

The specific procedures developed to guide us through invention are called *heuristics*. The root for the term is the Greek word for inventing or discovering. A heuristic establishes specific steps and activities to lead us to discover solutions to a problem. Although there are many heuristics, and some are very complicated, we will consider only four, and we will consider them only in their most basic terms. These four will provide a wide range of approaches to invention and allow you to discover and shape ideas for almost any writing task.

Pay close attention to both invention and heuristics; they are elaborations of how the human mind works. Understanding invention and heuristics will give you insight into the basic modes of thinking and will train you to be more creative and more analytical. If you want more detailed work with creativity and problem-solving, consult Koberg and Bagnall, *Universal Traveler* (Los Altos, CA: William Kaufmann, 1981), which provides a systematic and thorough approach to the general subject of creativity and problem solving.

Discovering Relations: Brainstorming and Bubbling

Brainstorming

After receiving a writing assignment, your first task is to determine what you already known about your subject. Brainstorming is a good way to get started with any writing assignment. When you brainstorm, you list whatever comes to mind about your subject in short, informal phrases. The effect of a brainstorm is to get material out so you can see if you can use it. It is much easier to work with something than with nothing.

Brainstorming works best when you follow a few guidelines:

1. As you brainstorm, *don't analyze* or attempt to figure out the why and how of a word or phrase that comes to you. Just get it down on the list and move to the next word or phrase that comes to mind. Brainstorming works by free association,

not by conventional logic. Writing one idea down jogs an association between that idea and another which may or may not seem immediately related to it. Analyzing relationships between ideas *while* you are brainstorming slows you down, perhaps preventing you from getting to the idea that will finally solve your problem. The whole point of brainstorming is to generate a surplus of ideas—many more than you can use. Later you will come back and evaluate them, develop what seems important, and discard what is irrelevant.

2. Set a *time limit*, perhaps ten minutes, and stick to it. The time limit is a way to give yourself both a sense of urgency and a sense of relief. You must get this task done, but there is a limit to the time you can spend on it. You work harder when you know the job will soon be done. Setting the time limit is a way to manage and motivate the creativity on which brainstorming depends.

3. Give yourself a *focal word* and build your brainstorm around it. The focal word can be the key word in the problem or question you are considering. It is the subject. The focal word will provide you with an immediate stimulus and direction that will help you get to work. It is the shove that gets you started in the right direction. For example, you are writing an essay examining the concept of freedom. "Freedom" becomes the focal word, and you brainstorm on any associations the word triggers in your mind. The focal word will help you discover material to define, illustrate, contrast, or analyze any subject.

LOG EXERCISE: Brainstorming

To gain some experience with brainstorming as a systematic means of generating ideas, work with one of the following subjects: loneliness, parenting, or snow skiing. Follow the advice on analysis, time limits, and focal words provided above. Complete this exercise in your Learning Log before proceeding any further in this section. You will need the brainstorm to complete subsequent exercises.

Remember the golden rule of brainstorming: your purpose is to generate as much material as possible. Do not analyze. Associate!

Bubbling

Bubbling helps you make sense of a brainstorm. It forces you to discover or create relationships among the various items on the brainstorm list. The bubbles are merely circles you draw around the items and connect them with other lines to help you see relationships. Through bubbling, the ideas in a brainstorm become material you can begin to shape into logical patterns.

The trick to bubbling is determining how certain items in the brainstorm relate to the focal word and to one another. For example, a brainstorm on snow skiing generated the following odd mixture of items. Do not be surprised by the variety of these items; brainstorming works by free association whose ways we do not always understand.

Snow Skiing

blinding snow and sun	running
broken shoulder	hockey
Maine	swimming
softball	sailing
Rich Flinn	camping
bindings	fishing
crutches	trout
fireplace	hamburgers
horse racing	ribs
fear—out of control	barbecue
falling off the mountain	sausage
mountain's majesty	picnics
Sierra Blanca	Frank
the desert	snow-covered cactus

When we bubble after brainstorming, our job is to determine which of the items on the list are related to one another and how. To simplify organizing the list, we will consider ideas to be (1) coordinate (equal to one another), (2) super-ordinate (one greater than another), (3) subordinate (one a part of another), or (4) irrelevant (not related to one another).

In the example brainstorm, you can see that there are chains of associations. The string of ideas in the second column beginning with swimming and continuing through fishing, is obviously an associative chain. They are all parallel and equal to one another—*coordinate*. Thus to represent them in bubble form, we put each in its own bubble, line them up horizontally, and connect them to show their coordinate stature:

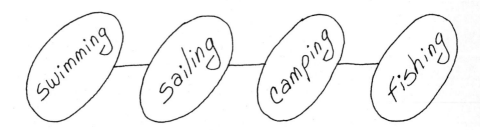

Continuing the process of bubbling, we consider other potential relationships among the sports on the list. We note that they are sports generally associated with warm weather. To show that they are all related—*subordinate*—to the concept of warm weather sports, we add a bubble to illustrate the *superordinate* nature of warm weather sports:

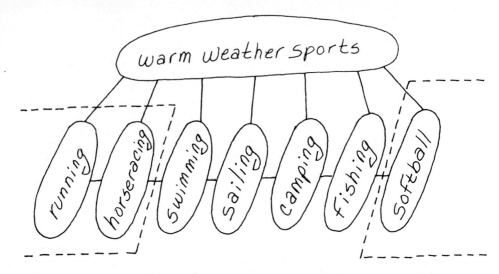

Notice that we have added new coordinate bubbles to include softball, horse racing, and running. They come from different places in the brainstorm list, but they nevertheless fit into the category of warm weather sports. Note how the superordinate has provided a way to organize a large number of the brainstorm items. Various lines now connect the bubbles to indicate relationships: a vertical line up connects a coordinate with a superordinate, a vertical line down connects a coordinate with a subordinate, and horizontal lines connect coordinates.

Analyzing the brainstorm further, we find all kinds of potential connections. We could list snow skiing and hockey as coordinates under a new superordinate, cold weather sports. The new category would itself be coordinate to warm weather sports.

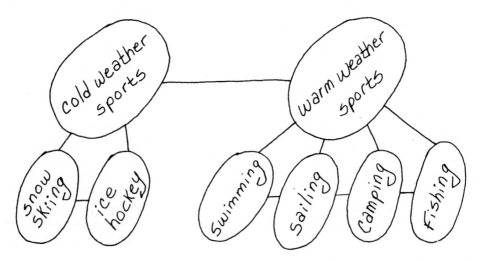

To complete the procedure, we look for a final, all-encompassing superordinate to bring the bubbles into relation. Initially "sports" seems to be the most general category. But this is inaccurate. What all the sports listed have in common is that they generally take place outdoors. That is why weather is one of the primary considerations. The superordinate for these bubbles would be "outdoor sports," which in turn would be coordinate to "indoor sports" represented by the subordinates basketball and gymnastics. Then we might be able to use "sports" as the final superordinate, though sports as classified by playing location would be even more precise.

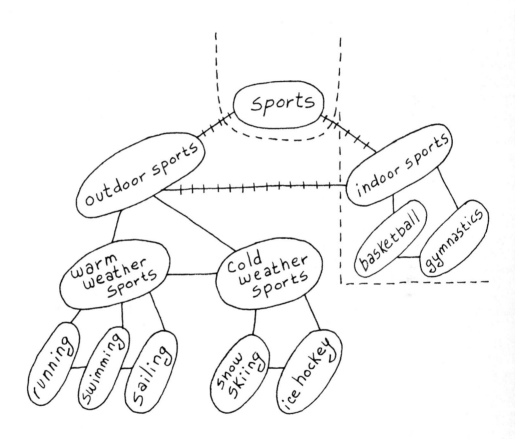

Obviously, we could categorize the elements of this brainstorm in many other ways, but this example should make clear the power of bubbling when organizing material generated by brainstorming. Brainstorming and bubbling have provided not only raw data for an essay, but they have also suggested a pattern of development. To write an essay defining snow skiing as a sport, we could contrast it with the other kinds of sports listed. In fact, we would have too much information. When writing essays, however, we are better off having to eliminate irrelevant material than being stuck for ideas.

LOG EXERCISE: Bubbling

In your Learning Log, bubble the brainstorm you completed a short while ago. Start by selecting a chain of associations, indicate their relation to one another (superordinate, coordinate, subordinate) by positioning the bubbles in relation to one another. Complete the exercise using data available from the brainstorm or stimulated by the bubbling sequence.

Remember that not all the information on your brainstorm list will apply to the particular organizing/categorizing system you develop. You are developing only one of the many potential patterns of organization in the brainstorm.

Finally, speculate on what kind of essay you could write based on this information.

Varying Perspectives: Particle, Wave, Field Analysis

Brainstorming and bubbling provide an easy way to generate some ideas about a subject, but they lack the direction and purposefulness that many writers need when they begin a writing task. A second invention procedure, particle, wave, and field (PWF) analysis, first developed by Young, Becker, and Pike in *Rhetoric: Discovery and Change* (NY: Harcourt Brace Jovanovich, 1970), provides considerable direction. PWF analysis considers any subject, either a physical entity or an event, first as a particle—a single, isolated entity or act—then as a wave—one of several items in a class—and finally as a field—its relation to many other items. PWF analysis works by considering interrelations among phenomena. Rather than discovering these interrelations haphazardly, however, PWF analysis presents a systematic procedure for viewing any subject from these multiple perspectives.

Particle

The first task in PWF analysis is exploring a subject as an individual entity, a particle with unique characteristics unto itself, with a specific identity. What are these characteristics and functions? Whether person, place, or thing, it can be described.

Going back to our earlier brainstorming subjects, consider snow skiing as an isolated discrete entity, a particle. Snow skiing is a outdoor winter sport that can be enjoyed by people of almost any age, as long as they are reasonably healthy and in good physical condition. There are certain prerequisites for snow skiing, including obvious ones like needing an open space and snow, as well as some less obvious ones like having access to adequate equipment including skis, boots and bindings, poles, and appropriate clothing. Snow skiing can be either downhill (alpine) or cross-country (nordic), and these require different kinds of equipment and clothing.

In addition, snow skiing is both pleasurable and dangerous. The pleasure comes from enjoying the crisp, cold air and the natural splendor of a snow-covered mountain. There is joy in the various sensations of speed and fluidity that come from gliding down the hill and feeling more a part of it than merely on it. Pleasure is also available through the social aspects of skiing including meeting people of like mind who have escaped to the alpine heaven for a holiday and have come together to have fun and relax.

Of course, there is also danger involved with snow skiing since speed, surprises on the hill, and other skiers getting in the way can lead to falls and collisions which in turn can result in strained muscles, sprained joints, and broken limbs. Social activities associated with skiing can result in hangovers, colds, and who knows what else. In short, skiing can be a hazardous physical undertaking. These are just a few of the many aspects of snow skiing that can open up as we examine it from the particle perspective.

Wave

The second task in PWF analysis is understanding a subject as a wave, something that is changing and evolving over time, a dynamic object that is part of an ongoing process or larger class.

For snow skiing, we could examine several perspectives. In terms of process, we can consider snow skiing as a range of skills and activities beginning with the rudimentary balance and control required to start down the hill, involving the concentration and control that lets us build speed and deal with curves and turns, culminating in the grace and physical prowess that allows us to change direction quickly to approach and conquer a mogul. We ski over it, extending our bodies and sailing through the air. Finally, we land, regain our balance, control, reestablish direction, and prepare for the next challenge the hill may offer. We also need to know how to use our leg and arm muscles and the ski poles to push ourselves back on our skis after a particularly nasty fall. And we must also remember how to herringbone up the hill to pick up the goggles we lost during that last tumble. Any one or all of these subprocesses of snow skiing could receive attention while we work through the wave element of PWF analysis.

In addition, we might consider snow skiing as a phenomenon that has developed over time. We could write with success about the evolution of equipment including the development of sophisticated bindings that greatly reduce the chances of injury, changes in ski design to increase speed and improve control, changes in the nature of ski resorts, whatever. The choices seem endless. Many alternatives arise when we begin to consider snow skiing from the vantage point of a wave, part of a continuum or process that develops over time.

Field

The final task in PWF analysis is viewing a subject as part of a field. Here the subject becomes an entity or activity within a network of interrelations, part of a system that is itself part of even greater systems.

As we write about snow skiing from this perspective, we have to decide how it fits among others of its kind. As a sport, how does snow skiing compare with hiking or bicycle riding? As a form of exercise, how does it compare with aerobic dancing or running? As a form of leisure activity, how does it compare with going to a football game or sunning on the beach? As part of the economy of the forest, how does it complement or compete with other activities like wood cutting, mining, or hunting and trapping? As we consider a subject from the field perspective, we begin to understand and appreciate the many systems of which it is a part.

Recognizing Limitations

As we examine subjects from the particle, wave, and field perspectives, we learn more and more. Our quick analysis of snow skiing has shown us what we could write. But another important benefit of PWF analysis is that as we learn about our subject in each context, *we also learn what we do not know but should look into before we begin to write.*

To complete our consideration of snow skiing as a particle, we may need to consult other skiers, experts, or books and magazine articles available in the library to determine how important physical conditioning is to the skier. Are there people who absolutely should not ski because of the sport's physical demands? Should people with back or joint problems or people with asthma who are acutely sensitive to cold air be encouraged to ski? How can we find out? Perhaps an interview or a visit to the library is in order.

In wave analysis we must recognize the limitations of our knowledge and supplement it. How do we find information about old-time bindings and other equipment? As part of wave analysis, where must we go to find how skiing affects the economy of the forest? All these are questions we can ask and, with a little effort, answer by completing a PWF analysis of snow skiing. We have discovered not only what we know, but also what we do not know and must learn before we can write effectively. PWF analysis can help us determine our readiness to write about almost any subject.

LOG EXERCISE: PWF Analysis

Use the procedure presented above to complete a PWF analysis of one of the following subjects: a favorite book, the seashore, or the American dream.

As you proceed through the analysis make sure to attend to the following:

1. PARTICLE: What is it by itself? Describe its individual characteristics. What makes it what it is?
2. WAVE: What process or sequence of events is your subject a part of? In this respect, how has it changed through time? What does it contribute to the larger process?
3. FIELD: In what larger context or field does your subject belong? How does it affect that context? How does the context affect it?

If you get stuck in any of the perspectives, return to the example of snow skiing for clarification. Complete the PWF analysis in your Learning Log.

After you have completed your PWF analysis, consult with someone who worked with the same subject. Consider what your analyses have in common and how they differ. Try to account for these similarities and differences. Are they attributable to individual experience, or are they a result of the nature of the subject? Did you miss any important information? How can you expand your perspectives next time to avoid missing important information? Spend time thinking about and discussing these problems to help make your next experience with PWF analysis more productive. Be prepared to share your PWF analysis with the class.

Considering Context: The Journalistic Questions and Burke's Pentad

Another simple but effective means of discovering information about a subject—uncovering what you know, discovering what you do not know, and determining ways to find out what you need to know—are the five questions journalists use when investigating a story:

Who	Who are the important characters playing a role in the event or subject you are investigating?
What	What happened? What was the significant outcome?
When	When did it happen? Did the time of the occurrence affect the outcome or significance of the event?
Where	Where did the event take place? Did the location influence the event or its significance?
Why	What caused the event to occur? What motivated the actors? What was their purpose? What effects did the event cause?

The framework supplied by these journalistic questions can provide a wealth of information you can use while writing. The procedure is a simple one that you have probably completed many times before. It can be an effective way to get started and gain momentum when writing.

Kenneth Burke, a contemporary rhetorician and philosopher, designed a more elaborate application of the journalistic questions. His procedure, called the Pentad because it uses five factors in its analysis, allows a writer to probe a situation or subject in terms of its dynamics. An action or event is like a drama unfolding over time which is influenced by its participants' motivations and purposes. Specifically, the Pentad considers these five factors:

1. The action: What happened?
2. The actors: Who played a part in the action?
3. The scene: Where did the action take place?
4. The means: What was used to complete the action?
5. The purpose: What did the actors hope to accomplish?

As you may have already noticed, the journalistic questions and the Pentad differ in kind from either brainstorming and bubbling or PWF analysis. Rather than being applicable to general activities or concepts, these heuristics are situational and help us analyze particular events. While brainstorming, bubbling, and PWF analysis lend themselves to analyzing the fixed elements of a subject, like the bindings used on snow skis, the journalistic questions and the Pentad lend themselves to analyzing the evolving or dynamic aspects of a subject, like a ski race or serious skiing accident.

The point is that heuristics are not universally applicable. Each has its own advantage, which is why writers need to understand and be able to use several. Writers need a variety of heuristics to deal with the variety of subjects they will confront. The Pentad can help us understand events in history, in literature, or in contemporary politics.

Applying the Pentad

To give you a sense of how productive the Pentad can be as a means of discovering information and meaning, we will put it to work on Theodore Roethke's short poem, "My Papa's Waltz."

MY PAPA'S WALTZ

The whiskey on your breath
Could make a small boy dizzy;
But I hung on like death:
Such waltzing was not easy.

We romped until the pans
Slid from the kitchen shelf;
My mother's countenance
Could not unfrown itself.

The hand that held my wrist
Was battered on one knuckle;
At every step you missed
My right ear scraped a buckle.

You beat time on my head
With a palm caked hard by dirt,
Then waltzed me off to bed
Still clinging to your shirt.

At first glance, the poem seems a description of an insignificant incident in the life of a child. Working through the Pentad, however, we will find that this simplicity belies a deeper significance. Responses to the first three elements of the Pentad come easily from a close rereading of the poem.

Action: The poem describes a scene in which a child dances with his father, the dance finally ending with the child being "waltzed" off to his bed. A frowning mother witnesses the dance.

Actors: There are three actors. The boy is small, dwarfed by his father's size and actions, and he must hold tight through the "romp" despite having his ear scraped by the belt buckle. The boy is also the narrator of the poem. Papa is the second actor. He seems to be a hard-working man. The description of his mud-caked hands and battered knuckle suggests that he is a working man, perhaps a laborer. He has had a few whiskeys while relaxing after a day's work. He dances his son joyfully around the kitchen and off to bed. The mother is a third, silent actor whose frowning countenance does not seem to compromise the father's joy.

Scene: The poem takes place in a working-class home, between the kitchen and boy's bed, probably on a weekend. The kitchen is a significant room in such households. It is the center of the house, the place where the family spends most of its time together. Typically, the kitchen is associated with the pleasures of living, like good meals and good talk in front of steaming coffee cups. Note also how the dance ends with the boy clinging to Papa's shirt. Does he cling because he is afraid of being dropped or because he does not want to let go and let the vital dance be ended by quiet sleep?

Means: Here is where the Pentad begins to take us more deeply into the poem. We find that there are two levels at work here. On the surface level, we might respond that the means of the action were the whiskey that loosened Papa up and the invisible music of the waltz that may have been supplied by an unmentioned radio or phonograph. The poem is a simple vignette of working-class life. On another level, though, we become aware that the incident is related by a narrator who is no longer a child, who is remembering a joyous dance on a night long ago and far away, if not in real space, at least in the sense of psychological or life space. The poem is the means by which the boy who is now a man brings his father back to life.

We realize that details have been purposefully chosen. The first stanza sets up what could be a frightening scene with the potential to bring harm to the child: the child hangs on like "death." But the poem ends with the boy seeming not to want the dance to come to an end; he wants to be with Papa, not to go to bed. The second stanza reinforces this irony. The mother worries about the pans sliding off the shelves. These pans, the kitchen—the center of her world—are being jeopardized for a time by the crazy waltz. No wonder she frowns. If she wanted to smile and laugh, she probably could not because she is so busy worrying.

All this is to say that at least two levels are at work in the poem. The first is the level of detail and plot—what seems to be happening. The second is the level of significance or interpretation—the meaning the poem holds for writer and reader. Interpretation is what the final elements of the Pentad probe. We are forced to go back through the earlier elements in order to add more information than we previously had. The Pentad works back on itself, helping us discover more and more significance in the poem.

Purpose: Again we see the Pentad's richness. Stated most simply, Roethke creates a fond remembrance of childhood, a time forever gone, which, as a consequence, must leave a bittersweet taste in his mouth and ours. Gone are those simple days. Dead are those wonderful people. The poem should not make us morbid; it should take us back to similar times in our own lives to remember them fondly. Perhaps the poem will remind us to tell those who mean much to us and who will not live forever that we love and appreciate them.

Heuristics and the Problem of Complexity

As mentioned earlier, the Pentad is a powerful system writers can use to discover information about an event. Although we have applied the Pentad to a poem, it is as effective when used to analyze a historical event. The Pentad can help us discover what happened and why, how the various elements in a situation work together to invest events with significance.

Take the United States' involvement in Vietnam, for example. Through researching and reading about the war, its actors, and its consequences, we can use the Pentad to unmask the complexity of seemingly simple facts. Consider the 58,132 names covering the Vietnam memorial in Washington. Each name seems a simple fact, a victim of the war. But each name hides a drama that can become available to us through interest, energy, and a system like the Pentad.

There is a double edge to the problem of complexity. As a writer, you want to avoid the trap of single-issue responses and oversimplification, the kind of response that would call "My Papa's Waltz" a frightening memory of spouse and child abuse attributable to alcoholism. At the same time you must also avoid being deluged, overwhelmed, and ultimately frustrated by the amount of information that invention techniques can produce. A complex system like the Pentad can help you survey a broad territory and stake a claim. When you write, however, you must limit your subject and direct yourself to an area in which you can make an effective point or communicate important information. You must protect yourself from areas so vast that you can wrestle no manageable point from the complexity.

With very complicated subjects such as the war in Vietnam, you can use the Pentad to discover and limit the broad subject to a specific one that is interesting to you and to your readers, and one that you can manage. The trick is to focus on a particular event related to your area of interest, for example, the fall of Saigon. Working systematically through the Pentad focusing on that event—the scene, the actors, the means and motivations—and following various leads through reference materials such as books and articles, interviews with participants and so forth, will give you more than enough information to create an interesting and informative report, a thoughtful and suggestive commentary, or whatever type of final written product you want. You have limited the topic and gotten your information from the heuristic and the areas it directed you to explore. That is its purpose.

Varying procedures to meet the demands of varying subjects and writing assignments is an important lesson. We must not become slaves to heuristic procedures. We must use them to liberate ourselves from ignorance and purposelessness. If you can see the value and application of these various heuristics as strategies to help you discover what you know and what you need to find out, then you have come a long way down the road to becoming a good writer.

LOG EXERCISE: Using the Pentad

Choose a significant historical or contemporary event and use Burke's Pentad to discover what you already know and what you need to find out in order to write a report on the issue. Events as large as the Vietnam War and the *Challenger* space-shuttle disaster, or as limited as a minor argument between friends, can be fruitfully analyzed by applying the Pentad.

Note, however, that complex subjects sometimes offer quick and simple, single-issue answers. Such answers are generally inadequate and require systematic analysis and research based on the procedures we have practiced.

Complete this exercise in your Learning Log. Be prepared to share your results with your classmates.

The Topoi: A Knowledge Nautilus

There is one more system, another set of questions or activities, to consider before ending our discussion of invention. Though we discuss it last, it has been around the longest. Since Aristotle of classical Greece and before, rhetoricians have trained their students in the use of the *topoi* to discover information about a subject. *Topoi* means places or locations; they are like rooms in the brain where particular exercises or activities take place. Imagine them to be like a mental Nautilus exercise center, a gymnasium for the mind, where various machines are available whose correct use can produce total intellectual fitness. In terms of invention, total fitness is coming to a complete understanding of a subject.

What is most interesting about the concept of the *topoi* is that, as a set of rooms or places where particular intellectual activities take place, they are comprehensive and complete. Theoretically, if you take your subject systematically through all the rooms and complete all the exercises, you will know all there is to know about that subject. In fact, some rhetoricians believe that the *topoi* reflect the fundamental ways humans think. Working through the *topoi* guarantees that the writer has thought about and come to know a subject in all the ways a human can. Obviously, using the *topoi* is a very powerful invention system.

You already have experience with some of the *topoi* because they are part of the heuristics we have practiced. We will discuss them here only briefly and consider them as a checklist you can use to evaluate your knowledge of a subject. If you work through one of the rooms, then you will know something about a subject. But do not not trust yourself to write then because such partial knowledge often generates poor writing. You may embarrass yourself through ignorance. If you work through several of the rooms, then you know the subject well enough for your writing to accomplish a particular and limited purpose. If you work through all the rooms, then you have a rigorous and comprehensive intellectual understanding of a subject. You are equipped to write about it.

Here are the *topoi*, selected and adapted for our purposes and accompanied by questions that will help you begin working through the rooms and the mental exercises required in each. In each instance we will develop questions from the *topoi* designed to help us inventory our knowledge of hats. Though the subject may seem trivial, working it through the *topoi* will illustrate how much there is to know about hats and how significance can lurk behind the obvious. Get yourself a hat to put before you as we work through what the *topoi* can teach us about hats.

Description

To describe an object, we must observe its minute details; then we must mentally organize these details according to a scheme that allows us to visualize or recreate the object we are describing.

Can you describe your subject precisely in terms of its shapes, colors, and textures—its physical essence? Can you list its qualities and characteristics? Can you determine what makes it what it is?

Completing the first parts of the description come easily. You have the hat before you. What shape does it have? Pointed? Floppy? Whatever. Consider colors and textures. A woolen watch cap is scratchy because of its material and its knit. Most often these caps are made in dark colors like red or blue because such colors absorb heat—the primary purpose of the watch cap. What about baseball caps? Why do all baseball caps have brims that stick out in front? How do form and function work together in making a hat what it is? These are just a few of the questions that the description element of the *topoi* helps you generate. Discover the details and organize them so you can recreate the object.

Process Analysis

To complete a process analysis, we must study our subject and determine how it was made and what it can be used to do. Often, such analysis uses a step-by-step reconstruction of the object.

Can you explain how your subject was made or how it works? Can you break it down into its various parts and subprocesses and explain how they work together? Can you establish the larger system of which it is a part and how it contributes to the working of that system?

In the case of the hat, answers to the first question are not difficult. A baseball cap provides shade from the sun. The hard hat provides protection. But how exactly do they do this? This is what you would pay attention to in process analysis.

What does your hat do? Often a hat will have multiple functions and be part of several processes. Hats have not only utilitarian purposes like providing shade or protection. They can also contribute to style and personal identity. How does this work? What about the recent popularity of painter's caps? What process is involved when you wear to an event a painter's cap that advertises a beer company, rock group, or professional sports team? Surely you are not worried that you are going to get paint drippings in your hair. It is important to see that process analysis works on several levels. Multilevel analysis reveals great amounts of significant information for a writer's use.

Comparison/Contrast

To compare and contrast something, we must first establish similarities between objects; then we must point out differences between them. Apples and oranges are both classified as fruits, but what other similarities do they share? Both have skins, but how do the skins differ from each other in texture, function, and so forth?

Can you show how your subject resembles other subjects like it? Can you show how it differs from them? Can you show how these similarities and differences are responsible for its uniqueness and value?

Look at your hat. Find another one. Compare the two. In what respects are they similar? How different? What significance does the comparison suggest? The painters' cap and the baseball cap have roughly the same shape, but the materials used to produce them and the manner in which they are put together differ greatly. Do the differences have anything to do with the purposes they serve? How?

Cause and Effect

To consider cause and effect, we must look at our subject and determine what events or circumstances caused it to come to be, and what events and circumstances it, in turn, has caused to come into being. The wheel was invented in order to move objects from one place to another to help us organize commerce and construct large buildings. In turn, the wheel created the possibility of carts, bicycles, automobiles, and many other vehicles that have resulted in great changes in human existence.

Can you trace the development of your subject to show how it got to be the way it is? What *caused* your subject to be what it is?

Consider again baseball caps. How have they changed? How have the new synthetic materials produced by technology affected baseball caps? How have styles changed? Are the changes a result of technological development only or do they reflect a fundamental difference in the nature of baseball?

Can you show how your subject's nature and identity influence—*affect*—other subjects and activities? What does your subject cause to happen? What does it bring into being?

Why do the police wear hats shaped as they do? These short-brimmed hats do not provide much protection from the sun or elements. They do not seem to protect the head from violence. And they do not seem to be comfortable. Most of the time the hat sits next to the officer on the front seat of the patrol car. When the hats are worn, they always seem ready to fall off. Despite the bother and seeming purposelessness, police still wear these outmoded hats. Why? Do they wear the hats because they are a part of a uniform designed to command respect and influence the way people think and act around them? Think about it. What is the consequence of the police wearing those hats? What is the significance when you wear your hat? Plenty of valuable information becomes available through this element of the *topoi.*

Application

To consider application, we must have an idea of what an object is and what it is used for. Knowing that, we speculate on other possible uses or designs for the object, or we evaluate whether the object is doing what it is supposed to do as well as it can. Finally, we imagine changes and what effect the changes would have on the object or its use.

Can you show what various functions your subject plays in the world? What is its purpose and use? How would you change it in order to have it do its job more effectively?

For example, redesign the police officer's hat trying to incorporate all the functions, real and symbolic, it must serve. What shape would it take? What materials would you use? How would it serve all its functions? Would the changes affect how the police feel about themselves or how citizens feel about the police?

LOG EXERCISE: The *Topoi*

Use the various activities and questions of the *topoi* as a checklist to systematically determine how much you know about a subject and how ready you are to write about it. As a Log Exercise, select two subjects, one concrete such as the hat example, and the other abstract such as the concept of patriotism. Work through at least three of the *topoi* for each. In doing both subjects, vary your approaches so you get practice with all five of the elements of the *topoi* we have discussed. Compare your responses to those of others in your class.

Conclusion

The *topoi* and other heuristics presented in this discussion of invention provide plenty of ways to overcome inertia and the terror of the blank page, which often confront writers when they begin to write. Invention procedures help us get started.

But once started, how do we know when to stop inventing and start writing? Understand that the distinctions between inventing, writing, and other aspects of the writing process are largely artificial; they are conveniences we use to help us talk about the whole process of writing. Once we start "writing," we surely do not want to stop inventing ideas to use in our assignments.

So when do we really start "writing?" Experienced writers sense when they have enough information to get started, and they start. Good writers also use intuition to know when they have reached a stuck point that requires them to cycle back to invention. Through frequent writing, you will develop these intuitions.

ON WORDS

THE WRITER'S DILEMMA: NOT ENOUGH WORDS

Student writers today have more interesting and complex ideas than ever before, but many do not have the words to match their ideas. They must approximate, trusting readers to somehow discover their exact meaning. Well-conceived ideas and essays, however, can be only as interesting and effective as the words used to express them. The problem of a limited vocabulary that limits choices needs attention.

Writers depend on words because they are the units that combine into sentences to make meaning. And good writers love words. They love the instruments of their art the way home-run hitters love baseball bats, the way concert masters love violins. As you grow in skill, you will learn to love words.

Have you ever thought about words, about their sounds, sources, and meanings? Have you ever wondered why there are so many words that can be used to mean the same thing or approximately the same thing? What is the difference between car, auto, automobile, and passenger motor vehicle? Which do you consider to be more abstract or concrete, formal or informal, distant or familiar? Respectively, you are considering abstraction, usage, and tone. Other distinctions can be made. Good writers deal with such distinctions as they write, striving always to make the most appropriate selection among many choices. But previous to this analytic understanding, good writers have a feeling for words, a *curiosity and wonder*.

The subject of words is in itself fascinating. Consider a book and all the word choices that were available to its author. It's mind boggling. So much of language comes so easily and naturally to us that we do not think about it. But often the word does not come automatically; it must be chosen from an army of possibilities as *the* word for the occasion. Stop and try to put yourself in a writer's place; reconstruct the scene and try to imagine all the possibilities that were eliminated in the act of choosing a particular word. Think also how some words are so wonderful and striking that whole poems get written around them. Think of Edgar Allan Poe's "The Bells" and how the words themselves transport us to another world:

> To the tintinnabulation that so musically wells
> From the bells, bells, bells, bells,
> Bells, bells, bells—
> From the jingling and the tinkling of the bells.

What about the sources of words? Modern American English is not the only language that is spoken or has ever been spoken in this world. Through linguistic reconstruction, scholars can trace Modern English back to Middle English and before that to Anglo-Saxon and before that to a Germanic source and before that to an Indo-European source. After the Norman Conquest of the British Isles, Middle

English exploded with foreign words, especially French and Latin words that expanded and changed the English word stock. English continues to explode: "input that data-string into your mainframe!"

Science and commerce contribute new words to English every day. Do you know the source of RADAR? How did it come into the language? How about the soft drink, coke? Is coke a word or brand name? Or both? Do you know about dialects and regional vocabulary? Why is a certain sandwich called a "grinder" in New England, a "hero" in New York City, a "hoagie" in Philadelphia, and a "poor boy" in New Orleans? These are all fascinating questions about words, and answering them, even beginning to pay attention to them, will increase your sensitivity toward language and allow you more choices when you write. These choices help you to use language rather than allowing language to use you. Get interested in words!

Dictionaries

Whether lover of words or struggling writer, your primary reference tool for words is the dictionary. The dictionary can answer a great many questions about words. For example, a good desk dictionary will have in its introductory materials a concise history of the English language. In that section you will learn about the sources of English and the dynamic through which it grew and continues to grow. English is indeed a living language and is always changing. New words are introduced, old words die from lack of use, and rules of usage change—even as you are reading this sentence. The dictionary can inspire you to love words and provide references for more detailed study.

The dictionary's introductory material also contains important information about its organization and use. It explains the information each entry contains including syllabication rules, pronunciation keys, etymology (word history), part of speech, definitions and the rationale for their listings, usage labels (whether the word is colloquial or informal, slang or obsolete), and lists of synonyms and antonyms. The introductory material will help you use the considerable information each dictionary entry contains more effectively.

Turning to the entry on "radar," we discover that it is an acronym, a word made from the initials of the words of a phrase, in this case RAdio Detecting And Ranging. Its source is obviously science and technology, and its entry into the language is recent, about 1940. And we find that "coke" is a slang term for a variety of soft drink and a trademark. We can answer questions about language quickly and accurately by referring to a good dictionary.

Dictionaries range in quality from the cheapest paperbacks available in the supermarket, through the substantial "college" dictionaries available in good bookstores, to expensive unabridged reference dictionaries available mainly in libraries. As writers, we need speedy access to several dictionaries.

For example, we may keep a small paperback dictionary for quick reference to determine correct spelling, to check the appropriate form of an irregular verb, to find common synonyms for frequently used words, or to check the meanings of uncommon words we encounter while reading. However, small dictionaries are often condensed versions of larger dictionaries. Because information is frequently omitted, we cannot be sure whether we are getting complete information.

For more information, we need easy access to a "college" dictionary. The following are frequently recommended:

The American Heritage Dictionary

Funk and Wagnalls Standard College Dictionary

The Random House College Dictionary

Webster's New Collegiate Dictionary

Webster's New World Dictionary.

We can use these dictionaries to solve problems the smaller dictionaries cannot. We can check the complete meanings of words to make sure we are using them accurately. The college dictionary not only provides more listings, but also more information, including examples of words in specific contexts, and their etymologies. The college dictionary will also include more complete biographical and geographical references. Thus the college dictionary serves as a much broader and complete reference tool.

LOG EXERCISE: The College Dictionary

Complete the following exercise in your Learning Log in order to become familiar both with the organization and use of a college dictionary.

1. Examine the table of contents of your dictionary to become familiar with its special features and their location. For example, some dictionaries include brief handbooks of usage, maps, tables of measure, and so on. You need to know all the different kinds of information available to you. What special features does your dictionary have?

2. Examine the introductory materials in your dictionary. Become familiar with the dictionary's plan, abbreviations, arrangement of word entries, and so forth. What does the introductory material of your dictionary consist of?

3. Use the information contained within your dictionary to answer the following questions. In each instance note where you found the information, in the introductory materials, alphabetical listing, appendices, and so on.

  a. What are the approximate dates of the Middle English period?

  b. What principle (frequency, historical origin, degree of formality, or combination of these) is used to organize the listing of definitions within word entries?

  c. What are the plural forms of the following words?

    tableau   genius   elite   zero   phenomenon

  d. What are the singular forms of the following words?

    criteria   dice   data   species   analyses

  f. How many pennyweights comprise an ounce? a grain?

4. Look up the following words:

    ingenuous   badger   wife   stiff   effect

Use the entries to provide the following information for each word and answer the questions about a writer's need for the information:

    a. *syllabication* (When do writers need this information?)

    b. *word construction* (What are the prefixes, roots, and suffixes?)

    c. *etymology* (What is the significance of each word's origin?)

    d. *part(s) of speech* (When do writers need this information?)

    f. *special usage labels and restrictions* (What significance?)

    g. *synonyms* (Are there significant differences in connotation?)

Word Choice and the Dictionary

We can use the college dictionary to search for the precise word. We can use the dictionary to rip the curtains of vagueness away from our writing by using it to find the exact word that will make our point.

If you find yourself stuck with only a vague sense, an approximation, of the word you need while you are drafting an essay, here is a procedure to follow:

1. Find the word in the dictionary you think you want, and look at the list of meanings and synonyms.
2. Find the specific meaning that you want. For example, you might discover that the third meaning listed is the one closest to your exact intent. With that particular meaning, the dictionary may list a synonym.
3. Look up that synonym, check its meaning, and examine any others that might be provided. Do not stop until you are sure you have uncovered the word that best expresses your meaning.

Following this procedure allows you to compile a list of choices, a set of alternatives, that you can use to choose the exact word you want.

The Thesaurus

You are probably familiar with the thesaurus, an alphabetical listing of words with synonyms. Like the dictionary, the thesaurus includes introductory material explaining its organization. Take some time to familiarize yourself with the thesaurus to see how you can use it most productively.

The thesaurus can be a handy and quick way to generate a list of synonyms. The problem with the thesaurus, however, is that many writers use it to find impressive-sounding words in order to compensate for weak vocabularies. They do not take the time to crosscheck the information provided by the thesaurus against the more precise and complete information provided by the college dictionary. This can lead to embarrassing mistakes.

Stuck with the word "cheap" as a label for someone who is less than generous with money, an inexperienced writer might pull down the thesaurus, look up "cheap," and find the word "churlish." Now there is an impressive-sounding word! The writer does not know exactly what it means, but it sounds good, and the thesaurus claims it is a synonym for "cheap." So, in an essay, the writer labels a friend who is not generous but cheap a "churlish fellow." That the friend has become a "fellow" is another example of the desire to sound impressive. In fact, neither of these impressive-sounding words contributes to the meaning.

After getting critiques back from peers that flag this odd and high-sounding phrase as a trouble spot, the writer finally goes to the college dictionary and discovers that churlish means "like a peasant, surly, miserly, or intractable." Surely, the writer did not really want to call the friend "churlish." The writer was trapped between a desire to sound impressive and the responsibility to use language precisely and write effectively, regardless of sound. In this instance, the writer failed. Had the writer used the thesaurus in conjunction with a college dictionary, the outcome would have been different. The thesaurus can provide a list of alternatives, but the dictionary allows you to check the meanings of words to make sure your final choice is appropriate. Remember: learn words to use them, not to be used by them.

Through time, moreover, the dictionary will contribute substantially to your education as a writer. The dictionary will help you learn new words, increase your vocabulary, and provide you with more and better choices among words. Do not ignore the real help a thesaurus can provide as a reference, but use it in conjunction with a desk dictionary.

Reference Dictionaries: *The Oxford English Dictionary*

Several unabridged reference dictionaries will be available in your college library. Two of the most current are *The Random House Dictionary* and *Webster's Third New International Dictionary*. But of all the complete dictionaries of the English language, *The Oxford English Dictionary* (OED) is the greatest. In addition to providing a complete list of the words that have been used in English writing, it also provides extensive information about each individual word.

As noted in its Preface, the aim of the OED is to present "the words that have formed the English vocabulary from the time of the earliest records down to the present day. . . . It embraces not only the standard language of literature and conversation, whether current at the moment, or obsolete, or archaic, but also the main technical vocabulary and a large measure of dialectal usage and slang." These meanings and examples are drawn from more than five million excerpts from English writing.

Reading an OED entry is like taking a linguistic journey. For example, looking up "churlish" in the Compact Edition of the OED (a two-volume, reasonably priced, micrographic version of the twelve-volume-with-supplements complete OED), we discover that the source of "churl" is the Anglo-Saxon word "ceorl," which traces all the way back through related Germanic languages and simply meant "a man without rank, a common man." It is also the source of the name Carl and probably Charles.

The OED also lists the earliest use of the word in preserved writing. In our case, "churlish" dates to 1000 AD when it appears in a book of laws, Ine's *Code*, originally issued from 688 to 694. This is the earliest preserved West Saxon prose. In addition, the OED includes quotations illustrating differences in the meaning of the word as it developed over time. The OED may not solve any immediate writing problem for you, but reading through it is like visiting the Great Temple of English Words.

Developing Vocabulary

As a writer, you need some practical advice about expanding your vocabulary and empowering yourself to make effective word choices. When you are writing, make sure to have a thesaurus and desk dictionary available and use the procedures explained here to solve problems. What follows is a program for systematically developing your vocabulary over time.

First, you need to discriminate the kinds of vocabularies you have. Sometimes even though you encounter a word for the very first time, you know what it means from its context. When you hear a word in conversation or read it in a paragraph, you use the abundance of information surrounding it to establish an approximate meaning. In addition, you have heard many words used several times and have read them frequently enough to be able to recognize and understand their meaning even though you would never use them yourself. In both instances, approximate meanings are sufficient.

These many words whose meanings you can guess from context or that you know only vaguely comprise your *passive vocabulary*. Passive vocabulary contrasts with *active vocabulary*, those words whose meaning you know well enough that you use them frequently and accurately in your speech and writing. Your passive vocabulary is considerably larger than your active vocabulary. The aim here is to learn a way to add to your active vocabulary.

Adding to your active vocabulary requires a sense of need and a procedure. If you have ever experienced frustration at being unable to find the right word, you know the need. But need goes for nothing unless you have a program.

As you know from your work with dictionaries, words themselves include information about their meaning. Prefixes and suffixes combine with a base to create a word's meaning. Thus, by knowing what some common prefixes and suffixes mean, and knowing a few bases, you can master many words. Showing how words are built from common prefixes and suffixes is how most commercial vocabulary development programs work. Look for one of these vocabulary development programs and work through it. Near the dictionaries and reference books in your college bookstore, you will find a self-help or self-instruction section that will include books on vocabulary development.

One of the most effective of these programs is also one of the oldest. Its longevity reflects its effectiveness. The program, Norman Lewis' *Word Power Made Easy*, uses the base, prefix, suffix approach and organizes itself around frequently used Latin base words. Whole classes of words come from a single Latin base word. In addition, certain disciplines, like the sciences, have developed large parts of their specialized vocabularies from a few base words. *Word Power Made Easy* introduces the bases and the contexts they appear in most frequently and provides information on how prefixes and suffixes add or qualify meaning.

Whatever program you choose, remember that your aim is not to learn to throw around impressive-sounding words, but to discover meaning and communicate it effectively through words you have understood and mastered. And remember that studying and practicing with new words will not pay off until you move these new words from your passive vocabulary into the active vocabulary of your writing. The test is in the using.

A Reading and Vocabulary Development Program

As effective as any commercial program, the following procedure will make each time you read an opportunity to increase your vocabulary. You will need a pencil, a pocket-sized notebook that you can keep with you whenever you read, index cards, and a college dictionary. The procedure requires you to mark and save new words, define them, quiz yourself to make sure you understand them, and use them in your own writing.

In order for this approach to work best, you should be reading a wide variety of materials—from novels to psychology articles to science books—as well as intellectually stimulating general readership magazines like *Atlantic Monthly*, *Harper's*, *New Yorker*, *Scientific American*, *New Republic*, and so on. But the program can help you even with popular magazines such as *Time*, *Newsweek*, or *Sports Illustrated*. Use whatever you are currently reading, but think about trying some more challenging materials. They provide the greater payoff for vocabulary development.

Follow this procedure to begin building your vocabulary through reading:

Step One: Mark Interesting Words

Whenever you read, keep your pencil and pocket notebook handy. As you are reading along at your normal pace, mark interesting words, new words, or words used in strange contexts. As mentioned earlier, you need not know every word to understand meaning, so do not stop reading when you find a strange word, just mark it in the margin, so you can go back later and find the word easily. Use pencil so you can erase. **Do not deface borrowed materials or library books.**

Step Two: Save the Word

After you have finished reading, look back over your marks to remind yourself of the words and the contexts in which they are used. If a word piques your curiosity, record it in your pocket notebook. To help yourself remember the word, write not only the word but also the sentence in which it appears. Record any other information—page number, author, title, library call number—that will help you find it again.

Step Three: Define the Word

When you have time, transfer each word onto its own three-by-five-inch index card. On the front of the card, write the word in syllables as it appears in the dictionary. Break the word into its base, prefixes, and suffixes; this allows you to use your knowledge of words and the information in the dictionary to help you remember the word.

Then, on the back of the card, write the sentence in which the word appeared and its dictionary meaning. Paraphrase the definition from your dictionary, do not copy it. Paraphrasing helps you make sure you understand the word. Explaining the word in your own words helps you understand.

Step Four: Quiz Yourself

Assemble the index cards, alphabetize them, and study them until you feel familiar with the new words. Think of sentences using the words. Check the dictionary to make sure you are using the new words appropriately. Remember, the purpose is active, not passive, vocabulary development.

Every now and then, pull out all the cards and go through them, looking at the front and reciting the information on the back. If you cannot remember a word, take it out of the study pile and put it into a pile of those you have not yet mastered. Go through these cards frequently, until you learn the words and can use them appropriately.

Step Five: Use the Word

As you learn new words, put them to use in your writing. You will be rewarded by discovering that you have increased your choices and improved your chances of finding the best word to make your point when you write.

Though it may at first seem complicated, the procedure finally becomes second nature. Many writers find they cannot read without a pencil and notebook handy. They have boxes filled with pocket notebooks and index cards. They find themselves studying their new cards frequently.

Use this procedure over a length of time and you will be amazed at how much your active vocabulary increases. You will note an almost immediate impact on your writing.

ON GRAMMAR AND MECHANICS

GRAMMAR AND MECHANICS, AND PROOFREADING

We learn to write by writing; not by thinking or reading about it, not by listening to someone lecture about it, but by writing about meaningful subjects to real audiences. The more we write, the more we appreciate the importance of certain fundamentals. We learn through harsh experience that if we do not edit and proofread carefully, errors will appear in our essays. These errors cause some readers to assume that we are illiterate; as a consequence, they discount our ideas. Why should they take us seriously when we cannot even control the language? Errors compromise our ability to communicate with an audience.

The kinds of errors we are talking about include spelling mistakes, faulty pronoun reference, incomplete or improperly punctuated sentences, comma omis-

sions, and so forth. They fall into the general category of grammar and mechanics. Most of us are fairly familiar with the conventions of grammar and mechanics, so the first step in dealing with errors is proofreading. We must find our errors in order to correct them. But first, we need to consider how important and how difficult it is to proofread our own work.

Effective Proofreading Techniques

When we finally come to proofread an essay that we have been working on for some time, we have become so familiar with it that we often read without really seeing what we have put on the page. We skip over mistakes or fill in missing words. These oversights too often come back to haunt us.

We can do a few things to compensate for being so familiar with our writing. First, let some time elapse between typing the essay for submission and proofreading it. Taking time off allows us to return to our essay better able to see what is really there. Second, when proofreading, concentrate specifically on grammar and mechanics problems. Working through the writing process gave us the opportunity to write what we wanted the way we wanted. Now we must make sure our grammar and mechanics are correct. Third, use special tricks to counter the problem of over-familiarity. Check spelling by reading the paper from the last word to the first. Test sentences by reading them out loud.

Because effective proofreading is so difficult, another good idea is to have someone else proofread your writing for you. In most situations, you can exchange the favor by offering to proofread your peer's writing. Make sure you have already done the best proofreading job possible before giving your work to a peer. Then, ask your peer to read and mark the text lightly in pencil. Have your partner note obvious problems or put question marks near where there might be an error. When you get your writing back, make obvious corrections neatly, then check the question marks, determine whether there are problems, and make the appropriate corrections.

Remember, you are responsible for your work. Do not blindly accept all the suggestions your proofreader makes. Check them to make sure they are accurate. Most important, if you discover that you make a certain mistake regularly, learn how to correct it. There are so many rules and conventions that few of us write completely error-free essays. Nevertheless, it is our responsibility to master the rules and conventions of language. Let a proofreading exchange session become a practical lesson in grammar.

The Writing Handbook

One of our responsibilities as writers is discovering our limitations in grammar and mechanics and correcting them. One of the first steps in doing this is to become familiar with a major resource that deals with grammar and mechanics skills, the writing handbook. As valuable for writers as the college dictionary, it is a com-

pendium of information and advice on many kinds of writing; that is, it collects a wide range of information about language and writing in one place, including:

> The rules of grammar and mechanics
>
> Exercises designed to help you master those rules
>
> Procedures and conventions for completing and reporting research
>
> Specific formats for specialized writing including resumes and business letters

Designed for easy reference, the handbook can help writers solve many problems.

Many good college writing handbooks are available. You may have purchased one already as a supplemental text for this or another writing course. If you have not, you should buy one. Ask your instructor or a friend to recommend one.

Familiarize yourself with all the information your handbook offers. Examine the table of contents to locate the sections that deal with standard usage, business letter formats, and so on. Check the section on research to find how to use the library effectively. Read through the section on subject-verb agreement or another common grammar problem to understand how its explanations work. Complete one or two items in each of several exercises to see how they can help you master the rules and avoid subsequent mistakes. Take an essay you have gotten responses to, find a specific problem a peer or instructor noted, and look it up in the index. Good handbooks provide an exhaustive index as well as quick reference lists to help you locate information. Completing these activities will give you a good overview of all the information available in a handbook as well as a sense of how to use it.

LOG EXERCISE: Using the Handbook

In order to familiarize yourself with the materials in the handbook and their use, complete the following exercise in your Learning Log. Include the number of the page or pages on which you located the information for each question.

1. Write the complete bibliographic entry for your handbook. Use the MLA format.
2. What are the three usual types of cards contained in a library's card catalog? Does your college library use all three cards?
3. Who is the first author of *Literary History of the United States*?
4. What do the following abbreviations mean? *Cong. Rec.*, pseud., et al.
5. Define "plagiarism" and "abstract."
6. Should a resume list an individual's experience from most recent to earliest position or from earliest to most recent?
7. Should a letter of application for a job include a discussion of salary requirements?
8. What is a modified-block format for a business letter?

9. Correct the following mispellings and provide a reference to the rule each violates:

desireable   occurence   studied

10. Choose the correct word in the following sentences:

   a. Your/You're going to graduate soon.

   b. Do not give empty compliments/complements.

   c. Did the argument affect/effect your opinion?

11. Define and provide an example of a nonrestrictive clause.

12. Select the correct verb in the following sentences:

   a. Two-thirds of the project has/have been completed.

   b. Neither the fit nor the colors of the dress is/are appropriate for a court appearance.

13. Revise the following sentences to solve problems with placement of modifiers.

   a. The car only costs $100.

   b. Standing on the curbside, the taxi raced past the tourists.

14. Define "jargon" and "*ad hominem* argument".

15. What are the principal parts of the verbs *to lie* and *to lay*. What is the meaning of each, and how should it be used?

AVOIDING ERRORS

Handbooks provide access to the information that can make writing error-free. Conscientious use of your handbook, support and assistance from your peers, explanations from your instructor, and determination on your part are the keys to remediating grammar and mechanics problems and avoiding errors. The following advice will help you help yourself with grammar problems.

There are basically two causes of errors: carelessness and misapplication of rules. The techniques presented earlier for effective proofreading should help you eliminate errors due to carelessness. However, your essays will contain errors that you did not even suspect were errors. These errors result from the misapplication of rules. Misapplied rules create especially difficult problems. They cause errors that writers, regardless of effort, cannot find and correct for themselves. Here is where we need the help of experts and a self-development program.

Awareness of errors can help us begin to solve problems. Conscientious proofreading will help us identify instances of hesitancy and rule confusion. While you are writing, you are fairly sure that you know a rule and are writing correctly, but, while proofreading, you begin to doubt yourself. This doubt signals a need to work with the handbook. If you discover an error, correct it, and learn to avoid it in the future. If you cannot solve the problem yourself because you do not know where to look, consider asking a peer or your instructor, or make a quick stop at the writing lab where a tutor will help you. Such vigilance can help you eliminate many errors.

Despite all these efforts, your essays may still contain errors. Because instructors have a variety of ways of dealing with errors, it is your job to discover how your instructor does so and learn how to use that approach to your advantage. Most frequently, instructors use a set of editing or revising symbols keyed to the handbook used in the course. In this system, an instructor marks the symbol of an error near it or in the margin of the paper. The mark refers you to information available in the handbook.

The complete list of editing symbols appears on the inside of either the front or back cover of the handbook. The list includes all the symbols and marks. Each mark is followed by the error or problem it represents, and sometimes by a brief phrase explaining the problem or suggesting a correction, and a reference to the page or chapter in which the error is covered in detail.

You can use the list of editing symbols to test your knowledge of basic grammar rules and conventions. Look through the list and try to remember what errors specific symbols refer to. FRAG, for instance, refers to sentence fragment, an incomplete sentence. Try to remember how to avoid making that error. If you come upon a symbol unfamiliar to you or one that refers to a problem you cannot correct, check through the instructional materials, become familiar with the problem and its solution, and test your knowledge by completing the exercises the handbook provides. This preparation will help you avoid errors later on. Also, review the list of editing symbols just before beginning a proofreading session. This will help you focus by reminding you of common errors that may appear in your writing.

Instructors use this system in order to help their students find and correct errors on their own. The symbols are a convenient shorthand for communicating a great deal of information with minimal effort. More important, the editing-symbol system places the responsibility for developing grammatical skills on the writer.

You are involved in a writing course, not a grammar course. If you want to learn grammar, then take a grammar course. But understand that taking a grammar course will not necessarily make you a better writer. You learn to write by writing. By using the editing symbol system, the instructor is reminding you that the central focus of the course is your writing, that grammatical and mechanical errors are significant distractions that deserve attention only during proofreading, and that avoiding errors is your responsibility. The instructor will provide needed feedback and access to resources like the handbook, but learning the fundamentals of grammar and error is your responsibility.

In some instances, errors are so large a problem with an essay that an instructor will use another approach and refer you to the writing lab or tutoring center. For whatever reason you are referred to a writing lab, do not take it as an insult or a punishment. Rather, the lab referral offers the most effective way of getting you the help you need. Students who work in writing labs almost always report that they received the specific help they needed, as well as humane support from tutors. They report feeling a part of a community in which students, tutors, and lab staff worked together to the benefit of all. Even more important, these students report dramatic improvements in their writing. A little help was what they needed to become effective writers.

Grammar Logs: A Self-Development Program

However your instructor is dealing with errors, you need to develop a systematic procedure for correcting them and making sure you do not repeat them. Basically, you must

1. Focus on a particular problem.
2. Locate where that error most frequently occurs.
3. Learn the standard English rule you are misapplying.
4. Practice correcting the error.
5. Create a list of your common errors so you can check for them specifically when you proofread your essays.

One of the most effective procedures individuals can use to help avoid errors is a grammar log. A grammar log is a systematic procedure for noting the errors that are damaging your essays in order to eliminate them. It gives you a place and method to make sure you are learning the lessons your peers and instructor are offering.

Use the grammar log after you have had an essay returned with grammatical problems noted. Either your peer proofreader or your instructor has discovered that you are making a particular mistake. Sometimes you may get an essay back that has several different problems noted. When that happens, *focus* on the error that has the most negative effect on your writing. If there are seventeen errors in your essay, it will probably turn out that there may be three different punctuation errors, six spelling mistakes, and eight repetitions of the same error, such as faulty subject-verb agreement. In this instance, work on the problem of subject-verb agreement. Learning to correct and avoid subject-verb agreement problems allows you to eliminate half of the errors from your essay. Once you have solved that problem, then you can turn to others.

Now that you have selected the error you are going to focus on, the next step is to *locate* where that error most frequently occurs. Learn the error's neighborhood. In the case of the subject-verb agreement problem, the neighborhood is the space between the subject and verb of a sentence. If you can learn to identify the complete subject of the sentence and the complete verb of the sentence, then you can check whether they agree or not.

For example, consider the following sentence: "The team, whose players had had no rest, were preparing for the big game." The subject of the sentence is "team," and the verb is "were preparing." Because the clause "whose players had had no rest" intervenes between the subject and verb (in other words, invades the subject-verb neighborhood), the writer may have become confused, thinking that "players" is the subject and choosing a plural verb "were preparing" to agree with it. The real subject, "team," is a singular noun requiring a singular verb "was preparing." Learning the neighborhood will help you identify places where you need to look for potential errors.

Now that you have located the neighborhood for the error, your job is to check the handbook and *learn* the correct rule by determining what rule you are violating, learning the correction, and developing a trick that will help you remember the correction later.

For example, you write the sentence, "The team are preparing for the big game." You find that the correct sentence would read "The team is preparing for the big game." Your original sentence is incorrect because the singular subject, "team," must take a singular verb, "is." This is the standard English rule. The source of your confusion is that a team is a collection of people and you think of it as plural. You are not being illogical, you are misapplying a rule. In fact, in Great Britain you would be correct because the conventions for usage there require collective nouns to take plural verbs.

As you go through the handbook, you find that one of the rules concerning subject-verb agreement deals exactly with the problem of collective nouns and singular verbs. You have so far discovered the problem and the rule you are misapplying; now you must develop some personal rule that will help you translate your misapplied rule into the correct one. For example, if you can make a collective noun, a noun that refers to a group, plural by adding an s (team, teams), then you must use the singular verb whenever there is no s. This may seem complicated, and it is not completely correct, but it is adequate for solving the immediate problem at hand—subject-verb agreement. A point to remember is that a rule you create for yourself is going to be most effective helping you remember to avoid the error.

Once you have found a way to translate your rule to the standard English rule, you must *practice* making the correction so you can avoid the problem in the future. There are three ways you can practice. First, try to use your own writing to practice. Go through your papers, find subject-verb agreement problems and correct them. You are most likely to remember the correction if you are working with your own writing. Second, use the exercises provided by a handbook or writing lab. These are generally designed to make you see and correct all the various forms the mistakes can take. Thus, the exercises give you a complete sense of the problem and how to solve it. Finally, make up some of your own exercises. Write sentences with subject-verb agreement problems, then revise them so they are correct. This makes you process the information learned in the first and second steps and makes sure you have mastered the material so you can identify, correct, and avoid the error. The key here is practice, plenty of practice.

Is the problem solved now? Not yet. Keeping a grammar log requires one more step. After you have completed the practice steps, *list* the problems you have recognized and solved on a sheet of paper which you keep near where you write. Each time you go through the procedure, add problems discovered and corrected to your list. Keep the list handy when you proofread. It is a personal record of your errors. Where you have made an error in the past, you are likely to make the error again. You can avoid repeating the mistakes by referring to the list and proofreading your writing specifically for those problems.

Using the five-step grammar log procedure will give you a good chance at eliminating errors that can negatively influence an audience and limit the effectiveness of your writing. You know the resources available to you—the handbook, feedback from peers, the writing lab, and instructors, and the grammar log procedure. Now it takes motivation. You must decide that errors are a problem, that they are solvable, and that you are going to assume responsibility and beat them. Given the great confidence you will feel as you write by knowing that you are in control of grammar and mechanics, keeping a grammar log is surely worth the effort.

LOG EXERCISE: Sample Grammar Log Entry

Use the following format for Grammar Log entries in order to make sure you are completing all the steps and learning as much as you can from the procedure. Attach a sheet like this to each of your essays when it is returned to you. Collect both essays and Grammar Logs in your Learning Log.

GRAMMAR LOG

Essay:
Errors Noted:

Error Selected:
Example: (note "neighborhood" of error)

Rule Violated and Handbook Location:

Correction:

Rule Translation:

Practice: Completed Handbook Exercises No. _____, p. _____.
  Personal Examples:

Added to Proofreading List on: (note date)

ON SENTENCE STYLE

We will use the term "style" here to mean how a writer uses the elements of language. Sentences can be short, the words simple, the message direct. This is plain style. Sentences can be long and complicated, the words unfamiliar, perhaps exotic, and the message both dense and ponderous. This would be ornate style. Both illustrate the use writers can make of the elements of language.

When we move from smaller to larger concerns, from vocabulary and correct grammar and mechanics to assembling basic language units to achieve particular effects, then we enter the realm of style. When we begin to consider not correct or incorrect, but effective and more effective, we confront sentence style.

You are already a master at composing English sentences. When speaking, you recognize sentences that are ill-formed and revise them to be more effective, you create wonderfully complicated and graceful sentences, and you regularly shift from one structure to another in order to clarify or emphasize a point. What we have to do now is become aware of our sentence-making abilities, understand certain principles we are already using, and put them to work purposefully in our writing.

CLASSIFYING SENTENCES

In order to develop our sentence style, we need some basic vocabulary to talk about sentence structure. We can then practice manipulating sentences and developing our sense of sentence style. Most commonly, sentences are classified by their clausal structures that reflect the logical relations inside the sentences. These structures include the types of sentences: simple, compound, complex, and compound-complex. You probably recognize this system because most schools teach it. If these terms are totally unfamiliar to you, or if you want a more detailed discussion, refer to your handbook.

Simple Sentences

A simple sentence contains only one subject-verb (s-v) core, even though either or both the subject and verb can be compound. For example, the following are all simple sentences:

Yellow notepads clutter my desk. (s-v)

Yellow notepads, a pocket calculator, a stapler, and several books clutter my desk. (ssss-v)

Yellow notepads clutter my desk, interfere with my writing, and frustrate me. (s-vvv)

Yellow notepads and a pocket calculator clutter my desk and frustrate me. (ss-vv)

The basic point to remember about a simple sentence is that it has only one complete subject-verb core. Having a complete subject-verb is a prerequisite for making a grammatically complete sentence. Note also that variations within simple sentence structure (compound subjects and verbs, modification by adjectives, adverbs, and prepositional phrases) make the simple sentence a remarkably flexible tool, a true resource for writers.

Compound Sentences

The second sentence type is the compound sentence. It includes two or more independent clauses (a subject-verb core that could stand alone as a simple sentence) joined by a comma and coordinating conjunction (cc), a semicolon alone, or a semicolon followed by a conjunctive adverb (ca) and a comma. There are seven common coordinating conjunctions: and, but, for, or, nor, so, yet. Some of the most frequently used conjunctive adverbs include: consequently, furthermore, however, moreover, nevertheless, rather, therefore, and thus.

For example, the following are all compound sentences:

Tea and coffee contain the powerful stimulant caffeine, and tobacco contains the carcinogen nicotine. (ss-v, cc s-v)

Walt Whitman wrote some of America's finest poetry; Edgar Allan Poe wrote some of our finest short stories. (s-v; s-v)

The dancer strained her back muscles working out; therefore, she will not dance this evening's performance. (s-v; ca, s-v).

In each instance two clauses of approximately equal logical and grammatical value are joined into one sentence. In fact, each of the clauses could be separated into a grammatically correct simple sentence. Each could stand by itself. These clauses are coordinate; in other words, they are of equal value. The point is that only clauses that are coordinate, which can be equated logically, can be joined in a compound sentence. Consider this sentence:

Automobiles are the most popular form of transportation in America, and Buddhism is the most popular religion in Asia. (s-v, cc s-v)

Though its properly positioned comma and coordinating conjunction make it a grammatically correct compound sentence, the sentence fails logically and, therefore, should not stand as a compound sentence. Obviously, comparing automobiles and Buddhism in the same sentence is logically inappropriate. Although this may seem a gross example of inappropriate coordination, it should put you on guard that compound sentences involve more than grammar; they also involve logic.

Complex Sentences

The third type of sentence is the *complex* sentence. A complex sentence includes at least two clauses, one of which is dependent upon the other. For example, this sentence

sc s v   s   v
While she was waiting for her flight, she called her office. ([sc s-v], s-v)

contains two subject-verb cores, but we cannot break it into two separate and complete sentences as we could a compound sentence. Although "she called her office" could stand as a sentence, "while she was waiting for her flight," could not because it begins with the subordinating conjunction (sc) "while." It is a dependent clause, and it must be associated with an independent clause. Note that in the structural summary after the example the dependent clause is contained within brackets—[ ]—in order to emphasize that it cannot stand alone. If it were punctuated as a separate sentence, it would be a typical example of a fragment. Using the brackets demonstrates that a complex sentence contains a dependent clause joined by a subordinate conjunction to an independent clause.

Of the many subordinating conjunctions (sc), some of the most familiar include those signaling time relations:

after	before	once	until
when	whenever	while	

those signaling causal relations:

although	because	if	since
though	unless	whether	

and the relative pronouns (rp):

that	what	which	who
whoever	whom	whomever	whose

The complex sentence is one of the writer's most important tools; it allows writers to show logical relations within a sentence. The subordinate conjunction signals the relationship. For instance, in these sentences

Jon, who is my younger brother, visits me often. (s [rp-v] -v)

Poker, which is my favorite cardgame, is a game of skill and nerves. (s [rp-v] -v)

note that when a relative pronoun serves as a subordinating conjunction, it can also serve as the subject of the dependent clause. In both instances the relative clause provides information about the noun it modifies. The clause cannot stand by itself as a sentence.

Subordinating conjunctions, as noted in the previous list, indicate various logical relations. Some signal temporal relations; others indicate causality or consequence. But separating these subordinate conjunctions into temporal and causal groupings can be problematic. Many can represent both temporal and causal relations as in this example:

 sc   s   v   s   v
While he was dozing behind the wheel, his car ran off the road.
([sc s-v], s-v)

Although "while" generally signals time, there is also a causal relationship between sleeping at the wheel and running off the road. Both relationships are at work here. The meaning of the conjunction and the verb and the whole context of the sentence combine to establish the relationship. Good writers take advantage of the various elements and how they combine to make meaning.

Compound-Complex Sentences

The final sentence type is the compound-complex sentence. As its name suggests, it is a hybrid type, a compound sentence to which one or more dependent clauses are attached, such as

 sc   s   v   s   v   s
While the pizza was baking in the oven, John made the salad, and Frank

 v
set the table. ([sc s-v], s-v, cc s-v)

Compound-complex sentences are particularly valuable to the writer because they contain several logical relations. In the sample sentence, both a temporal and causal relation is signaled by "while." Of course, the pizza takes *time* to bake, but that time also allows or *causes* Frank and John to do something else. Both time and cause are at work here. There is obviously a coordinate relationship between making salad and setting the table; both are activities that must be completed in order to prepare dinner.

SENTENCE STYLE

Sentences often contain subtle relationships like the ones discussed here, and that is the real reason we need to pay attention to them. A good writer takes advantage of the potential within sentences to establish logical relations, create rhythm, and provide emphasis. Though you have already seen how both coordinate and subordinate relations can be established and how subordinate relations can include more than one logical consideration, understanding rhythm, emphasis and other aspects of sentence style may be a little more difficult.

Sentence style is the general term for a great many choices a writer makes while creating sentences. One aspect of sentence style is rhythm. Rhythm involves tempo, the speed and regularity of a sentence. Purposefully or not, writers create sentences with various rhythms. Some sentences rush along from beginning to end, gathering speed as they go along, ultimately crashing into the period at the end of the sentence like a wave against the seawall. Some move along at a steady pace, one part leading into the next, and that leading on to the next, until the period ends the leisurely tour, leaving both writer and reader to prepare for the next part of the journey. Some sentences, not many but a few, sometimes written by folks who do not really know what they are trying to say, are interrupted by so many qualifications and asides that they never seem to get started. The point is that writers can make choices and create sentences to control rhythm. They can use sentence style to help accomplish their writing goals.

Cumulative and Periodic Sentences

Considering sentence style leads us to another kind of sentence classification, one that describes sentences as cumulative and periodic. These types exist by contrast. Basically a *cumulative sentence* places the subject-verb core near the beginning of the sentence and then builds or accumulates modifiers as the sentence goes along. This sense of accumulating meaning as the sentence progresses results in the term *cumulative sentence*.

Most of our sentences in speech and most of the "natural" sentences in writing are cumulative sentences. They follow the normal pattern for making meaning. The speaker/writer states the subject and verb and then qualifies and elaborates the meaning. It is a particularly effective pattern for introducing basic information.

But the cumulative sentence also allows a writer opportunities to achieve special effects. Look at the following example:

> **The sailboat flew across the lake, sails close-hauled, bow crashing through the waves blown up by the stiff breeze, leeward deck heeled underwater, while the crew desperately tried to convince the wildly laughing skipper to head-up into the wind.**

Analyzed by sentence types, this is a complex sentence. But to label it a complex sentence only is to miss a great deal of the effect caused by its cumulative style. Note how the sentence starts with a rather tame and pleasant subject-verb core, "sailboat flew," which then develops into first an exciting and finally a terrifying scene with crashing waves, a desperate crew, and a maniacal captain. A reader could not have predicted the end of the sentence at its beginning but could only be taken on the journey by a clever writer trying to make the reader experience the sentence as well as understand it. The cumulative sentence allows for dramatic effect through the writer's control of information and rhythm and emphasis. The choice is there for the writer to make.

The *periodic sentence* exists by contrast to cumulative sentence; its modification precedes the subject-verb core. Note how the pattern is reversed in the following version of the sailboat sentence:

Sails close-hauled, bow crashing through the waves blown up by the stiff breeze, leeward deck heeled underwater, the sailboat flew across the lake.

In terms of sentence types, this is a simple sentence with only one subject-verb core coming near the end of the sentence after three bursts of modification. Withholding the subject-verb core is the key to a periodic sentence. Styling the sentence adds dramatic effect. The writer establishes certain details but does not bring them into resolution until the subject-verb core is finally introduced.

How the subject-verb core resolves or clarifies the meaning of the sentence is a key concept in periodic sentences. Notice how the revised sentence is energized by the three bursts of modification. The writer wonders whether a reader could process any more information without becoming confused. In a sense, this is a limitation. Periodic sentences can be graceful and emphatic, but they do not have the flexibility of the cumulative sentence that can almost turn around and go the other way. The writer cannot add details about a terrified crew and maniacal skipper without worrying that the sentence will dissolve into fragmented confusion.

Balanced Sentences: Parallelism

We need to note another concept at work in the periodic "sailboat" sentence. The three bursts of modification preceding the subject-verb core are grammatically parallel and demonstrate *balance*. *Parallelism* occurs when a writer takes several items and coordinates them by repeating the grammatical construction. The writer makes them parallel and in so doing establishes a relation of equality or logical sequence and emphasis. A good example comes from John F. Kennedy's "Inaugural Address":

Ask not what your country can do for you; ask what you can do for your country.

Notice how the same grammatical structure, the imperative beginning with "ask," is repeated to emphasize the contrast and make the point more dramatic.

You are also aware of a frequently remarked error called *faulty parallelism*. "Jon likes to swim, hike, and sailing," is a faulty parallel which can be corrected easily by repeating the grammatical sign [to + verb] consistently: "Jon likes to swim, to hike, and *to sail*."

But look at this sentence: "Jon likes swimming, sailing, and peanut butter sandwiches." There is obviously something wrong with this sentence. While it may seem this problem could be easily corrected by inserting the grammatical sign used to make the last item parallel, in this case [verb + ing], creating "Jon likes swimming, sailing, and *eating* peanut butter sandwiches," we discover that the problem is more than grammatical; it is logical. Eating peanut butter sandwiches is not of the same logical order as swimming or sailing and, therefore, cannot truly be paralleled with them.

The balance created through grammatical parallelism works well in the revised sailboat sentence. We see the boat's sails, then its bow, and then its leeward deck; each element contributes to the sense of "flying" across the lake. But balance achieved through parallelism is not limited to phrases. Any grammatical unit will work from adjectives:

Long and tall, chic and glamorous, the Parisian model swirled across the stage.

to prepositional phrases:

Across the river, through the forest, over the mountain, and beyond the glade, to Grandmother's house we go.

to participial phrases,

Walking slowly and talking ceaselessly, the old friends enjoyed their reunion.

to whole clauses as with the quotation from Kennedy's "Inaugural Speech."

While the examples provided so far illustrate balance achieved through precise grammatical parallelism, combinations of structures that are approximately rather than precisely parallel are also effective. Look at this revision of the sailboat sentence and note how precise and approximate parallelism work to balance the sentence:

Its sails close-hauled, its bow crashing through the waves, its leeward deck heeled underwater, the sailboat flew across the seas while the desperate crew tried to convince the wildly laughing skipper to head-up into the wind.

You know already that the three bursts of modification describing the sails, bow, and deck of the sailboat illustrate balance through precise grammatical parallelism. Note also how the modification before the independent clause balances the qualification provided after the independent clause by the subordinate clause. The sentence is constructed like a teeter-totter balanced by two children of equal weight sitting on either end.

But where is the approximate parallelism? To understand how it works requires a close reading of the sentence. The beginning of any unit sets up expectations for the rest of the unit. Violating expectations is the problem with the faulty parallelism—to swim, to hike, and sailing. Such a gross violation is an error.

But look at the dependent clause begun by "while" in the revised sentence. The subject of the clause is "crew" and the direct object is "skipper." How are they modified? The crew is "desperate." The skipper is "wildly laughing." They are not modified by the same grammatical structure. "Crew" takes a simple adjective while "skipper" takes an adverb and a present participle used as an adjective.

Is this an error? In a sense this shift of grammatical patterns violates the reader's expectation since "desperate crew" should be paralleled by "insane skipper" or "crazy skipper" or "maniacal skipper." But, by changing the pattern and violating the expectation, the writer emphasizes the madness of the skipper. The adjectives "insane," "crazy," and "maniacal" do not establish the skipper's madness as effectively as "wildly laughing" does.

This approximate parallelism, in contrast to the parallelism the reader expects as a result of the precise parallelism of the first half of the sentence, exemplifies how balance achieved through parallelism, or the purposeful violation of an expected parallel, can create emphasis and dramatic effect. Balance and its instrument, grammatical parallelism, are stylistic options good writers take advantage of frequently.

STYLE IN PARAGRAPHS

Remarking on the various capabilities of cumulative and periodic sentence styles and how balance is at work in both emphasizes the amazing flexibility of the English sentence and the wide variety of choices it affords a writer. However, these styles exist in a context; they do not have particular value in themselves. They most often function within paragraphs. The contrast of the styles and the manipulation of the parts within both the sentences themselves and the paragraphs they constitute make certain effects possible. This interaction is the essence of paragraph style. Watch how Edgar Allan Poe contrasts a long cumulative sentence woven together with various parallel constructions with a short, emphatic periodic sentence to create an unforgettable effect near the end of "The Fall of the House of Usher":

> For a moment she remained trembling and reeling, to and fro upon the threshold, then, with a low moaning cry, fell heavily inward upon the person of her brother, and in her violent and now final death agonies, bore him to the floor a corpse, and a victim to the terrors he had anticipated.
> From that chamber and from that mansion, I fled aghast. . . .

The last sentence of this excerpt is one of the two or three sentences from all of literature that haunts certain readers, sneaking up on them and echoing through their nightmares. The violent contrast of sentence styles that Poe creates by opposing the long cumulative sentence with the short periodic one makes the effect unforgettable. He builds through one paragraph and then whips his readers with the second. It is the work of an arch stylist at work. Poe uses words, grammar, and sentence style to create special effects such as emphasis and drama in the same way the film producer Steven Spielberg uses his technology to create unforgettable moments. As writers we, like Poe, need to use all the resources of language to produce an effect, to make our point. This is the purpose and the challenge of style.

Now and always, let your writing illustrate what you have learned about the writer's basic resources, about the love of words, about grammar and mechanics, and about the great potential of the English sentence.

LOG EXERCISE: Sentence Combining

You have been reading about and analyzing certain operations based on sentence style and sentence types. Now it is time for you to practice some of these operations. In the following exercises, you will combine several core sentences—short simple sentences—into longer sentences using coordination, subordination, and modification. Directions will instruct you to construct either a particular type or style of sentence; you will make certain core sentences the independent clause or the central idea as a result of grammatical structure or position.

Our purpose is not to exhaust all the possibilities each list of core sentences creates, but to understand that constructing sentences involves exercising control and making purposeful choices. You will discover some of these choices by completing the following exercises. This practice, along with some style-checking procedures to be presented shortly, will give you new ways to use the writer's resources when you are paying attention to the style of your sentences during revision. Record all your sentences in your Learning Log.

Exercise One

Following the directions below, use your knowledge of sentence types and style to create interesting sentences. One or two possible responses to each instruction will be provided as models, then you will write alternative versions.

Core Sentences

   A. Richard has only one leg.
   B. Richard is a long distance swimmer.
   C. Richard has a great heart.
   D. Richard has overcome his handicap.

   1. Using core sentences A and B, create a compound sentence using a conjunction that will emphasize B by establishing contrast, such as:

Richard has only one leg, yet he is a long distance swimmer.

   2. Using A and B, create a complex sentence with B as the independent clause, such as:

Although Richard has only one leg, he is a long distance swimmer.

Richard, who has only one leg, is a long distance swimmer.

   3. Using all the core sentences, create a compound-complex sentence with B and D as the independent clauses, substituting an appropriate verb when necessary, such as:

Although Richard has only one leg, with his great heart he has overcome his handicap, and he has become a long distance swimmer.

4. Using all the core sentences, create a complex sentence coordinating the verbs of B and D in the independent clause, such as:

Though Richard has only one leg, he became a long distance swimmer and with his great heart overcame his handicap.

5. Using all the core sentences, create a cumulative, simple sentence, such as:

Richard is a long distance swimmer despite having only one leg, a handicap overcome with his great heart.

6. Using all the core sentences, create a periodic, simple sentence, such as:

Overcoming the handicap of having only one leg, Richard, with his great heart, has become a long distance swimmer.

7. Using all the core sentences, write a simple sentence with parallelism to create balance.

Having only one leg but a great heart, Richard overcame his handicap and became a long distance swimmer.

Exercise Two

Core Sentences

> A. Pale light entered the room.
> B. A mourning dove cried.
> C. She finished the night's last dream.
> D. She woke up.

1. Using core sentences A, C, and D, create a compound sentence coordinating the verbs of C and D in one clause. (Answers appear at end of Exercise Two.)
2. Using all the core sentences, create a complex sentence with D as the independent clause.
3. Using all the core sentences, create a compound-complex sentence with C and D as the independent clauses.
4. Using all the core sentences, create a periodic simple sentence using grammatical parallelism to balance A, B, and C.
5. Using all the core sentences, create a cumulative complex sentence.

Some Suggested Answers

1. Pale light entered the room, but she finished the night's last dream and woke up.
2. As pale light entered the room and a mourning dove cried a finish to her night's last dream, she woke up.

3. While pale light entered the room and the mourning dove cried, she finished the night's last dream, and she woke up.

4. Pale light entering the room, the mourning dove crying, the night's last dream coming to an end, she woke up.

5. She woke up when the pale light entered the room, the mourning dove cried, and she finished her last dream.

Exercise Three

Core Sentences

A. New Mexico is a large state.
B. New Mexico has alpine mountains.
C. New Mexico has magical deserts.
D. New Mexico has good highways and tourist services.
E. New Mexico is a great place to visit.

1. Using core sentences A, D, and E, create a compound sentence with A and D in one clause.

2. Using core sentences B, C, D, and E, create two simple sentences with E as the subject-verb core, making one periodic and the other cumulative.

3. Using core sentences A, B, C, and D in one dependent clause, create a periodic complex sentence.

4. Using core sentences B, C, D, and E, create a simple sentence with paralellism establishing balance.

Some Suggested Answers

1. New Mexico is a large state with good highways and tourist services, so it is a great place to visit.

2. With alpine mountains, magical deserts, and good highways and tourist services, New Mexico is a great place to visit.

New Mexico is a great place to visit with its alpine mountains, magical deserts, and good highways and tourist services.

3. Because it is a large state with alpine mountains, magical deserts, good highways and tourist services, New Mexico is a great place to visit.

4. With alpine mountains and magical deserts, with good highways and superb tourist services, New Mexico is a great state to visit.

Exercise Four

Create at least five different sentences from the following set of simple sentence cores. Describe each sentence you create both in terms of its sentence type and style. Abbreviate sentence types using S for simple sentences, C for compound sentences, CX for complex sentences and CCX for compound-complex sentences. Identify each sentence's style as CM for cumulative or P for periodic.

A. Alyce is an investment counselor.
B. Alyce used to be an English teacher.
C. Alyce quit teaching English.

D. Alyce still relies on her teaching background.

E. Alyce now teaches people how to make their money grow.

Example:

My investment counselor, Alyce, used to teach English, and she still relies on her teaching background since she teaches people how to make their money grow. (CCX, CM)

Exercise Five

Create at least five different sentences from the following set of simple sentence cores. Describe each sentence you create both in terms of its sentence type and style.

A. Stella is a talented artist.

B. Stella studied and worked hard.

C. Stella persevered.

D. Stella is now a successful children's book illustrator.

Example:

A talented artist, Stella studied and worked hard, and, because she persevered, she is now a successful children's book illustrator. (CCX, CM)

Exercise Six

Create at least five different sentences from the following set of simple sentence cores. Describe each sentence you create both in terms of its sentence type and style.

A. Carl is an art historian.

B. Carl was a museum curator.

C. Carl programs computers.

D. Now Carl is making twice the money.

E. Carl misses caring for and preserving beautiful things.

Example:

Carl, an art historian and former museum curator, now makes twice as much money programing computers, but he misses caring for and preserving beautiful things. (CD, P)

Exercise Seven

Create at least three different sentences from the following sets of simple sentence cores and describe each.

1. A. Education is an investment.

   B. The investment has two returns.

   C. The first comes as one learns.

   D. The second comes as one earns.

Example:

Education is an investment with two returns: the first learning, the second earning.
(S, CM)

    2. A. Zunis are pueblo Indians.
       B. Zunis are peaceful.
       C. Zunis disdain modern American ways.
       D. Zunis prefer to make their living off the land.

Example:

Zunis are peaceful pueblo Indians who disdain modern American ways and prefer to make their living off their land. (CX, CM)

    3. A. The room was dark.
       B. The room was shadowy.
       C. The little boy was afraid.
       D. The little boy screamed.

Example:

In the dark and shadowy room, the boy, afraid, screamed. (S, P)

    4. A. He likes to read.
       B. He likes books about folklore.
       C. He likes books about religion.
       D. He remembers most of these books.

Example:

He likes to read books about folklore and religion, and he remembers most of what he reads. (C, CM)

LOG EXERCISE: Evaluating Personal Sentence Style

To gain some perspective and practice with sentence-level style, complete the following analysis in your Learning Log.

1. Select two paragraphs from essays you have completed. Make sure one paragraph is primarily discursive or argumentative in purpose; in other words, it states an idea and develops it logically. Argumentative and persuasive essays will be good sources for this paragraph. The other paragraph should be descriptive in purpose. The chronology of an event or the spatial relationships within a scene or an object should be the organizing

principle of the paragraph. Descriptive essays and personal narratives will be good sources for this paragraph. Also make sure the paragraphs are of sufficient length to make this analysis worthwhile. Try to find paragraphs of at least eight sentences.

2. Having selected the paragraphs, complete the following analysis concerning the LENGTH of your sentences:
Number each sentence in the paragraph.
Count the number of words in each sentence.
Count the number of words in the paragraph.
Find the average number of words in each sentence by dividing the number of words by the number of sentences. Round the average to a whole number.

Answer the following questions:
a. What is the longest sentence in the paragraph and where does it appear— beginning, middle, or end?
b. What is the shortest sentence in the paragraph and where does it appear?
c. How many sentences are long sentences? For our purposes, a long sentence is one-third or more longer than the average. Thus, if the average length is 15, then a "long" sentence would be 20 words (15 + [⅓ × 15] 5 = 20 words) or more.
d. How many sentences are short sentences? For our purposes, a short sentence is one-third shorter than the average. In the case above, a "short" sentence would be 10 words (15 − [⅓ × 15] 5 = 10 words) or less.
Briefly consider the relations between sentence length and variety in your paragraphs. Have you avoided problems of reader boredom by varying the length of your sentences? Does the rhetorical purpose of the paragraph, discursive versus descriptive or narrative, seem to have an effect on sentence-level style? What are the differences between the two in terms of sentence length?

3. Complete the following analysis concerning the texture of your sentences:
Using the abbreviations suggested earlier, identify each of the sentences in your selected paragraphs by type. Now answer the following questions:
a. What type of sentence do you use most frequently?
b. Are your sentences predominantly single-clause simple sentences, or multi-clause compound and complex sentences?
c. Have you varied the types of sentences to avoid the problem of boredom?
d. Have you used the structure of your sentences to avoid confusion through the use of subordination and coordination? Provide an example from each paragraph.

Finally, consider the rhetorical purpose of each paragraph and determine whether purpose affects sentence-level style and your use of sentence types. What conclusions would you draw?

4. Complete the following analysis concerning the style of your sentences:
Using the abbreviations suggested earlier, identify each of your sentences by sentence style. Style refers to whether they are cumulative (the subject-verb core comes near the beginning of the sentence and modification/elaboration follows)or periodic (the subject-

verb core comes late in the sentence). Note any instances of balance created by the use of grammatical parallelism. Answer the following questions:

    a. What type of sentence do you use most frequently?

    b. Is your style predominantly cumulative or periodic?

    c. Is there variety in your sentence style?

    d. Have you used balance? Provide an example.

    e. Have you used sentence style to create any instances of emphasis or dramatic effect? Provide examples.

5. Now that you are aware of the elements of sentence style and how sentences contribute to the effectiveness of your writing, revise *one* of the paragraphs you have analyzed. In your revision, do not change the purpose or substance of your paragraph. Rather, use your new skill with sentences to better accomplish the writing job you originally set out to complete. Use the analysis and evaluation questions to develop new strategies for improving the effectiveness of your sentence style. Learn to use sentences as another one of the writer's resources.

INDEX